BLACKSTONE'S
MODERN CARD TRICKS
AND
SECRETS OF MAGIC

BLACKSTONE'S
Modern Card Tricks
AND
Secrets of Magic

By HARRY BLACKSTONE

GARDEN CITY PUBLISHING CO., INC.

GARDEN CITY, NEW YORK

CL

PRINTED IN THE UNITED STATES OF AMERICA

PREFACE

THE PRESENT popularity of magic may be attributed to a new and wholesome trend; that of a general interest in smaller tricks suited to close range presentation. Subtlety as much as skill is the order of the day, and those persons interested in magic are therefore enabled to begin without the long and arduous practice of difficult sleights that were once considered necessary.

Card tricks offer the logical starting point, as they are suited to the impromptu performer, and are also demonstrated by more experienced magicians. Time spent on card tricks automatically benefits the student, and places him in a more advanced category. Hence, the first half of this volume is devoted to "Modern Card Tricks," and their presentation.

The reader is advised to study the introduction to "Modern Card Tricks" to familiarize himself with the fundamentals. He will then be ready to try the tricks themselves, and in connection with some, he will find reference to the section on card tricks that appears in "Secrets of Magic," the second portion of this volume.

In "Secrets of Magic," the card tricks described are a direct follow-up to those in "Modern Card Tricks," as they deal with sleight-of-hand methods that will be useful to any one who has accustomed himself to presenting such tricks as require very little skill.

The subsequent sections of "Secrets of Magic" are designed to lead, step by step, into the larger fields of general magic, from pocket tricks through magic with apparatus, up to the stage illusions which are seen in the more elaborate magic shows. A special section has been added covering mental mysteries and spirit effects, which are always popular; while the volume concludes with a chapter on how to present magic.

It should be mentioned that the tricks described in "Modern Card Tricks" have been adapted from tested methods used by capable performers. They all have been selected because of their practicability. Though both quality and quantity are present, emphasis has been placed on the former.

As for the tricks in "Secrets of Magic," many of them are performed with apparatus which may be purchased from magic dealers, thus rendering it unnecessary to have the appliances specially constructed. Such items are worth-while; otherwise they would not be on sale, and by first learning the secrets of these tricks, the reader can form an opinion before acquiring the apparatus.

There is a difference between merely knowing how a trick is done and knowing how to do it. This volume undertakes to elucidate both by explaining proper presentation, as well as actual method. Many magicians will find its pages profitable in that they reveal many effective phases of certain tricks which have too often been disregarded or overlooked.

HARRY BLACKSTONE

BIOGRAPHICAL NOTE

FOR MORE than a quarter of a century the name of Blackstone has been associated with Magic, until, to the American public, the terms have become practically synonymous. For the people of America, more than thirty million of them, have seen Blackstone and his Magic throughout those years. In New York he has played return engagements on Broadway, and his coast to coast tours have taken him to every sizable town in the United States and Canada, an uninterrupted record which truly defines him as the greatest of American magicians.

Born in Chicago in 1885, the future magician was thirteen years old when he witnessed a performance by Harry Kellar, then America's leading magician, at McVicker's Theatre. That experience determined Blackstone's career. His one ambition was to become a magician, with a show as great as Kellar's.

The style in magic was changing, and when Blackstone in his early twenties was ready for the stage, the trend had shifted from the full evening show to vaudeville. Nevertheless, it was still his desire to present a large and spectacular performance of magic. So he combined the best of large illusions, with his many sleight-of-hand tricks in which he is so skilled and in this way was able to keep within the time allotted to a regular vaudeville turn. Billed as Harry Bouton and Company, the act became an immediate success and was headlined over the largest vaudeville circuits.

By 1914 Blackstone was more than ready to embark with a full evening show. He adopted the name of Blackstone—the family name of one of his grandparents—and made his debut with a road-show of two hours' duration, requiring more than a dozen assistants and tons of apparatus. It was with this performance, interspersed with his own deft specialties in sleight-of-hand, that he appeared in the Mason Theatre in Los Angeles during his first season.

After the first act of Blackstone's Los Angeles performance, a visitor came backstage to see him. He was none other than Harry Kellar, whose wizardry had so inspired Blackstone sixteen years before. Retired and living in Los Angeles, Kellar had come to see Blackstone's performance, and on this occasion it was the old master who acclaimed the new. So pleased had Kellar been with the first act, that he could not wait until the finish of the show to congratulate Blackstone. The two were friends from that meeting, and Kellar not only predicted that Blackstone would eventually become the greatest of modern magicians, but privately resolved to furnish him a legacy which would be a fitting tribute.

In the years that followed, Blackstone did many things in magic. He initiated a type of performance peculiarly his own, the hour show, combining the speed and precision of the shorter vaudeville turn with the large spectacle of the road show. This not only enabled him to play many theatres where a combination of motion pictures and stage shows was the policy; it gave Blackstone the added opportunity of replacing older methods with new. Thus, in each circuit of the country he presents a different performance, appealing to those who have witnessed his work before.

During the twenties Blackstone invented and presented such spectacular illusions as the "Vanishing Horse," the "Vanishing Automobile," and the "Vanishing Camel," which were followed by his famous "Cannon Illusion," wherein, at each performance, he was tied to the mouth of a huge cannon and fired into nothingness, only to reappear as the man who had fired the cannon itself!

Space does not permit the cataloging of the many other magical effects which he has produced, but no matter how large his show becomes, Blackstone never omits the small, deft tricks before the curtain, which mark him as the all-around magician who can mystify at the closest range as well as upon the full stage.

Chief among his smaller specialties is the "Flying Bird Cage" mystery. In this surprise a bird cage and the canary occupying it disappear instantly from Blackstone's finger-tips. He immediately repeats the trick with another cage while members of the audience are holding the cage along with him, only to find that it is gone from their very hands!

Unlike many magicians who have traveled in foreign lands, Blackstone has remained constantly in America, for the simple reason that the public here want him. Through the thirties he continued his nation-wide tours spending only the brief summer months at his home in Michigan, not for vacations alone, but to construct new illusions for each coming season. Having his own work-shop and trained crew, Blackstone has for years been equipped to produce the best in magic.

Then, with another decade almost past, came the legacy from Harry Kellar.

During his professional career Kellar had presented one illusion which outshone all others: "The Dream of Princess Karnac," which brought into actuality the fables of the East. This was the levitation of a girl who floated in mid-air away from all scenery while Kellar passed a solid hoop about her. When Kellar retired and turned over his show to a successor, the levitation went with it. But Kellar, though he had spent thousands of dollars upon the illusion, had not regarded it as perfected.

In retirement, Kellar began work upon a new levitation, and concentrated all of his magical knowledge upon that one theme. Before his death, he finally perfected it and willed the illusion to Blackstone. After many delays, the masterpiece finally reached its intended recipient, and Blackstone publicly presented this absolute in magic.

From that day he has performed the Karnac levitation in every show and always will. One must witness Kellar's greatest creation, as demonstrated by Blackstone, to realize how the art of the modern magician can render the impossible real. Shown on a fully lighted stage under conditions that no one ever before dared the "Dream of Princess Karnac" is more than Kellar's tribute to Blackstone. It is the ultimate in mystery.

Perhaps Kellar foresaw that this new inspiration would press Blackstone on to further achievements in magic. Certain it is that Blackstone today will accept no limitations in the field that he has so ably represented. To start his new quarter-century, Blackstone has cracked the greatest riddle of the Orient, the "Indian Rope Trick." Many have talked about it, and some magicians have attempted to produce it, but always with limitations, until Blackstone at last presented it in accordance with the descriptions of those few who have claimed that they actually saw it.

In full light a rope rises from a basket and hangs suspended in air, the top of the rope quite visible. To the accompaniment of Oriental music, a boy climbs the rope, and hangs from it in view. Blackstone fires a pistol shot; there is a puff of smoke, and the boy is gone. Only the rope remains, still suspended, until—and this is a real Blackstonian touch—the white-haired wizard fires another shot, whereupon the rope, itself, drops to the stage.

Such are the high-lights of the Blackstone show today. The show fills two baggage cars and requires a company of thirty people, to say nothing of the "Vanishing Horse" and the multitudes of rabbits that accompany this extravaganza. Though Blackstone's adventures have been many, he measures them in terms of his performances, which in turn may be subdivided into tricks and methods.

It is Blackstone's firm belief, as warranted by experience, that the art of the magician depends upon personal ability, as much as method. Therefore, it has been his policy to initiate others into the craft, that they, through knowledge of tricks such as those explained in this volume, may test their own ability in the art of magic and be qualified to seek success in the fascinating field of modern magic.

WALTER B. GIBSON

CONTENTS

Book One: Modern Card Tricks

MODERN CARD TRICKS

INTRODUCTION

IT IS NOT DIFFICULT to perform tricks with cards. The old idea that considerable skill is necessary is now obsolete. Once, card tricks could be divided into two grand divisions—simple tricks and difficult tricks. The simple tricks were scarcely worthy of notice; the difficult ones were hard to learn. But that time has passed.

Many new and ingenious methods of card magic have been evolved. Older tricks have been improved beyond recognition. Some of the simpler sleights, formerly used but seldom, have now become adapted to newer purposes.

A certain amount of skill is required to do card tricks well. But it is a fact that such skill is scarcely more than is required to handle a pack of cards smoothly. Anyone who aspires to do card tricks at all will readily understand that the ability to shuffle a pack neatly and well is certainly a requirement.

Some of the cleverest tricks are really very simple. To make them effective, the magician must present them in a convincing fashion. If he appears clumsy, spectators will take it for granted that the tricks are simple. If he appears clever, spectators will believe that the tricks are the result of superior skill.

The essential thing, then, in learning card tricks, is to first familiarize oneself on the handling of a pack of cards. The beginner should spend some time in learning to shuffle rapidly—either by the dovetail method or by the overhand system, both of which are used by card players.

He should also try to deal cards smoothly and rapidly; learn to riffle the end of the pack; to spread the cards between his hands, or sweep them along the table. All these little points add to the effectiveness of a performance with cards.

It may be assumed that the average card player already knows how to handle a pack. If the reader possesses what we may term normal skill, he is ready to utilize the information which this book contains.

In the first section, we have introduced a number of sleights which will prove useful. Each one is included with a definite purpose—it has some use in connection with the tricks that appear in later sections. The reader should study it as preliminary work. He will find that most of the methods are merely ideas in card handling that will come easily to him. His study of that section need not be a long one. He can go on to the tricks that follow and refer back to the first section as needed.

The old idea of explaining card methods was to bewilder the student with some of the most difficult of all sleights, stating at the beginning that these must be learned in order to do card tricks. Such is not the plan in this book. The most difficult sleights are not included at all. The reader will find them in some of the older standard works on magic, if he chooses to look them up. They are useful to the expert card worker, but they are not needed by the average performer.

The right way to learn card tricks is to begin by doing them. This book follows that plan. At the same time, we advocate preliminary work with the cards themselves in order to present card tricks most effectively.

The first section—that of preliminary sleights—has been mentioned. The second section is a very useful one. Many good card tricks depend upon the location of a card which has been selected by a member of the audience. So our second section deals entirely with card locations. The performer can use whatever method he sees fit, choosing his favorite locations. Some are very easy of accomplishment and will enable the beginner to start using locations right away.

The third section covers card discoveries—unique ways of producing cards after one has been selected and located. It naturally follows the second section in logical sequence. The remaining sections involve tricks which do not require the usual locations and discoveries. Here the reader will find a varied array of card magic. The final section of the book covers tricks that utilize certain elements of skill, mostly referring back to the first section.

Special attention is called to the fourth section, which is devoted entirely to "spelling tricks"—a variety of card magic that has come into popularity during the past decade.

HARRY BLACKSTONE

BOOK ONE
MODERN CARD TRICKS

CHAPTER I

PRELIMINARY SLEIGHTS

BLACKSTONE'S CARD TRICKS

HERE THE READER will find useful methods in card handling that he can apply constantly in card tricks. The first of these are false shuffles and false cuts—always of value.

The other sleights in this section have been included because they are of use in certain tricks which could not otherwise be performed successfully. With the present trend of card magic, there is no purpose in utilizing all sorts of manipulations. Nevertheless, certain tricks require the introduction of some bit of skill.

The reader should familiarize himself with all of the methods given in this section so he can refer to them as he proceeds. If he likes a particular trick that depends upon the "glide" or the "palm," he can then spend time in practicing the sleight.

Any feats of skill with cards are useful, as they represent a definite step in the smooth handling of cards. At the same time, the old idea of practicing sleights that had no practical use is something which can scarcely be recommended. The sleights in this section were placed there after the major portion of the book had been written and they were found to be necessary for reference in certain tricks.

I. FALSE SHUFFLES

False shuffles are useful in connection with many card tricks. Through their aid, the performer can keep a card on the top or bottom of the pack; or can retain the entire deck in its regular order.

Such shuffles are not difficult to learn, although they should be practiced frequently. They must simulate genuine shuffles; therefore, some of the best false shuffles are patterned directly after ordinary ways of shuffling the pack.

In Blackstone's "Secrets of Magic," we outlined a false shuffling system for use with the "Card Control." Other methods of false shuffling are given here, with a few references to the system described in the previous book. There is no reason why any performer should attempt to utilize a wide variety of false shuffles. The shuffle is simply used to mix the cards—and it is natural for a person to shuffle the cards in one way. The magician, therefore, is apt to bring suspicion upon himself if he shuffles differently each time he handles the cards.

Most persons, however, utilize both the dovetail shuffle and the overhand shuffle, as well as cuts, when they are mixing the cards. Therefore we are giving practical methods of false shuffling both dovetail and overhand, with a section on false cuts in addition.

2. DOVETAIL FALSE SHUFFLES

In the dovetail shuffle, the executor simply divides the pack into two portions and riffles the ends, allowing the two sections of the pack to interweave. In doing this, it is best to let the inner corners of the packets run together, under control of the thumbs.

In many tricks, the magician desires to keep the top card in its position; in others, he may wish to keep the bottom card in position. This is easy with the dovetail shuffle—in fact it is so natural that there is virtually no falsity about the shuffle.

To keep the top card in position, simply dovetail in the usual fashion, but be sure to retain the top card until after all others have fallen. By this method, one can keep a dozen cards or more on top of the pack. Presuming that the upper portion of the pack is taken in the right hand, it is desirable that the upper portion should be slightly larger than the lower. By riffling the lower portion more rapidly than the upper, the left hand finishes with its cards while those in the right are still being riffled. The top cards remain on top.

To retain the bottom cards in position, they are simply allowed to fall first. In this case, the left hand, with the bottom heap, runs ahead of the right, dropping a number of cards before the right hand begins its release.

Retaining cards on both top and bottom is simplicity with the dovetail shuffle. Dividing the pack into two equal heaps, the left hand lets the lower cards go first; then the right hand follows and when the left hand packet is exhausted, the right hand is still riffling cards.

The ordinary false shuffle by the dovetail method is scarcely more than an imperfect shuffle which the performer turns to his own advantage. Yet the spectators, unsuspecting of his purpose, have no idea that he is deliberately controlling the cards.

3. COMPLETE PACK CONTROL
(*With the Dovetail*)

The apparent shuffling of the pack without disturbing the arrangement of a single card may be accomplished with the dovetail shuffle. This is a real false shuffle. It will require considerable practice, in order to render it deceptive.

The right hand heap represents the upper portion of the pack. It should contain fewer cards than the left hand heap. Cards are riffled first from the left hand, giving that packet a start. Following, the right hand ends with some of its cards on top of the pack.

Up to this point the shuffle is genuine. The spectators are allowed to see that the inner corners of the pack are actually dovetailed. Only the very corners are interlaced, however. As though to complete the shuffle, the performer swings his fingers together. As he does so, he bends the outer end of the right portion upward. The fingers come together and by a slight drawing of the thumbs, the interwoven corners of the pack are separated.

The upward bend of the outer corner of the right heap enables it to slide up on top of the left heap and thus the hands come together, simulating exactly the completion of an ordinary dovetail shuffle. The fingers prevent anyone from observing that the shuffle is not bona fide.

This shuffle should be practiced until it is natural. It reaches a point where just the slightest twist enables the magician to change a genuine shuffle into a false one. By using this mode of shuffling regularly, he can make the movement highly convincing, no matter how closely the observers may happen to be watching.

4. OVERHAND FALSE SHUFFLE
(To Control Bottom Cards)

In the simplest and most natural form of the overhand shuffle, the shuffler holds the deck in his left hand and peels off several cards with the thumb. The remainder of the pack is brought down by the right hand and more cards are peeled off. This is continued until all the cards have been shuffled off.

To control bottom cards during a normal overhand shuffle, the performer simply grips them with the tips of his left fingers when the left thumb peels off the first layer of cards. Result: the bottom cards are retained beneath the top ones. The rest of the pack is shuffled on top and the bottom cards are not disturbed.

By this method the performer can control a single bottom card and also bring a card from the top to go with it. He does this by peeling away the lone top card and shuffling the rest of the pack on it. He retains the bottom card when he draws down the top one. This shuffle is executed with the left side toward the audience.

5. OVERHAND FALSE SHUFFLE
(To Control Top Cards)

In this false shuffle, the performer stands with his right side toward the audience and holds the pack in his left hand. The top of the pack is against the fingers of the left hand.

In shuffling, the pack is lifted by the right hand. The left thumb peels off a few of the bottom cards, while the left fingers retain some of the top ones. The pack is brought toward the left

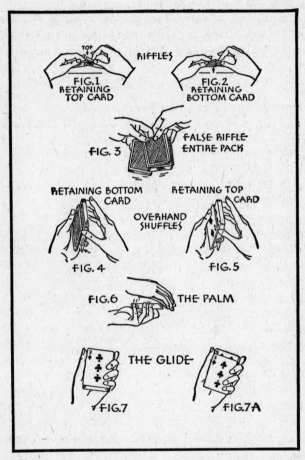

The diagrams show the correct positions for various preliminary sleights explained in Section One.

thumb, which peels away cards and adds them to the bottom of the cluster held in the left hand. This is continued until the right hand has shuffled away all its cards.

By this method, a bottom card may be made to join a single card at the top. Simply peel away a top card and a bottom card together, clipping them and shuffling the pack upon the bottom card.

6. TOP AND BOTTOM SHUFFLE

Assuming that the magician has two cards on the top of the pack and wishes to transfer one to the bottom, he does as follows: Holding the pack in the left hand, with thumb on the bottom, he peels a few cards from the bottom while the left fingers draw down one top card. He then shuffles away until only one card is left in the right hand. That card drops on the bottom of the pack. One of the top cards is still on top; the other on the bottom.

Presuming that one of two bottom cards is to go to the top while the other remains on the bottom, the magician holds the pack in his left hand with thumb on top. He peels off some top cards and draws a single bottom card beneath them. He then shuffles the pack from the right hand until only one card is left. It goes on top. Thus one bottom card is on top; the other remains on the bottom.

7. OVERHAND SHUFFLE WITH COMPLETE PACK

This is the method whereby none of the cards are disturbed during an overhand shuffle. Hold the pack in the left hand with the thumb on top. Peel off about a dozen cards with the left thumb. Bring the pack down on top of those cards and remove no cards whatever—although the motion makes it appear that you do.

Now bring the pack beneath the left hand cards and peel off some with the left thumb. Once more come on top with the right hand but leave none. Go beneath and leave some. Continue thus as though you were leaving cards on both top and bottom. Actually you are leaving them on the bottom only. In this way the entire pack is shuffled off—right back to its original condition, without a single card being disturbed.

This shuffle naturally keeps top and bottom cards in position, so it can be used for that purpose as well as for an entire deck shuffle.

8. FALSE CUTS

A false cut serves the same purpose as the false shuffle—an apparent mixing of the pack without the mixing taking place. The usual false cut is designed to preserve the entire arrangement of the pack.

It is a simple fact that a single cut does not disturb the order of the cards, even though it does change the position of the top card. Therefore false cuts are designed to appear more thorough than a single cut but to do no more than cut the card once.

Many of the tricks in this book involve selected cards that are on the top of the pack or the bottom; therefore the false cuts have been specially arranged so that they do not make any change at all. Despite their appearance, they leave the pack exactly as it was before the cuts were made.

Therefore these cuts, when learned, can be applied in any trick. The card conjuror may at any time give the pack a series of cuts and be sure that he is not injuring his chances of doing the trick successfully.

Many magicians neglect false cuts. This is a mistake. In all legerdemain with cards—particularly when tricks are performed at close range—false cuts add that degree of emphasis that makes the magician's work seem amazing. Furthermore, false cuts can be learned easily and done with great rapidity—even by the beginner.

9. SIMPLE FALSE CUT
(With Three Heaps)

Lay the pack on the table. Lift off about two-thirds of the cards and lay this portion six inches to the right. Lift off half of this portion and place it in the center. This makes three piles.

Put the right pile on the left. Put the center pile on top. This brings the pack back to its original position. The following table shows the piles as they are made:

1	3	2
(Bottom)	(Top)	(Middle)

2 goes on 1 and 3 goes on 2. The pack is unchanged. This is ordinarily done with one hand. With two hands, form the piles with the right hand only. Then reach across with the left and pick up heap 2, dropping it on heap 1. The right hand immediately picks up 3 and puts it on 1 and 2.

10. ANOTHER FALSE CUT
(*With Four Heaps*)

Lay the pack on the table and lift off most of the cards, leaving a small heap. Drop a dozen more from the bottom, to the right of the first pile. Drop a dozen more below the first pile and put the remainder at the right. Thus:

1	2
(Bottom)	(Lower Middle)
3	4
(Upper Middle)	(Top)

Gathering: Place 3 on 2; put 4 on 2 and 3. Lay all on 1. With two hands, the left hand picks up 3, dropping it on 2; the right hand picks up 4, gathers 2 and 3 beneath it and transfers all to the top of 1.

11. SPECIAL FALSE CUT
(*With Five Heaps*)

This time four heaps are formed about the pack as a center, making five heaps in all. The mode of cutting is different at the start. A few cards are lifted from the pack and laid at the upper left corner of an imaginary square. Some more are taken from the pack and put at the upper right corner. Another group from the pack is placed at the lower left; a fourth group at the lower right.

This is the arrangement:

| 1 | 2 |
| (Top) | (Second) |

*
(Pack)

| 3 | 4 |
| (Third) | (Fourth) |

Gathering: Drop 2 on 3. Drop 1 on 2 and 3. Drop 4 on pack. Place 1, 2, 3 on 4 and pack.

With two hands, the left drops 1, the right 2, the left 3, the right 4. Picking up; right places 2 on 3; left puts 1 on 2; right places 4 on pack; left puts 1, 2, 3 on 4 and pack.

12. SHUFFLE CUT

This cut has the appearance of a shuffle and certainly gives the impression of a mixing of the cards. It may be performed

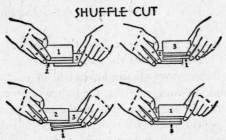

SHUFFLE CUT

The positions of the pack during the stages of the Shuffle Cut. 1 shows the original top section; 2 the center; 3 the bottom.

either with the cards on the table or with the cards held by the hands alone.

The hands hold the ends of the pack. Fingers are at the far side; thumbs at the near side. The right hand draws off cards from the bottom, pulling them away between the thumb and forefinger alone. Moving above the pack, carrying its heap, the right hand grasps some of the top cards between the tip of the thumb and the second finger.

These are drawn off to the right also—the position enables the right hand to keep the two groups separated. The left hand now holds a group of cards—those which constitute the center portion of the pack.

The left hand comes above and places its cards upon the upper group held by the right hand. The left draws away both groups as one. The right hand then lays its only remaining group upon the cards that are in the left hand.

With a little practice, this procedure becomes simple. Learn to do it rapidly and it is very effective. It can be repeated time and again, for it brings the pack back to the starting point. No change whatever in the order of the cards.

13. FALSE CUT SHIFT

In this method of locating a chosen card, a false cut serves the purpose of a pass. The cut is very similar to the "Shuffle Cut" elsewhere described. It is given here in detail and the reader will note the similarity.

The pack is held between the tips of thumbs and fingers. The right hand is near one end of the pack; the left near the other.

The right hand draws off the lower half of the pack between the thumb and forefinger, inviting the return of the selected card, which is placed on the lower half of the pack.

The right hand then moves above the pack and draws off the upper portion between its thumb and second finger—below the portion already held. These sections of the pack are kept separate.

Left hand is now holding the center portion of the pack between thumb and forefinger. It comes above and with thumb and second finger draws off the upper of the two groups held by the right hand. It keeps its groups separated.

The right hand drops its one remaining group of cards upon the upper group held by the left hand and pulls away both groups as one. This leaves the left hand with its lower, single group, which it drops upon the cards in the right hand.

This puts the selected card on top of the pack, in spite of the confusing shuffle cut.

14. THE REVOLVING PASS

The sleight known as the "pass" is nothing more than an invisible cut used by the magician to transpose two portions of the pack. It was for many years the recognized method of bringing a chosen card to the top of the pack.

REVOLVING PASS

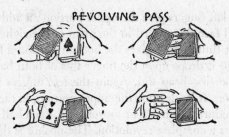

The upper half of the pack is dropped face up on the right fingers. Note how the left fingers flip it over. The lower diagrams show the other half of the pack following.

The difficulty of learning the "pass" is out of proportion to the value of the sleight, so far as the average card performer is concerned. With all the modern card detections and locations that have been devised, the "pass" is necessary only on rare occasions.

There are various forms of the "pass"—and the really good ones are hard to learn. But there are also certain "false passes" which accomplish the same purpose. The one we are about to describe is easy to do and is, at the same time, deceptive. It would not be a good sleight to use repeatedly; but it is excellent when performed occasionally.

It is included in this book so that the reader may have it available when the "pass" is actually required in any particular trick, unless he happens to be familiar with some other form of the "pass" which he finds suited to his purpose.

Hold the pack in the left hand, thumb on top, fingers beneath. The little finger is inserted in the pack at the lower right corner, holding the two portions of the pack separated. Thus, if a chosen card has been replaced in the pack, that card is just beneath the tip of the left little finger.

The right hand approaches the left. The left hand tilts toward it and lets the upper portion of the pack fall face up upon the tips of the right fingers. The left side of the portion is resting on the tips of the left fingers also (with the exception of the left little finger, which, with the left thumb, holds the lower half of the pack).

Now the left fingers give the upper portion an added flip, causing it to fall face downward in the palm of the right hand.

The right thumb now gives the bottom portion a flip from beneath so that it drops upon the finger tips of both hands, face up —just as the first heap did. Again the left fingers flip, turning this heap over. It lands upon the upper portion, in the right hand.

The procedure requires four movements. Each half of the pack, in turn, does a complete revolution. The upshot is that the lower heap is on top of the upper heap. The "pass" has been accomplished.

The effect is highly deceptive. There is no attempt to conceal the motion. On the contrary, it should be done boldly, in full view. It appears to be a fancy action like a riffle—a bit of jugglery that adds to the trick and seems a display of skill. It has a peculiar effect, no one realizing that it actually cuts the pack.

In using this revolving pass, the performer should first square up the pack at the front, so no one will notice the little finger of the left hand, inserted at the inner end of the pack. Then the right hand riffles the outer end of the pack, to indicate that all is fair. Immediately after the riffle comes the revolving pass.

There is no great skill needed; but the move should be practiced until the four motions blend into one, making a very pretty continuous effect. It is quite possible to throw the cards from hand to hand, letting each portion revolve as it goes from left to right. This is also a pretty effect.

The important point to remember is that the movement is actually used to transpose the sections of the pack; and it serves that purpose admirably. By using fancy cuts and riffles in other tricks, the magician can lead his observers to expect little flourishes that have no particular bearing on the trick; and when he uses the revolving pass, they will be taken entirely unaware.

15. THE PALM

One of the most useful of all card sleights is the "palm" by which a card is removed from the pack and secretly retained in the right hand. Sometimes two or more cards may be retained in this manner.

The simplest palm for a single card is the following. Hold the pack in the left hand, flat and back upward. Place the right forefinger against the outer left corner of the pack. The joint of the finger should touch the corner of the card.

The right fingers are all together. Lined in this fashion, they move forward, taking the card with them. The hand closes slightly and the fingers point downward as they go along, so that the end of the pack presses against the end of the card and it is forced tightly into the right hand.

The hand should be kept in a half-closed position, retaining the palmed card. This method enables the hand to get a firm hold on the card. The pressure should be light at first, however, so that only one card will follow the right hand.

To palm one card or more—a required number—the left thumb first pushes the cards to the right side of the pack. As the right hand covers the pack, as though to square the cards, the second finger of the left hand pushes upward from beneath and forces the cards into the right palm. This must be done neatly, to make sure that the cards are well hidden in the right hand.

16. THE GLIDE

The "glide" is a very old sleight—but a very useful one and a very easy one. It was first described many years ago and it served its purposes then; however, newer tricks have utilized this sleight and it is because of this that we recommend the method to the reader.

The "glide" is actually a "second deal" in which the cards are drawn from the bottom of the pack instead of the top. It is of use only to magicians and it takes the place of a card "change."

There are two methods for the "glide." The first is the neater; the second the easier.

First Method: Hold the pack in the left hand, the thumb at the right side, the fingers curled beneath, at the left. The bulk of the hand is above the pack, which is face down. Show the bottom card by tilting up the pack. Hold the pack face down, while the right hand approaches the outer end to draw off the bottom card.

At this point, the left third finger gets busy. It moves inward and slides the bottom card along with it. Hence the right hand, in drawing off a card, is able to take the second card from the bottom—not the bottom card itself. The right hand deals the card face downward on the table and everyone supposes it to be the card that was shown on the bottom of the pack.

Moistening the left third finger will facilitate the operation of the "glide."

With this sleight, the magician can "change" a card or he can make a chosen card appear at any number from the bottom of the pack, simply by holding it back while others are drawn forth.

Second Method: This time, the right fingers do the work. The right hand approaches the outer end of the pack. The thumb rests on top; the fingers beneath. The right fingers push the bottom card back; then draw off the next card.

In both methods, the card can be drawn, when required, by the right fingers. If they want the pulled-back card, they simply stretch to get it and bring it out.

The "glide," while an easy sleight in either form, should not be neglected in practice. Its effectiveness depends upon doing it neatly. Fumbling will spoil any trick, and simply because the sleight is not hard to learn is no reason for performing it crudely.

17. THE FALSE COUNT

A very simple and useful sleight. The performer wishes to count off some cards from the top of the pack and to actually take less than the audience supposes.

He does it thus. He draws off one card, saying "one." He places the card back on the pack and removes another with it, counting "two." The left thumb pushes each card to the right to assist the right hand in the removal.

In taking a third card, the magician simulates the previous movement, but he simply brushes the right hand cards upon the card that is on the pack, without removing it. The left thumb, at the same time, pulls back the card.

By this procedure, the magician can apparently count off twelve cards, really taking only nine. Three times during the course of the counting, the false motion is made.

With nine cards in his hand, the magician can count the packet to make it appear as twelve. He simply counts off three cards normally; makes the false count on number four; actually counts off the next card; then the false count; counts off another; then the false count; and finally counts off the remainder.

Make sure of the position of the cards, remembering that they are backs up. Practice the sleight, until you can do it naturally and easily. You will be surprised how simple it is—and how deceptive.

CHAPTER II

CARD LOCATIONS

IN LOCATING CARDS, there are certain points to be considered. A card, having been selected and replaced in the pack, is presumably lost. The chances of finding it again are—from the spectator's view—just about one in fifty-two.

It is true that very many tricks begin with the old formula: "Take a card." Perhaps the phrase has become hackneyed. Nevertheless, it is the usual beginning of many good tricks. If people want to see card tricks, they should expect to take cards.

After the card is taken, it is up to the performer to find it when needed. Card locations solve that problem. There are various types of locations. We can consider them in three groups.

First: The learning of a card. Through some method, the performer discovers the card by glancing through the pack after the card has been returned. This type of location is sometimes termed a "detection." It is not so effective as the controlling of a card, but it serves as well in certain tricks.

Second: The control of a card. The performer, by some system, keeps the card under his control, bringing it either to the top or the bottom of the pack. He does not necessarily know the name of the card. This type of location is usually followed by false shuffling.

Third: The forcing of a card. In this type of location the magician knows beforehand what card the spectator is going to take. The "force" serves purposes all its own. By use of it, the magician can predict the name of a card which is to be selected. The "force" also serves as a location, however, for it enables the magician to find a card any time after it is returned to the pack.

The special advantage of the "force" in locating cards is that with it, the spectators may be allowed to shuffle the pack themselves, thus strengthening the performer's own position when he shuffles for himself. This is also possible with a form of location known as the "glimpse," which is explained in this section.

Often, when the performer knows the name of a card, he can find it by the simple expedient of shuffling the pack dovetail fashion. He riffles the end of the pack that is toward himself and thus sights the card as it comes along. Cutting at that point, he can keep the card on the bottom or the top as he prefers.

This is a useful point to know in connection with card tricks where the performer is using some form of location other than the actual control of a chosen card.

I. THE DIVIDED PACK

This is one of the simplest forms of card location ever devised. In fact, it is so simple that it has been relegated to beginners and its real merits have been forgotten.

Red and Black

To explain the method in its primitive form requires only a few words. The pack is cut into two heaps. A card is selected at random from one heap. It is placed in the other heap. Looking through the second heap, the magician discovers the chosen card.

This is easy to do when one knows how the pack is divided. One heap contains red cards; the other heap contains black. Simple, isn't it? A red card shows up among the blacks or a black shows up among the reds—as the case may be.

Note that each heap may be shuffled prior to the drawing of a card. But should any spectator chance to look at the cards in his heap, he would easily find a clue to the trick.

Mixed Suits

When we consider this idea in its more subtle forms, we discover real merit in it. The first stunt is to use the spades and hearts (mixed) in one heap; the clubs and diamonds (mixed) in the other. This means that a much closer inspection is necessary on the part of the spectator.

Odd and Even

A further improvement is to pay no attention to suit whatever. Use all *odd* cards (ace, three, five, seven, nine, jack, king) in one heap; use all *even* cards (two, four, six, eight, ten, queen) in the other. That makes detection highly unlikely.

Mixed Odds and Evens

In its most elaborated form, the trick utilizes the *even* spades and hearts and the *odd* clubs and diamonds in one heap; the other heap consists of the *odd* spades and hearts and the *even* clubs and diamonds. This makes the system virtually undetectable.

For practical purposes, however, the use of odds in one section and evens in the other will be all that the performer may require.

Now it is obvious that the trick will work both ways: given two heaps of different kinds of cards, one or more cards may be transferred from heap A to heap B; or from heap B to heap A. Examination of both heaps will show any "strangers" in their midst. Thus the performer is not limited to the choice of a single card.

Complete Pack Method

Let us consider the two-heap idea with the pack all together. The top portion of the pack consists of, say, odds. The lower portion consists of evens. Spreading the pack, the magician requests the selection of a card. If one is taken from the top half of the pack, he keeps on spreading and allows the card to be put back in the bottom part. If one is taken from the bottom portion, the pack is closed and spread again near the top, so the card goes in there.

This is done with two or more cards; then the pack is cut a few times. Upon looking at the faces of the cards—even while the spectators are watching—the magician can immediately find the chosen cards.

Complete Pack with Shuffles

To make the trick more deceptive, we shall explain a way of using this principle in which the pack is genuinely cut in four heaps before the selection of cards; and actually shuffled in dovetail fashion after the chosen cards are replaced!

Arrange group A (consisting of even reds and odd blacks) on top of group B (consisting of odd reds and even blacks). Remember the bottom card of group A—say the ten of diamonds. Or the joker may be placed at that point.

Spread the pack slightly and cut at the key card. That makes two heaps, A and B. Cut each of those heaps, making two A heaps and two B heaps. In assembling, gather the heaps A, B, A, B from bottom to top. The A heap with the ten of diamonds should be the upper A heap. Also note the bottom card of the upper B heap.

Now cards are selected and replaced. This time, you are dealing with four groups. They must be considered as the cards are replaced. Simply see to it that the card goes in a group of the other variety.

When the chosen cards are back in the pack, spread a trifle to find the ten of diamonds and cut there. Now, in dovetailing, let the right hand cards drop more rapidly than the left. As soon as the bottom card of the upper B heap (say the four of spades) appears, retain it and let the left hand cards fall until they are well exhausted. Then finish the shuffle. This simply segregates the A and B heaps. You are ready to look for the chosen cards.

2. THE NEW PACK

This is one of those opportune tricks that no card conjuror should neglect when the occasion permits it. It is particularly useful when performing at a card table. A new pack is often presented to the magician and then he has his chance.

A pack of cards is taken from the case. It is spread along the table. Persons are asked to draw cards. The magician's head is turned away. As soon as cards have been removed, he closes the pack without looking at it—sweeping the cards together.

Again he spreads the pack and asks for the replacement of the chosen cards. This being done, he sweeps the pack up without even glancing at it.

Nothing could seem fairer than this. The magician does not even know how many cards were chosen. But by spreading the pack before him and concentrating, he manages to remove several cards, which he lays faces down. The chosen cards are named. Those cards are turned up. They are the chosen ones!

New packs are always arranged in sequence of suits. Nowadays the suits are usually in order from ace to king. Thus when cards are taken—the pack closed—the pack reopened—the selected cards naturally go back at new positions and it is a simple matter to learn their identity by simply looking through the pack! For they are out of place.

The pack may be cut once or twice during the trick; that does not disturb the rotation. Afterward, the pack should be shuffled immediately to dispose of the clue that would give away the method.

3. EASY LOCATIONS
(With Puzzling Additions)

Bottom Card Location

This is one of the oldest types of card location. We are describing it, however, because it has many useful variations and can be made to deceive the shrewdest spectator if handled in the proper manner.

Basically, the trick is simply a division of the pack into two heaps. A card is taken from the top of the lower heap, noted, and transferred to the upper heap. The cut is then completed. After a few cuts of the pack, the magician looks through the cards and discovers the selected one.

This is accomplished by first sighting the bottom card of the pack. When the selected card is transferred from the lower heap to the upper and the cut completed, the known (bottom) card naturally comes on top of the selected card. Cutting does not separate those two cards. It is easy for the magician to discover the chosen card.

Top Card Location

Now let us note some variations to this idea which the average man of a few card tricks does not know. First is the subterfuge of noting the *top* card of the pack instead of the bottom. To facilitate this, the magician may actually note the bottom card and shuffle it to the top before placing the pack on the table. The pack is cut; it is divided into two heaps. A card is noted while being transferred from the lower heap to the upper. The magician tells the spectator to complete the cut—and requests him to mix the cards of the lower heap before he does so!

The shuffle puts the bottom card out of commission and kills the spectator's pet theory (if he has it) that the bottom card is of help to the magician.

Top and Bottom Location

Another factor which is not realized—even by magicians—is that the pack can be shuffled when the bottom card or the top card serve as locators. Yes, it can be shuffled—if you pick your shuffler.

The average person does not shuffle a pack thoroughly. Noting such a person, the magician can give him the pack for shuffling and the chances of the two cards (locator and chosen) being separated is very slight. This applies to those who shuffle by the overhand method. The dovetail shuffle, if thorough, is more apt to spoil the trick.

But this leads us to the combined location in which the magician knows *both* the top card and the bottom one. When the pack is cut into two heaps and the chosen card transferred from lower to upper, the completion of the cut puts it *between* two known cards.

The magician can either find it as the card above the original top card or the card below the original bottom card. In other words, the wizard has caused the formation of a little cluster of three cards—the center one being the selected card.

Ordinary shuffling is not apt to disturb this group. Upon looking through the pack, the magician will usually find the desired card right between the other two. But supposing the shuffle is quite a thorough one. The chosen card may drift away from one of its locators, but it has very little chance of leaving both of them.

For instance: let us consider a group formed by the six of spades, ace of hearts and six of diamonds (from top to bottom). The six of spades is the original bottom card; the ace of hearts is the chosen card; the six of diamonds is the original top card. If the cards appear in that position after the shuffle, it is obvious that the ace of hearts is the card the magician wants.

Now suppose he finds the two locating sixes well apart. Beneath the six of spades is the king of clubs; above the six of diamonds is the ace of hearts. He knows that the chosen card is either the king of clubs or the ace of hearts. The magician then uses both those cards in whatever trick he is performing. For instance, he can slide one card to the top of the pack and the other to the bottom. Then he strikes the pack and turns up the top card. If it is recognized as the chosen card, well and good. If not, the magician "remembers" that the blow knocks the card to the bottom—not to the top, so he shows the bottom card to be the chosen one.

4. THE MASTER CARD LOCATION

This trick was highly advertised when it appeared a few years ago and it is still known to only a very few. It is a most convincing method of discovering a chosen card. The pack is shuffled by a spectator. The magician spreads the pack face down. A spectator touches a card. Before he has a chance to remove it, the magician puts the pack right in the spectator's hands and lets him turn up the card while the pack is in his own possession. He does not even remove the card from the pack. Then he cuts the pack as often as he wishes; yet the magician, looking through the pack, learns the name of the selected card.

The operation is quite ingenious. Upon receiving the shuffled pack, the magician notes the bottom card by turning the pack slightly toward himself. He begins to spread the cards from hand to hand. He counts them as he does so. Thus, when the spectator touches a card, the magician knows just how far down it is from the top.

He gives out the pack with impunity. For so long as the spectator cuts the cards with single cuts only, the selected card will always be the same number below the card that was on the bottom of the pack—the number counted from the bottom!

All the magician has to do when he gets the pack is spread the cards with the faces toward himself. He looks for the card he knows (the original bottom card) and counts down to the selected card. If he comes to the bottom of the pack during his count, he continues the count from the top.

Cutting the pack—in single cuts—does not change the rotation and the relationship of the known card to the chosen one will remain a constant number.

In utilizing this card location, the performer should practice counting cards as he spreads them. There is much to be gained by doing the counting in a rapid, smooth manner. With a little practice, it is quite an easy matter to count the spreading cards by threes instead of singly. The magician begins his counting as he tells the spectator to touch any card. As a result, the selected card will be well down in the pack.

If desired, a spectator may be allowed to simply peek at the corner of a card and the magician may slide the cards along further, allowing a choice of a second card. In this case he starts a second count or continues the first one. This is one of the best of all methods for determining the name of a selected card.

5. THE SLIDE OUT

While this form of card location is an old one, it is virtually unknown to the present day magician. We are describing it here, with improvements, because it is a good, reliable method of con-

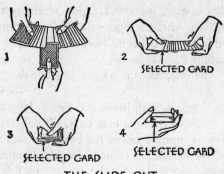

THE SLIDE OUT

(1) Selected card returned to the pack. (2) The selected card drawn beneath the spread. (3) The selected card at the bottom. (4) Final stage of the sleight.

trolling a selected card. It serves the same purpose as Blackstone's "Card Control."*

A certain amount of skill is necessary in the maneuver, as it brings a selected card to the bottom of the pack. Nevertheless, the movements are so natural and so simple that the method is by no means difficult to learn.

Simply spread the pack between the hands and ask that a card be selected. This card is returned to the center of the pack. Then the left thumb draws a few cards to the left so that they cover the selected one, as though making sure that it is lost in the middle of the pack.

The spread, at this juncture, is quite wide. The pack has been opened slightly to admit the return of the chosen card. The right fingers, reaching beneath, slide the chosen card to the right. This

*Explained in Blackstone's "Secrets of Magic."

is hidden by the cards which the left thumb has drawn over the chosen one. A short pull by the right fingers and the chosen card is clear of the pack—beneath it.

Now the pack is closed by bringing the hands together. It is no trick at all to let the selected card glide along the bottom as a free agent until it safely arrives on the bottom of the pack.

The maneuver may be repeated with another selected card— in fact as many cards may be used as required for the particular trick. Each one glides to the bottom. There they may be easily controlled.

Some readers may prefer this system to the Blackstone "Card Control," although the "Card Control" is unquestionably the superior method. It is interesting to compare the two, however, and good results may be obtained by alternating them.

In the "Slide Out," the magician may start to close the spread by pulling a few cards to the left; then he can begin to spread the cards again, telling the chooser to note that his card is actually in the center of the pack.

What the spectator sees is one of the cards which the left thumb drew over. Seeing only the back of the card, he takes it for granted that it is really his card. By diverting attention in this manner, the magician has an excuse for spreading the pack, which facilitates the sliding of the chosen card to the right. Then the pack is closed with a quick movement and the selected card goes to the bottom.

6. THE PUSH THROUGH

A card is selected from the pack. The magician holds the pack in his left hand and squares it so that all the cards are well together. He riffles the outer end of the pack so that the selected card may be inserted. This card projects—so the magician pushes it squarely into the pack.

This being done, he divides the pack into two heaps and proceeds with a dovetail shuffle. Everything is natural—in fact, the magician goes to great pains to show that there is no possible way for him to control the chosen card. Yet that is exactly what he does.

It's all in the "push." When the chosen card is inserted, the end projects, as has been mentioned. The magician pushes the card into the pack; in doing this, he strikes it rather forcibly. As a result, the card now projects from the inner end of the pack, where it cannot be seen by the spectators.

When the pack is divided into two heaps for the shuffle, the magician simply uses the projecting end of the selected card as

THE PUSH THROUGH

Left: Selected card returned and left projecting. Center: The right hand strikes the card into the pack. Right: The chosen card projecting at the back.

a tab by which he can lift the upper portion. In shuffling, he lets this card fall first, thus placing it on the bottom of the pack.

If the cards are held slightly loose, the card will push through more readily. Remember that the strong part of this trick lies in its apparent fairness. It may be done deliberately, with good effect.

7. THE PUSH BACK

A very neat form of location. Riffle the pack and allow a card to be selected. Raise the upper portion of the pack with the right hand so the card may be replaced upon the lower heap. Now comes the important move.

In setting the upper portion on the lower, bring the inner end down first. Let the tip of the right thumb rest upon the chosen card.

As the top portion of the pack is a trifle advanced, the hand is naturally drawn back so that the front edge of the pack will be even. Due to the pressure of the thumb, the chosen card moves backward as this action is performed.

The entire movement is covered by the upper heap. The front of the pack is tilted a trifle upward. The chosen card projects half an inch at the rear of the pack, but it is not observed.

The right hand squares the pack very carefully. With the pack squared and the chosen card presumably safely buried, the per-

THE PUSH BACK

How the right thumb pushes back the top card of the lower heap (the selected card) while placing the upper half of the pack in position.

former is ready to execute the dovetail shuffle. He can bring the selected card either to the top or bottom. For the bottom, he lifts its projecting end when he cuts the pack. For the top, he lifts all cards above the projection.

8. A NEAT LOCATION

A card having been selected, the magician squares the pack and holds it for the reception of the chosen card. He lifts up a large portion of the pack and invites the chooser to return his card. When this is done, the magician drops the rest of the pack on top.

In this natural procedure, he keeps the location of the chosen card. When he drops the upper portion, he lets it fall slightly toward himself, so the upper section projects inward. He immediately tilts the hand forward so the cards slide flush at the front.

But the card directly above the chosen one will not slide forward. It will remain, projecting inward. When the magician shuffles by the dovetail system, he uses this tab to lift off the upper half of the pack.

In shuffling, he lets the top card of the lower half be among the last to fall. It being the selected card, the result is that the performer brings the chosen card to the top of the pack where it is in just the position where he can use it.

9. THE FAN LOCATION

In this location, the pack is fanned or spread in the customary manner for a person to select a card. When it is replaced, the magician uses a very clever subterfuge. He holds the pack fanned

THE FAN LOCATION

Selected card inserted in the fan, is pushed in almost flush. The squaring of the pack leaves it projecting.

rather closely, in the right hand. Thus it is impossible for the spectator to push the card entirely into the pack.

The magician may use his left hand to help—if the spectator pushes the card only about half way in, the performer can remark that it should go farther in, suiting the words with the action.

When the card is nearly in the pack, the magician turns slightly to the left and closes the fan by striking the left edge of the pack against the palm of his left hand. Even though he has pushed the chosen card well in, it will still project slightly. It forms a tab which can be easily located.

Note that at this point, the end of the pack from which the card projects is turned away from the spectators. The magician simply takes the pack and shuffles it in dovetail fashion. He catches the projecting card with his right thumb, separating the pack at that point. Letting the chosen card fall first, puts it on the bottom of the pack, from which position it is easily controlled.

10. A CARD DETECTION

This is a simple method of learning the name of a chosen card. It is particularly useful as it leaves the card in a very advantageous position—on the bottom of the pack, where the magician may learn the name of the card and reveal it as he sees fit.

Give the pack to a spectator. Tell him to shuffle it. Tell him to deal off any number of cards, faces up, one by one, making a heap —and to note the last card dealt. You turn your back while he does this. Suppose he deals eight and the last card is the five of spades. You do not know this and you tell him to replace the cards on the pack, remembering both the card and the number.

You turn away with the pack and work with it a few moments. Then you return it to the spectator, saying that you have mixed the cards but have not discovered the chosen one. Ask him to deal the same number that he dealt before—faces up—but not to remember any new card—to keep the name of the old card constantly in mind.

He does this while your back is turned and you ask him to replace the dealt cards upon the bottom of the pack. He is apt to notice that his card does not appear this time; that is natural, because you mixed the cards.

Again you take the cards and mix them, either by looking at them or by holding them behind your back. Then you discover his card—either by showing it to him on the bottom of the pack or by producing it in some clever manner.

How do you get the card? Simply enough. Suppose the spectator dealt twelve cards and put them on the top; then dealt twelve and put them on the bottom. The twelfth—chosen—card would naturally wind up on the bottom of the pack. That's the way you do the trick—but you do not work it so baldly.

When you first receive the pack, count off a number of cards from the bottom and put them on the top. That is done after the spectator's first deal. Remember the number of cards you use—say sixteen. After the second deal by the spectator, count off the same number of cards—sixteen in this case—but this time take them from the top of the pack and put them on the bottom.

This has the same effect as the simple procedure described above. Perhaps, in reading it, you may think it won't work. But it does work—every time—and that is the beauty of it. Just follow the directions as specified and you will get the chosen card on the bottom of the pack where you want it.

II. THE PICK-UP HEAPS

This is a bold form of card location, but a deceptive one, if properly practiced. The magician divides the pack into three heaps—or allows someone else to do so. A card is selected and placed on one of the heaps. The magician drops that heap on another heap and drops the third heap on top. He appears to bury the selected card in the pack.

Actually, he is bringing the card to the top. It is done this way. Pick up the heap with the chosen card and drop that heap on another heap. As you do so, retain a few of the top cards between the tips of your thumb and fingers. In reaching for the odd heap, simply carry those extra cards along (the chosen card being on top of them) and let them fall on the final heap as you carry it to the pack.

This requires smartness of action, even though no special skill is necessary. There is an important point that adds much. If you intend to use your right hand, make sure that the spectators are mostly to your right. Your hand, tilting slightly in their direction, covers the carried cards very effectively.

If the spectators are on your left, use the left hand to execute the three-heap pick-up.

12. SURPASSO

This is the title of a remarkable card detection that is one of the newest and best ideas in card conjuring. It approaches the impossible when well performed; and the trick is not difficult, although it requires close attention to detail.

Anyone removes a pack of cards from its case and gives the pack a shuffle. Then the person selects a card and puts it face down in the case. Following the magician's instructions, the

SURPASSO·

Left: Selected card is first placed in case. Center: Then the pack itself is inserted. Right: Selected card discovered projecting.

person then inserts the pack, seeing to it that the selected card is buried amongst the others. This is accomplished by making a little space in the pack to receive the chosen card.

The magician takes the case as the spectator closes it and retires to the opposite side of the room. He looks at the case; then at the spectator. He removes the cards from the case, runs through the pack and produces the selected card!

The secret is a simple one. Using the usual style flap case, the pack, when pushed in, has a tendency to shove the single card further down. To make sure of this, the magician should approach and take the pack just as soon as the spectator has the pack well in. If the pack fits the case rather tightly, so much the better.

Across the room, the magician inverts the case and taps the flap end against his hand. This evens the pack a bit. When he removes the pack from the case, the magician grips it firmly and he will discover one card projecting a fraction of an inch from the lower end. That card is the selected card. He takes it from the pack.

The use of the case makes the trick good, because no one can see the projecting card.

13. AN EASY FORCE

This idea has many uses. It is explained here in a simple and effective form. The magician lays a pack on the table. He writes something on a sheet of paper. He asks someone to cut the pack at any point. The paper is laid between the two portions.

AN EASY FORCE

TOP HALF

BOTTOM CARD

TOP HALF

Known card on bottom of pack. Top half removed; lower half placed on it. Bottom card arrives at the center, ready for selection.

When the upper half of the pack is lifted, the spectators are asked to note the card on its face—suppose it is the queen of clubs. The paper is unfolded. It bears the name "queen of clubs."

This is accomplished by simply noting the bottom card of the pack after a shuffle. That is the name which the magician writes on the sheet of paper. It does not matter where the pack is cut. The magician simply picks up the lower half of the pack and completes the cut by dropping it on the top half—but he inserts the sheet of paper as he does so.

Thus it is the bottom card—the known card—which comes on top of the sheet of paper. But the method is so natural and so subtle that persons will be positive the magician put the paper at an unknown spot near the center of the pack.

For ordinary forcing or location purposes, the magician may note secretly the top card of the pack; then ask someone to cut the cards and to complete the cut by leaving the upper portion at an angle. Then a spectator is allowed to look at the card immediately below the break. This is the card that the wizard knows;

but people will not realize it. That card can be discovered later
—after a shuffle.

14. THE JOKER FORCE

This is by no means a new idea; but it is a very useful one. It
enables the magician to learn the name of a card before the card
is drawn.

It begins after a borrowed pack has been shuffled. The magician
takes the pack, turns the bottom card toward himself and remarks
that he must remove the joker. He spreads the cards from the
bottom; when he reaches the joker, he discards it and lays the
pack face down upon the table.

The pack is now cut into three heaps. Choice is given of one.
The top card of the heap is noted by a spectator. Strange though
it may seem, the magician knows that card and no matter how
often the pack may be shuffled he can always look through and
find it.

The trick begins with the removal of the joker. As he runs
through the bottom cards of the pack, in his search for the joker,
the magician slyly slides the top card a trifle to the left—just far
enough so he can see its index corner. After removing the joker,
he squares the pack and divides it into three heaps. He lifts off
two-thirds of the face-down pack and places the large upper
portion to the right of the lower. He then lifts half of the upper
portion and puts it between the two heaps.

This tricky cut is seldom noticed. It puts the top of the pack in
the middle of the heaps, although one would normally suppose
the top portion was at the right.

When the magician asks that a heap be chosen, the spectator
usually obliges by taking the center one. He is told to look at the
top card of the heap—the very card that the magician knows.

Suppose that the center heap is not chosen? Very well. The
magician tells the person who takes an end heap to remove it.
Then he remarks that there are two heaps left. One must be
eliminated. Which does the person want?

If the desired heap is touched, the magician says: "You want that one? Well, that eliminates this one." If the wrong heap is indicated, the magician's response is: "So that's the one you want eliminated. Well, that leaves this one."

An interesting trick performed by the joker force is to ascribe wonderful powers to the joker itself—a good excuse for removing it from the pack. When the center heap is chosen (whether the spectator wants it or not!) the magician tells the chooser to push the top card off the heap and on to the table.

Then the card is touched with the joker. The magician pretends to hold conversation with the joker. It tells him the name of the card and the magician announces that name. To prove the joker was correct, he uses the joker to flip the single card face up on the table and the statement is seen to be true.

15. THE FORCE LOCATION

This form of card location involves a simple type of card force. It is designed to work to the performer's advantage whether or not the right card is actually selected by the spectator.

Briefly, the magician spreads the pack and asks that a card be selected. This card is removed and replaced in the pack, which is fairly closed. The magician later discovers or names the selected card.

The first thing the magician does is to note the bottom card of the pack. He draws off the lower portion and transfers it to the top, keeping the two sections slightly apart so that he can handle the known card.

In spreading the pack, he pushes this card a trifle forward so that it projects more than the others and is the logical card which the average person would select. If that card is taken, well and good. Everything is as the magician wishes it.

Now suppose the known card is not selected. In most instances the chooser will pick a card quite close to it. The magician can visually count to the card that the spectator draws. It may, for example, be three cards below the known one—or five cards above. It may often be the card next to the known one.

Under such circumstances, the magician says to the spectator: "Don't remove the card from the pack—just look at its corner." This enables the magician to close the pack, holding the chosen card at its relative position from the known one. Needless to say, the chosen card may be easily discovered by looking for the known card and counting to it. The pack is not shuffled—unless a false method is used.

Should the spectator pick a card well away from the card which the magician desired to force, another procedure is available. The performer lets the spectator take the card clear of the deck. When it is about to be replaced, the wizard raises the pack at the known card, forming a space for the return of the selected one.

This brings the chosen card next to the known card and the matter of locating the chosen card is simplified. In a great percentage of cases, the known card will be the one selected and in such instances, this additional action is not necessary.

Nevertheless, it gives the magician an excellent way of avoiding the embarrassment that follows the selection of the wrong card when a force is attempted. The old style procedure was to do another trick when the force missed; but it is much more satisfactory to utilize the forcing card as a locator when the emergency calls for it.

16. BEHIND THE BACK

This is an excellent method for forcing a card. The magician holds a shuffled pack behind his back. He lets a person lift off some cards. The magician asks that the next card be noted. This is done. The card is then replaced; the pack is shuffled by the audience..Nevertheless, the magician knows the name of the card.

He manages this by removing the card from the pack *before* he begins the trick. If the magician simply wants to know the name of any card that the audience may take, he removes any card and notes its identity. If he wants a certain card taken, he removes that card from the pack. The magician tucks this card beneath his belt, behind his back, the face of the card being outward.

Tricks are performed while that card is missing from the pack, no one realizing that it is absent. When the performer wishes to have the card selected, he turns his back and tells someone to put the pack face down in his left hand; then to lift a number of cards.

As soon as the cards are raised, the magician swings toward the spectator, with some pertinent remark, such as: "You took off some cards, didn't you?" This hides the left hand momentarily. Raising the hand to his belt, the magician draws away the hidden card so that it lies on top of the cards that are in his left hand.

Turning away again, the magician extends his left hand behind his back and asks the spectator to look at the next card—that is, the card now on top of the left hand packet. Inasmuch as it is totally impossible for the magician to have seen the card, there is no suspicion. This card is noted; then the pack is shuffled.

In brief, the magician has simply added his held-out card in such a way that it is logically selected and he can proceed with the trick without danger of detection.

This method can be used in a different way, however. When the spectator lifts a bunch of cards, the magician can turn and tell him to glance at the bottom card of the group he has taken. While the spectator is doing so, the magician adds the extra card. Turning his back, he asks that the spectator's group be replaced. This is done. The chosen card is now directly above the card that the performer knows. Hence the discovery of the selected card is not a difficult matter.

In this method, the pack should be cut a few times behind the magician's back—not shuffled. This is merely a variation of the forcing idea and is mentioned because it has occasional use.

17. THE GLIMPSE

This maneuver is aptly named, because in practice, the magician glimpses the index corner of a card after it has been returned to the pack. Thus learning the name of the card, he can allow the pack to be shuffled, yet can find it when he wants it.

First Method: Simply insert the left little finger beneath the card after it has been returned to the pack. The finger is at the right, inner corner. Raise the upper portion of the pack slightly and shift it a trifle to the left. At the same time bring the left edge of the pack straight up. Note the index corner with a downward glance and immediately close the pack, removing the little finger from between the two portions.

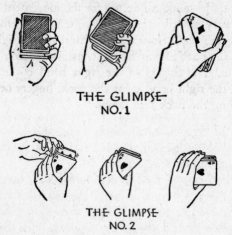

THE GLIMPSE
NO. 1

THE GLIMPSE
NO. 2

The methods of glimpsing a card in the center of the pack are depicted here.

Second Method: Riffle the front edge of the pack and ask a person to insert his finger. When he does so, tell him to note the card above his finger. Let the rest of the pack fall with a quick riffle, but press the ball of your left forefinger against the outer right corner so a space remains there.

The left thumb, on top of the pack, pushes the upper portion a trifle to the right as the left hand turns the pack face up, toward yourself. This gives you a glimpse of the selected card and the right hand immediately takes the pack, bottom up, closing the space. The right hand offers the pack to a spectator for shuffling.

Third Method: This is for sighting the top card of the pack, after the cards have been shuffled. It is useful in certain tricks.

Hold the pack in the left hand. The fingers are beneath; the thumb is across the top.

During a gesture of the left hand, the thumb pushes the top card a fraction of an inch to the right and a trifle forward. The left hand turns the end of the pack almost straight up and the index corner of the top card is sighted.

A good finish to this movement is to square the pack by tapping it upon the table—a logical excuse for the movement of the pack.

Another way of utilizing this glimpse is to perform it while transferring the pack from the left hand to the right. The left hand turns the pack almost face upward, the thumb pushing the top card out. The fingers of the right hand cover the tell-tale corner and the right hand grips the pack, fingers below, thumb above, turning the pack face down.

CHAPTER III

CARD DISCOVERIES

AFTER A CARD has been selected and replaced in the pack, the performer naturally discovers it in order to complete the trick which he is exhibiting.

The simplest form of card discovery is to pick the card out of the pack. That is effective when the spectators are sure that the magician has no way of finding the card. To discover one card out of a possible fifty-two is a good trick in itself.

But to get effective results in card magic, the performer should utilize various surprising methods of producing a chosen card after it has been lost in the pack. Such methods are known as card discoveries.

This section includes a list of effective discoveries following the selection of a card. The reader may choose those which interest him the most and by using them in connection with locations, he will be able to form a most surprising repertoire.

The usual steps before a card discovery are: the selection of a card; its replacement; its control or location by a method known to the magician; the shuffling of the pack (by false shuffles or cuts). Then the stage is set for the surprising appearance of the selected card.

I. THE KNOCK OUT

An effective conclusion to a card trick. This method is well-known, but is mentioned here because it is always good and also because of its variations. Note the points of difference in the methods.

The magician holds the pack in his left hand. He strikes it with his right or allows a spectator to perform that action. The result: the only card that remains in the magician's hand is the one that was selected beforehand by a spectator.

First Method: The selected card is brought to the bottom of the pack. Hold the pack firmly in the left hand, fingers beneath and thumb on top. Hold it at one corner. The pack is face down. When the cards are struck, all are knocked from the hand except the bottom (selected) card.

Second Method: This time the selected card is brought to the top of the pack, which is held face up. The blow works the same, but the selected card is face up, staring at the spectators. This is a better effect.

Third Method: The card is brought to the top. The pack is held face downward. The spectator is asked to strike the pack *upward*. As a result, cards are scattered everywhere. The magician's hand goes upward with the blow so that only the selected card remains, facing the spectators.

2. CARD FROM THE POCKET

This is an old method of discovering a selected card; but it is given here with a puzzling addition. The pack is placed in the performer's inside pocket. Someone is told to reach in and draw out a card. He does so—and he brings out the selected card!

The answer is that the selected card is on top of the pack. By hurrying the person, the magician causes him to draw off the top card—the only one which he can easily and naturally grasp. The top of the pack is outward in the pocket.

Now for the improvement. Two selected cards. The magician shuffles the pack and puts it in his pocket. Reaching in, he draws out one of the selected cards.

Then, as an added feature, he takes the pack from his pocket and lets anyone shuffle it. Back it goes in the pocket. A spectator is told to seize a card from the pack. He does so—out comes the second selected card!

How does the magician get around the shuffle? Simply enough.

He has both selected cards on top. He draws out one himself. When he brings out the pack to be shuffled, he leaves the other selected card in his pocket. It goes on top of the pack again, when the magician replaces the pack. That's why the grabbing spectator gets it.

3. ANY NUMBER

Here we make a chosen card appear at any number in the pack after the pack has been shuffled. Suppose nine is the number given. The chosen card is on top of the pack, brought there by the magician. He counts off nine cards one by one—this count reversed their order. He shows the ninth card. It is not the chosen one. So the performer puts the nine cards back on the pack.

He recalls that he forgot the magic riffle. So he riffles the pack and again counts to nine. Due to the reversed order, the chosen card shows up at the required number—in this instance, just nine cards from the top of the pack.

Now for an improvement on the old idea. Suppose nine is given, with the chosen card on top. Count off eight (reversing their order). Drop the ninth on the table and ask the person to look at it. While attention is directed there, the eight cards are brought back to the pack by the right hand. The right fingers push the chosen card forward. The left hand, tilting to the right, allows the card to come face-up on the rest of the pack; rather, the left hand puts the pack face down on the chosen card. Swinging to its normal position, the left hand receives the other cards on top of the pack, as they should be.

The performer does this automatically. It is all finished by the time the spectator has discovered that the ninth card is not the one he selected. So the magician puts that card on top of the pack and resorts to his magic riffle.

Then comes the surprise. Counting slowly to nine, the magician reveals the chosen card at the desired number and furthermore the chosen card is face up—just a little token of the potency of the wizard's riffle!

One important fact should be noted—for this trick and all

others that involve reversed cards. Only perform such effects with packs that have a white margin on the backs. Otherwise, there will be difficulty. Most good packs have the required white margins.

Any slight unevenness of the pack will not betray a reversed card, if white margins are used. But with packs that have a design running solid to the border, reversed card tricks should be avoided.

4. A REVERSED CARD

A card having been selected and returned to the pack, the magician starts a search for it. He finds a card and lays it face upward on top of the pack.

"That's your card, isn't it?" he asks.

"No," is the reply.

"What!" exclaims the mystifier. "Not the six of spades? I'll have to try again."

He removes the seven of diamonds and thrusts it back into the pack, which he shuffles. Then he turns the pack face downward and spreads it. One card appears face up. It proves to be the card selected.

The Method: The magician easily finds the chosen card by whatever system he chooses to use. But he draws it from the pack in back of the six of spades—that is, he holds the two cards as one and instantly lays them face upward on top of the pack.

Finding that the six of spades is not correct, the magician tilts the pack upward so that only the faces of cards can be seen. He takes the six of spades from the top of the pack and puts it properly among the other cards.

But this time, he manages the six of spades alone—leaving the chosen card face up on top of the pack. A short easy shuffle—keeping the faces of the cards toward the spectators—puts the chosen card in the midst of the pack—face up, ready for the finish.

5. ONE REVERSED CARD

An easy reversed card trick, depending upon one simple move which can be made slowly without fear of detection. A chosen card is brought to the top of the pack. The magician shuffles with

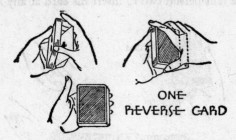

ONE
REVERSE CARD

Movements of shifting the top card of the pack so it lies face up on the bottom.

the faces of the cards toward the spectators and he keeps the chosen card on top of the pack.

Completing the shuffle, he grips the top card with the fingers of his left hand. At the same time, the right hand (thumb at one end, fingers at the other) lifts the pack a trifle upward and forward and turns it face down.

The left hand goes flat as the pack is turned, so the magician simply lays the pack on that single, face-up card. All that is now necessary is to cut the pack; then spread it on the table. The chosen card will be seen face up in the midst of the face-down cards.

6. THREE REVERSED CARDS

This is a very bewildering card trick. The magician apparently causes three selected cards to reverse themselves so they lie faces up at different parts of the pack.

The first card selected is brought to the top of the pack. The magician places it face up on the bottom (as described in the preceding "One Reversed Card" trick). He leaves the card on the bottom.

Now he spreads the pack (watching the bottom card) and has two more cards taken, by persons well apart. Squaring the pack he walks from person three to person two. As he does so, he turns the pack over in his left hand, so the single card is face up on bottom. He tells person two to insert his card at any spot, calling

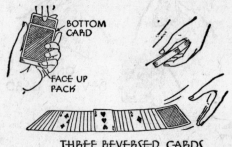

THREE REVERSED CARDS

Upper Left: How the pack is held face up, with one selected card inverted upon it. Second card is being inserted.
Upper Right: Third selected card projecting on the top of pack.
Bottom: The result—three cards faces up.

attention to the fact that the pack is squared so the card's position cannot be noted. The card goes in face down. Thus, like the card on the bottom, it is inverted or reversed.

Going back to person three, the magician, with a swing of his hand, brings the real top of the pack uppermost again. He lifts a few cards off with his right hand and transfers them to the bottom, saying: "When I cut like this, put your card on."

Lifting a few more, the magician allows the placement of the third chosen card. He drops the right hand cards upon it and immediately brings the card to the top of the pack.*

The result now is that one chosen card is on top of the pack. The others are reversed but buried. The magician holds the pack across his right hand, with the thumb on top. He pushes the top

*The "Revolving Pass" is useful at this point.

card slightly forward and lets the pack slide along the table—or better, along the floor.

This maneuver, if properly done, causes the top card to turn over on the pack, due to the air pressure. It travels along with the pack and seems to bob out from some unexpected spot. At the same time, the spreading pack reveals the other two chosen cards, each lying face up amidst the pack.

It looks like a triple reverse and the fact that the cards are far apart has a marked effect upon those who witness it. This trick should be carefully rehearsed, as it contains many points that must be remembered, even though it has been simplified in method so that any performer of ordinary ability can demonstrate it without recourse to unusual dexterity.

7. OUT OF THE HAT

This is a great finish for a card trick. Cards are selected and replaced in the pack, which is shuffled. The magician handles the deck a while; then spies a felt hat, into which he drops the pack. He holds the hat with the brim upward. He flips the crown of the hat with his forefinger. Out come the selected cards, sailing toward the ceiling!

There is no great difficulty in this trick. It may be performed with one or more selected cards. They are brought to the top of the pack or to the bottom. In either instance, the magician is set for the hat trick. When he drops the pack into the hat, he keeps the opening of the hat toward himself. He lets the pack go into one section of the hat; but he retains the selected cards and slides them into the other section of the hat.

Holding the hat above the spectators' line of vision, the magician makes a sharp flip against the crown of the hat. But he chooses the side where the selected cards are located. The force of the flip causes the cards to fly out of the hat in a most mysterious fashion. The hat is immediately tilted forward and the rest of the pack is allowed to slide out on the table.

8. BLACKSTONE'S CUT TRICK

This is one of the finest of all card discoveries. Two cards are selected by the audience. The magician shuffles the pack after the cards are returned. He riffles the end of the pack and asks a third person to insert another card, face upward, at any point in the pack.

This is done. The third person retains his hold on the face-up card. The magician withdraws the entire pack, with the exception

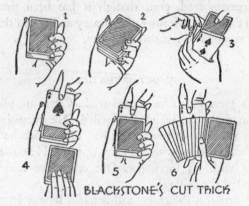

BLACKSTONE'S CUT TRICK

(1) Pack with one chosen card on top; other on bottom.
(2) Pack cut. Little finger retains the break.
(3) Riffling for the face-up insertion of an odd card.
(4) Drawing off from the break, showing face-up card.
(5) Top half replaced upon the lower.
(6) Pack spread to find inserted card between chosen ones.

of two cards—the one above the inserted card and the one below.

Holding these three cards, the conjuror calls for the names of the selected cards. The names given, he turns over the three cards in his hand. This reveals the two selected cards! The spectator has thrust his face-up card between them!

The Secret: The two selected cards are first received in the pack and one is brought to the top; the other to the bottom. This is done by a card location system and is aided by false shuffles.

Now the magician cuts the pack by drawing off some of the bottom cards, to the rear, with his right hand. He puts the lower half on the upper half. This brings the selected cards together, but the left little finger holds a space between them. The cut should be made so that the two cards are fairly near the bottom of the pack as it now stands.

Riffling the pack at the outer end (with the right fingers) the magician invites the insertion of the odd face-up card. If it happens to go in the space between the two selected cards, well and good. But the magician is riffling rapidly to reach that space and the card often goes in above it.

With his right hand, the magician simply grips the upper portion of the pack (all cards above the break held by the left little finger). His right thumb is below; fingers above. He draws back the entire portion of the pack until it is free of the face-up card which the spectator is holding. Then he slaps that portion down upon the face-up card.

This movement is natural, sure and undetectable. It brings one chosen card directly above the inserted card; the other directly beneath. The rest of the pack is spread out and drawn away, leaving only the three cards—two selected and one inserted between them.

The same trick can be performed with the aid of a knife, which is inserted instead of a face-up card. The procedure is exactly the same, the knife-blade serving as the indicator in this instance.

9. CARD IN CIGAR BOX

A great trick. A chosen card is replaced in the pack, which the magician shuffles. The wizard then empties some cigars from an ordinary cigar box. He shows the box empty. He closes it and lays the pack on it. A mystic pass; the box is opened—the card is round therein.

The card actually goes into the cigar box—but before the spectators suppose. The magician gets it to the top of the pack. He palms it off and in going to the cigar box, keeps the card in readiness. The cigars are emptied—in drops the card from the wizard's palm.

The regulation cigar box is lined with paper—and the paper overlaps along the bottom. When the magician drops the card in the box, his hands are free and as he picks up the box to show it to the spectators, he tilts it so the selected card slides under the overlapping paper.

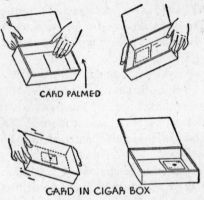

CARD PALMED

CARD IN CIGAR BOX

The diagrams illustrate the routine of the card in the cigar box.

This enables him to show the box absolutely empty and to let the spectators close the box. When the box is shut, the magician sets it on the table, tilting it as he does so. The card drops from its hiding place. It is then in the box, ready for its mysterious appearance.

By using a duplicate card, the magician can have one already hidden in the box. He must then force that card upon the audience and later remove it from the pack.

10. CARD ELIMINATION

A card having been selected and returned to the pack, the magician offers to determine its identity by a process of elimination.

He takes eight cards and holds them faces down. Showing each card, he deals four on the table. None is the selected one. He deals two of these on the table. Neither is the one chosen. Then one card is left; it proves to be the chosen card.

This trick depends upon the sleight called the "glide."* The selected card is actually among the eight—which the magician does not show. The card is second from the bottom.

Here is the procedure. Holding the cards faces down, the magician shows the bottom card and asks if it is the chosen one. The spectator says that it is not. So the magician apparently deals it face down on the table. Actually he makes use of the "glide" and the chosen card is the one dealt.

The performer says he will put the next card back in the pack, eliminating it. So he draws off the bottom card of those in the little packet and replaces it on the pack without showing it. He shows the next card, however, and actually deals it face down. Then another on the pack, alternating thus, so there are four cards faces down on the table—the chosen card among them.

The magician gathers the four cards and sees to it that the selected card is again second from the bottom. He shows the bottom card and apparently deals it. Actually the chosen card is dealt—the "glide" again. The bottom card is then replaced, unshown, upon the pack. The next card is shown and dealt face down. The fourth goes into the pack.

The elimination has left only two cards—neither of which is supposed to be the chosen one. The spectators are wondering what the magician is about. He asks a person to place a hand on either card. Suppose the person touches the chosen card. The magician picks up the other card, shows its face and says: "Of course this is not your card," and replaces it in the pack. That leaves only one card. Turned up, it proves to be the chosen one.

Of course there is a possibility that the spectator will decide to touch the card which the magician wishes to eliminate. That makes no difference. He is simply told to turn up the card and look at it—not the chosen card, of course. It is put in the pack. That leaves just one card—which proves to be the chosen one.

*Explained in Section One.

Artfully done, this trick is surprising at the finish, because the performer seems to be dealing with cards other than the chosen one. The appearance of the selected card comes as a real bit of amazement. The trick must be done neatly—but very little skill is needed.

CHAPTER IV

SPELLING TRICKS

THE ORIGINAL spelling tricks were simply "spelling bees" performed with a set of cards. Then came the use of the spelling idea for the discovery of a chosen card.

There are now various good tricks which involve the spelling of a chosen card and this section includes the best of them. It logically follows card discoveries as some of the spellers are discoveries in themselves.

Others form complete tricks, from beginning to end, including the location of the card which is to be spelled. This section represents the latest development in up-to-date card magic.

The spelling trick is so novel that it invariably calls for a repetition; hence the various methods given will be useful as they enable the magician to employ the spelling in different ways.

The novel application of the spelling principle, revealing a selected card by dealing with each letter of the name, will be appreciated fully through a careful perusal of the tricks in this section. They show how the spelling method simplifies certain tricks instead of complicating them.

I. SIMPLICITY SPELLER

This begins like the usual card trick. The magician takes a pack of cards and spreads it between his hands, running the cards from left to right. He asks a person to select a card and to remove it from the pack. That having been done, the magician lifts some cards so that the chosen one may be replaced.

Riffling the pack, the magician states that he will make the card choose its own position. He asks the spectator to name the card. We will suppose that it is the five of hearts. The magician commences to deal the cards, spelling: "F-I-V-E-O-F- H-E-A-R-T-S—" a letter for each card. With the final "S," he turns up the card. It proves to be the five of hearts.

The important method of the trick is quite simple. In running the cards from the left hand to the right, the magician counts them. He does not give anyone a chance to take a card until he has run eleven cards along the fan. He pushes the cards more slowly after the eleventh, keeping a slight space between the eleventh card and the twelfth.

When a card is removed, the magician invites its replacement, by lifting the eleven cards at the top of the pack. As a result, the selected card takes the position of number twelve.

Now it is not at all difficult to spell to the chosen card after it is named. Simply count the letters to oneself. If the card is spelled with eleven letters, spell it and turn up the twelfth. If twelve letters, end the spelling on the twelfth. With thirteen letters, leave out the word "O-F." Example: queen of hearts. Spell: "Q-U-E-E-N-H-E-A-R-T-S" and turn up the next card. With fourteen letters, leave out the word "O-F" and turn up the card with the final letter of the spelling.

There remain only two possibilities: ten-letter cards and fifteen-letter cards. These are a minority. With a ten-letter card, the magician turns the top card of the pack face up and appears surprised because it is not the chosen card. He lays that card aside; thinks a moment; then brightens and spells the name of the card, turning up the card after the last letter.

With a fifteen-letter card, the magician spells very slowly. He says (for example): "Your card was the seven of diamonds? I shall spell 'S-E-V-E-N.' The suit? A diamond? Very well: 'D-I-A-M-O-N-D'."

He turns up the card on the final "D" and reveals it as the seven of diamonds. Thus by a little ingenuity, the chosen card can be spelled every time. This is one of the most practical and effective versions of the spelling trick. It requires some amount of rehearsal in order to be presented convincingly, but the actual skill involved is negligible.

2. SPREAD-OUT SPELLER

There is a certain similarity between this effect and the trick we have called the "Simplicity Speller." The reader should compare the two methods, for a reason which will be mentioned later.

A shuffled pack is spread along the table. A card is chosen from any spot. Only the person selecting it sees it. The card is

SPREAD OUT SPELLER

Noting thirteen cards above selected one. Making break at that point. Shifting extra cards to bottom. Also the final position.

replaced from where it was taken. The performer picks up the pack and requests the name of the card. He spells the name, dealing a card with each letter. The spelling ends by the turning up of the chosen card.

It is all a matter of careful counting. The pack is spread clear along the table. As soon as the spectator touches a card, the magician counts along the line to a spot thirteen cards above the chosen one (beginning the count with the touched card).

As the spectator replaces the card he took, the magician still keeps his eye upon the place to which he has counted. He has spread the cards from left to right. Sliding them up with his left hand, he holds a break with his left thumb when he reaches the spot to which he has counted. The right hand simply transfers all cards above the break, putting them on the bottom of the pack.

Thus the chosen card is thirteen from the top. The wizard asks its name and spells in such a manner that he ends with the chosen card.

For instance, if the card has only ten letters, he adds the word "T-H-E" before it. Example: "T-H-E-A-C-E-O-F-C-L-U-B-S." With eleven letters, he removes the top card from the pack, strikes the pack with it, and thrusts the card into the pack at the center. This by-play disposes of an odd card. It leaves only twelve to deal. The magician spells with eleven cards and turns up the *next* card.

Twelve letters is a simple spelling, turning up the next card; thirteen letters spells right to the card itself. With fourteen letters, eliminate the word "O-F" and turn up the card after the spelling. With fifteen letters, eliminate "O-F" and turn up on the final letter.

There is another method of gathering up the cards from the table—simply a variation of the one described. Sweep them up with the right hand until the desired spot is reached. Then transfer those cards to the left hand and use them as a lever to gather up the cards from left to right. This puts the chosen card thirteen from the top.

In comparing this method with the "Simplicity Speller," note that here the chosen card is set at thirteen; with the other method, it is set at twelve. There is no reason why the reader should not adopt one standard for both methods. Either keep the chosen card twelve from the top or put it thirteen from the top and act accordingly. Both systems are explained here, to show how flexible the spelling can be.

3. FOUR HEAP SPELLER

This is one of the most interesting versions of the spelling trick. It can be demonstrated with an ease of action that defies detection. It requires boldness more than skill.

A spectator is asked to shuffle a pack of cards and to cut it in half. He is then requested to cut each half into two equal portions. The result: four heaps.

He is told to look at the top card of any heap and to place it on any other heap. This done, the magician gathers the heaps, burying the chosen card in the pack.

The card is named. The magician proceeds to deal cards off, faces upward, spelling a letter as he deals each card. "F-O-U-R-O-F-H-E-A-R-T-S—" he spells and on the letter "S" he is holding the four of hearts!

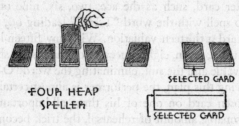

FOUR HEAP SPELLER

SELECTED CARD

SELECTED CARD

Left: Division of pack in four equal heaps. Right: One heap placed on selected card. Final position before the spelling.

It so happens that the separation of the pack into four approximately equal heaps puts about thirteen cards in each heap. Thus, when a card is selected from the top of a heap, it is quite possible to put that card just about thirteen from the top when the heaps are gathered. Merely drop a single heap upon the chosen card.

Let us suppose, by way of example, that the chosen card is just about thirteen from the top of the pack—the exact location being unknown. When the cards are spelled, they are dropped faces up, each letter being given just before the card is tilted into view.

The count, or spelling, is rapid at first, but it slows appreciably. "F-O-U-R-O-F-D-I--A--M--O--N--D—"

On the final "D," we have reached the zone of the selected card. If it turns up on the letter "D," the magician smiles and holds the card out for all to see. He has completed the spelling! If it does not show up, he drops the card; then, he deals another card saying "S." This is likely to be the chosen card—if so, the trick is done. If it is not the chosen card, he simply drops it and deals off the *next* card very decisively, turning it up to reveal it as the four of diamonds.

In brief, the magician has *three chances* of hitting the chosen card and any one will bring the trick to a successful finish.

It is wise, in picking up the heaps, to drop a slightly undersized heap on the chosen card. The heaps should be almost equal. They seldom are exact, however. It is advisable to put *ten* or *eleven* cards on top, in preference to a larger number.

The magician must act carefully when he begins to spell. With any ten-letter card, such as the ace, two, six, nine of clubs, he does best to spell with the word "T-H-E" leading off, giving the particular card a thirteen valuation. With any fifteen-letter card, such as the three, seven, eight, queen of diamonds, he should spell simply the value and the suit, eliminating the word "O-F."

By following this plan, the performer is almost certain of striking the chosen card on one of his three all-important chances. With a reasonable amount of rehearsal, the trick becomes almost certain of success. The performer may, if he wishes, form the four heaps himself, thus increasing the chances of exactness.

The four heap speller may be extended by having two cards selected and placing the heap with one selected card upon the heap that has the other. Then a heap on top of both. This leaves everything set to spell to the second card after the discovery of the first. This additional effect should only be utilized when the heaps are almost identical in size, as it is then possible to depend upon the number thirteen.

There is another way of using the four heap idea. Tell a person to cut the pack in half; then lift half of the top portion and glance at a card, replacing the cards just as they were. Then the pack is taken by the magician who spells to the chosen card. This is simply an artifice that causes the spectator to look at either the thirteenth card or a card about thirteen from the top of the pack. The dealing and spelling are the same as in the four heap method.

4. EASY SPELLING TRICK

This is simply a new form of an old card-counting trick. Nevertheless, it makes a good speller. The effect is that a chosen card is returned to the pack. The magician asks its name. He spells it, a card being dealt for each letter. He turns up the last card of the deal. It is not the chosen card.

Perplexed, the wizard recalls that he forgot to riffle the pack. He does so. More than that, he puts the pack in the hands of the person who chose the card and lets him do the spelling. This time it arrives on the chosen card.

The chosen card is on the top of the pack when the first spelling begins. It is brought there by whatever method the performer prefers. In spelling, the performer peels off the cards one by one, holding each face down. He draws the second card on to the first; the third on to the second and so on.

Of course the spelling does not work; but when the dealt off cards are put back on the top, it is all set, for the chosen card is now the bottom of the dealt group instead of the top. The performer has reversed their order in spelling so when the spectator goes over the ground, his spelling ends upon the selected card.

5. THE MENTAL SPELLER

The magician takes a pack of cards and opens it some distance from the top, spreading a series of cards so that they come into view when the front of the pack is fanned before a spectator's eyes.

The onlooker is told to make a mental selection of any card. The wizard closes the pack and riffles it. He asks the name of the card. Whatever it may be, the magician promptly spells to the chosen card. He may then repeat the trick with another person.

The secret lies in the special arrangement of seven cards. It will be noted that each of these cards is spelled with a different number of letters; the sixth and seventh are the same, but there is a simple way of giving an extra value to the seventh.

S-I-X-O-F-C-L-U-B-S	10 letters
A-C-E-O-F-H-E-A-R-T-S	11 letters
Q-U-E-E-N-O-F-C-L-U-B-S	12 letters
E-I-G-H-T-O-F-S-P-A-D-E-S	13 letters
K-I-N-G-O-F-D-I-A-M-O-N-D-S	14 letters
S-E-V-E-N-O-F-D-I-A-M-O-N-D-S	15 letters
T-H-R-E-E-O-F-D-I-A-M-O-N-D-S *	16 letters

The asterisk (*) indicates that a card is turned up *after* the spelling is completed. In the other instances, the spelling ends with the final letter in the name of the card.

Based on this simple formula, the magician is ready to mystify.

He arranges his seven pet cards and places nine indifferent cards upon them. The entire group goes on top of the deck. Performing, the magician casually counts nine cards down and spreads the pack at that point, so when he turns the faces toward the audience, only seven cards are in view—the seven arranged cards.

It makes no difference which one is selected. The magician simply spells to it. Ten spelled letters arrive on the six of clubs; eleven on the ace of hearts; and so on—the only special instance being the three of diamonds. If it is the chosen card, the magician spells his deal and turns up the next card after he has completed.

Of course the trick can be repeated. This can be done with the same setup. It is an excellent idea, however, to have another group of cards arranged. Place nine indifferent cards under the three of diamonds; then set: ten of clubs, two of spades, seven of clubs, queen of hearts, jack of diamonds, three of diamonds, queen of diamonds.

After spelling to the chosen card of the first group, casually drop those cards aside; also the few more that may remain in the group. Again bunch nine cards at the top of the pack and give selection of the second setup.

It is merely a repetition of the trick. When only one group is being used, any borrowed pack may be quickly arranged as there are various options: ace of spades will answer for ten of hearts; three of spades for eight of spades, etc.

This cannot be regarded as a trick with a prearranged pack because the actual preparation is such a simple matter and may often be done in the course of other tricks. Even if the magician should pick his own cards, and someone comment upon the fact, he can easily explain it as a problem of psychology, stating that he will cause a person to pick a certain card, even against his will.

The "Mental Speller" is quite different from most of the other spelling effects and forms an excellent variation that will create much favorable comment among those who witness its performance.

6. THE PROGRESSIVE SPELLER

This form of the spelling trick requires some arrangement of the cards. That, however, should not detract from the effect, especially when the trick is presented at a small gathering where the magician appears as a special performer.

Several persons are handed packets of cards. Each is told to remember one card. The magician gathers each packet. He places all on the pack. He calls upon one spectator to name his card. This done, the magician spells to the card exactly. The effect is repeated with each of the other persons.

We have stated that "several" persons are handed "packets" of cards. In practice, the number of persons is exactly four; and there are just five cards in each heap. These cards are arranged progressively for spelling, as in the "Mental Speller."

Group 1: jack of clubs, four of hearts, queen of spades, five of diamonds, eight of diamonds.

Group 2: ten of hearts, eight of clubs, seven of spades, jack of diamonds, seven of diamonds.

Group 3: two of spades, queen of clubs, ten of diamonds, king of diamonds, three of diamonds.

Group 4: ace of hearts, king of spades, eight of hearts, four of diamonds, queen of diamonds.

These heaps are on top of the pack. If the magician indulges in cuts or shuffles before dealing, he must use false ones that do not disturb the order of the twenty cards. He goes to four different persons, dealing five to each in turn. He fans the cards for a selection and has the person hold his cards just as given to him—face down, after the mental selection.

Finishing with the four persons, the magician casually counts off two more groups of five, both as one, while he is talking. He is about to move to another person when he decides that four are enough. Holding the ten extra cards in his right hand, he presents the pack so that each person holding five can replace his group of cards. The magician remembers the order of the persons as they return their packets.

Noting the cards in his right hand, he throws them on the pack and gives the pack a riffle or a false cut. He calls upon the last person who returned the packet to name his chosen card. Given, the performer spells to it. The presence of the ten cards on top enables the magician to spell exactly to the mentally selected card, no matter which one of the five happened to be taken.

All dealt cards are immediately put back on the pack. The magician picks off the top five, fans them and reminds his audience that the selected card was chosen mentally from a group. He slides the five fanned cards to the bottom of the pack. He is now set to spell the card chosen by the third replacer, as he has ten indifferent cards upon that particular person's packet.

Repeating his previous maneuver, so as to replace ten cards, the magician spells the second replacer's card; and finally the first man's card.

This trick will be readily understood by experiment with the actual cards and the magician who uses it will find that it can be worked up to an excellent effect. It may be improved or varied by the use of a few false shuffles and great importance should be laid upon the fact that each chooser takes his card mentally from a group.

This trick is suitable for presentation with giant cards and should make a very fine showing on a small platform or stage. It is not essential to place the cards in the spectators' hands, although that facilitates matters when working with cards of ordinary size, at close range.

7. A SPELLING TRICK

This is an addition to a simple routine of spelling. The original arrangement is one used by Jack Gwynne, the well-known professional magician, who presents it as a short story with cards.

The performer offers to show just how the cards tell their own story. He takes a pack from his pocket and deals the cards faces down, one by one, spelling: "A-C-E--" turning up the third card to lay it aside. It is an ace. Continuing, he spells "T-W-O"—turning up a card and laying it aside on the letter "O." It is a two. He continues thus, turning up a three, a four, and so on. With "J-A-C-K--" he turns up a jack. With "Q-U-E-E-N--" and queen; and on the last letter—the "G" of "K-I-N-G"—he turns up a king, the final card of the pack!

Now for the addition. Thirteen cards are lying faces up, in order from ace up to king. The rest of the pack is back up, the cards together as they have been dealt one on the other. Picking up the face-up cards, the magician turns them face down and lays the packet on the other cards. He remarks that he has spelled values; he will now spell suits also.

"Take a king," he says. "The highest card—and hearts as a suit."

He deals the cards face down, spelling "K-I-N-G-O-F-H-E-A-R-T-S." He turns up the *next* card. It is the king of hearts.

"There are four suits," says the magician. "Four from king is nine. We have hearts; let's try diamonds—the nine of diamonds."

He spells the name of the card, dealing with it. He turns up the next card after the spelling. It is the nine of diamonds.

"Now for the blacks. Four from nine is five. We'll aim for the five of clubs."

The spelling follows. Right after the "S" the magician turns up the five of clubs.

"We have one more suit—spades. Four from five is one. Now for the ace of spades."

He spells down and when he finishes naming the ace of spades, letter by letter, the magician holds but one card. He turns it face up. It is the ace of spades.

To perform this trick, simply arrange the four aces on top of the deck; then four twos; four threes and so on. Note, however, the positions of four cards. The ace of spades should be the top ace of the aces. The five of clubs is the top of the fives; the nine of diamonds the top of the diamonds; the king of hearts on the very bottom of the pack.

The mere action of going through the deals as described, with their automatic card reversals, will make the trick work in the manner indicated.

8. AUTOMATIC SPELLING

The magician takes a number of cards from the pack. He gives the little packet to be shuffled. He asks a spectator to deal it into two heaps, one card at a time. The spectator is to look at the last card, remember it and lay it on either heap. The other heap is then dropped upon it.

We will suppose that the ace of hearts is the one selected. The magician takes the packet and asks for the name. It is given. He deals the top card of the packet face up, saying "A." The next card goes beneath the packet. Another is turned up, saying "C." Then one beneath. So on, spelling "E--O-F--H-E-A-R-T-S." When the magician announces the letter "S," he is holding a single card in his hand. He turns it up. It is the ace of hearts!

The secret depends upon the fact that when a group of eleven cards are spelled in this fashion, the sixth, or center card, will be the last one left. That is why the magician instructs the spectator to deal two heaps, look at the last card and lay it between the heaps, when they are gathered. It puts the chosen card right where he wants it.

All the cards in the packet must be spelled with exactly eleven letters. Here is a good line-up to use:

Ace of hearts, ace of spades, jack of clubs, six of spades, four of clubs, two of hearts, ten of spades, king of clubs, five of clubs, two of spades, ten of hearts.

There are just eleven cards in the group. Remember that those eleven are shuffled before one is selected. As a variation in the spelling, the magician may allow the person to spell mentally the name of his card, letter by letter, each time a card is dealt face up. The magician does not know the name of the card at all!

This is a trick that may call for repetition. Here is an interesting method that involves a different arrangement. The magician gives a cluster of cards to a spectator, tells him to shuffle the cards and to deal them into three heaps. Note—three heaps, instead of two. Then the person is told to look at the bottom card of any heap and to place the heap between the other two.

Once again, the magician gathers the packet and spells, turning up a card for each letter and putting one under after each letter. In this case he also arrives at the selected card for the grand finish.

In this method, twelve cards are utilized instead of eleven. They are all cards that may be spelled with twelve letters: for instance —five of hearts, queen of clubs, jack of spades, eight of clubs, seven of clubs, king of hearts, three of clubs, five of spades, jack of hearts, king of spades, four of spades, four of hearts.

With twelve cards, the eighth from the top will be the one left when the spelling deal is completed. By having the cards first dealt into three heaps, after the shuffle, there are three groups of four cards each.

The process of looking at the bottom card of any heap and placing that heap between the other two heaps automatically makes the chosen card lie number eight from the top. It is the most natural type of procedure. Yet all the magician needs to do is go through his spelling bee and he finishes with the desired card in his possession.

These two methods can be worked into a very effective combination. Take any pack and get eleven eleven-letter cards together; beneath them twelve twelve-letter cards. Deal off the eleven and emphasize the shuffle and choice of card after dealing two heaps. Spell to that card. Repeat the trick, letting the spectator spell silently. Shuffle the group back into the pack, or place it on the bottom and deal off twelve cards. Then use the three-heap method.

Never state the exact number of cards that you are using in the trick. Take them off casually and let the audience think that you are using a number at random. Persons attempting to duplicate the stunt will invariably get a mixture of cards that spell with varied numbers of letters.

This is one of the newest of all spelling tricks and one that affords real possibilities to the practical performer.

CHAPTER V

EASY CARD TRICKS

THE TRICKS in this section can be performed anywhere at any time—with any pack of cards. They depend upon clever secrets or systems unknown to the spectators. None of them require any particular skill.

There are certain formulas in some of these tricks that will do the work, once the performer understands them. Each trick is a good one and an excellent program of card magic can be arranged from this section alone.

Practically every trick in this group is a mystery in itself, not depending upon any other method. Those persons already familiar with card magic will notice some novel ideas that may prove quite surprising to them. Certain principles have been adapted to new use and a close perusal of this section will prove of value to all card wizards.

I. CARD FOUND IN HAT

Someone shuffles the pack and gives you half, keeping the other portion. Drop your half of the pack in a hat and begin to shake it; put another hat over the top so the shaking can be done very violently and the cards will be sure to mix.

After demonstrating this, let the spectator take three cards from his half and insert them one by one, face downward, between the brims of the hats. As each card comes in, you shake the hats to mix it with those that are already in. The spectator, of course, knows each card he pushes in between the hats.

After lots of shaking, you remove the upper hat and reach

into the lower, producing the chosen cards one by one—much to the astonishment of the chooser.

It's all done when you put your cards in the hat. Give them a good bend at the center. Best, shake them first, showing how they mix. Then gather them into a pack again and bend this time, the hat covering the movement.

The selected cards mix with the others, right enough, but they are straight while the others are curved and it is easy to distinguish them. Then, in gathering the remaining cards from the hat, bend them the other way to straighten them and no clue remains.

This trick mystified Blackstone when he first saw it performed —so the reader can be sure that it is a first class mystery when properly performed.

2. TWO NUMBER TRICK

A pack is shuffled. Any person takes it and notes a card a certain distance from the top—not more than ten or twelve cards down.

Taking the pack, the magician holds it behind his back and asks another person to name a number above twelve. The magician promises to put the chosen card at the new number—even though he does not know the chosen card nor its position!

He apparently does this, for when the cards are counted, the chosen card is at the new number.

There is a point to this trick that most persons fail to grasp. That is the method of counting. It begins not at one, but at the mentally selected number.

To make this clear, let us consider the trick just as handled by the performer. Suppose the fifth card is noted by the first party. Fifteen is the number named by the second person. Behind his back, the magician counts off fifteen cards, one by one, reversing their order. He drops them on top of the pack.

Giving the pack to the first spectator, he says: "Count to fifteen, starting the count with *your* number."

The person naturally counts: "five, six, seven," and so on until he says "fifteen." He will then be at the card he chose. This trick always works, no matter what the two numbers may be.

An interesting effect is to decide upon the higher number by using a pair of dice. Roll them often enough to get a total greater than twelve, adding the spots on each roll. Then proceed with the number thus determined.

3. BOTTOM TO TOP

This is a variation of the trick just described. It is given here as an alternate method. Many persons, seeing the two tricks, think that they are different in principle, whereas they are fundamentally the same.

Give the pack to a person. Tell him to pick any number less than ten and to remember the card that is that many from the bottom.

Take the pack and call for a number higher than ten. Suppose eighteen is given. Transfer eighteen cards from the bottom to the top, without changing their order. Move them in a group.

Now ask the first person's number. Suppose it is six. Counting from the top, begin with six. "Six, seven, eight—" a card for every number until you reach eighteen. That will be the card noted by the person as six from the bottom.

Let the man do the counting himself, if you wish, but always remember to have him start on his own number.

4. THOUGHT DISCOVERED

The magician spreads a pack so that about ten or twelve cards in the center are visible when the front of the pack is elevated toward the onlookers. A spectator is requested to note one of the visible cards mentally and to write its name on a sheet of paper.

The performer turns away while the name of the card is being written. The paper is folded and is given to another person. The magician shuffles the pack and gives it to the same person. The paper is then opened and the name of the mentally selected card is read. The person who has the pack looks through it for the chosen card. The card is missing—the magician immediately produces it from his pocket!

This is a very perplexing trick, yet it is not at all difficult. On the top of the pack the magician has ten or twelve cards that he has remembered—for instance: eight, queen, three, ten, two, seven, four, nine, king, ace.

This list, it will be noted, has no two cards of the same value—hence it is not necessary to remember suits. The magician may either arrange cards according to an order that he has previously memorized; or he can simply note the ten cards that happen to be on top of the pack, removing any that happen to be duplicated in value. Most persons will prefer to set up the cards to conform with their regular arrangement; then there can be no mistake.

At any rate, the magician cuts the pack by drawing some cards from the bottom and putting them on top. He keeps the two sections of the pack slightly separated and spreads the center cards—those which were originally on top. Thus the spectator must think of one of those cards.

The writing of the card gives the performer an excuse to turn away. He immediately lifts the cards that are above the known group and puts them back on the bottom; that is, he simply shifts the original bottom half of the pack back to where it belongs, so his ten known cards are again on top of the pack.

He then picks off at least ten cards and thrusts them in his pocket. Thus he has the ten known cards in his pocket—and one of those cards must be the one mentally selected.

When the slip of paper and the pack are handed to a spectator, the paper is naturally opened and read to learn the name of the missing card; while the spectator is looking for the card in the depleted pack, the magician simply puts his hand in his pocket and counts down to the required card. He, like the spectator, sees the name on the paper. Having his cards in a known order, he can easily find the right one. If the paper says "ten of spades," he counts eight, queen, three—*ten*.

He brings out the "missing" card and tosses it on the table, adding the additional cards to the pack at the first opportunity. The fact that the pack is depleted is never noticed.

5. TWENTY-FIVE CARDS

A great improvement over an older trick. A pack is shuffled. Five persons take five cards each. From his group, each person mentally selects a card. The magician gathers up the cards. He shows five cards and asks whose card is among them. A spectator says that he sees his card. The performer drops all cards but the chosen one. This is repeated until all five cards are discovered.

Here is the method. Let each person hold his group of five and remember one. He can shuffle his heap if he wishes. Go to the first person and ask for one card, face down. Then take a card from the second person, placing it on the card in your hand. Continue with persons three, four, five. Then go back to number one for another card.

You simply make the round, gathering cards one at a time until you have collected all twenty-five. But in this natural procedure, you have done something very important. You have arranged the cards in five groups: one, two, three, four, five—counting up from the bottom of the pack.

Now you take five cards from the top of those you hold. Fan them with the right hand. Although you alone know it, each of those cards has come from a different person. The card at the extreme left belongs to person one; the next to person two; three, four and five in order.

Show each person the fan. Ask if his card is there. If anyone says "yes," you immediately know which card it is, according to the person's number. Drop all cards but that one.

Now proceed with the next five cards—they will work just like the first five. Sometimes no one will have a card in the group. Just lay those cards aside. Sometimes two or three persons will see their card in the group. In that case drop one of the chosen cards, telling to whom it belongs; then drop the other and the third, if there is one.

Do all you can to make the trick effective. Do not even glance at the faces of the cards. That makes it so much the better. This trick, properly presented, will be a great mystery to those who witness it.

You are not limited to twenty-five cards. You can use thirty-six if you wish, involving six persons in the trick. You can also use forty-nine cards, with seven persons. Twenty-five is the best number for practical purposes as the trick goes more rapidly and is just as effective as when performed with a greater number of cards.

6. A DOUBLE PREDICTION

This is a very perplexing card trick. Read it carefully; then try it and you will be surprised to see how perfectly it works.

The magician takes twenty-one cards, among which is a conspicuous card—either the joker or the ace of spades. He writes two numbers—each on a separate slip of paper—without letting anyone see the numbers. He rolls up each piece of paper.

Someone removes the joker from the packet of cards and shuffles the cards. The performer spreads the cards. The joker is pushed into the heap. One person is told to remember the card just above the joker; the other person remembers the card just below.

Squaring the cards, the magician deals them into two heaps. He spreads each heap separately, asking the persons to note their cards but to say nothing whatever. He places the heaps together and again deals two heaps, each of which is shown, but no comment is asked.

The heaps are placed together; the cards are spread and someone removes the joker. The packet is now cut into two heaps, one of which is counted, to make sure that there are at least eight cards in it.

Now the papers are opened. One bears the number 6; the other the number 4. The chosen cards are named. One is discovered six from the top in one heap; the other is found four from the top in the other heap!

Let us explain. Read the directions carefully. After the two cards have been noted, one on each side of the inserted joker, the joker is left in the pack and two heaps are dealt, one card at a time, alternately, reversing the order of the cards. Both heaps are spread and shown in turn. In putting them together, be sure that the heap of eleven cards goes on top of the heap of ten.

Deal again—once more reversing the order of the cards—and show each heap. This time, again be sure to place the heap of eleven on top of the heap of ten.

Now fan the cards with the faces toward the audience and ask a person to remove the joker. Here is the important part. When the joker is removed, one chosen card will be exactly five cards above that spot; the other chosen card will be exactly five cards below.

Cut the pack at the place from which the joker is removed. You will have one card five from the top; the other card five from the bottom. Square up the pack and cut it into two portions, as near equal as possible. Count the cards in the bottom section, reversing their order as you do so. Result: one chosen card is five from the top in one heap; the other is five from the top in the other heap.

In this explanation, it is assumed that the two numbers written were 5 and 5—as that is the normal finish of the trick. But the reader will recall that in the description, we gave the numbers as 6 and 4. Certainly. They can be 6 and 4 just as well as 5 and 5. The crux lies in the cutting of the packet just after the removal of the joker. In cutting, draw one card from the top of the lower heap to the bottom of the upper, as you make the cut. Proceed just as with 5 and 5. But this time, the cards will turn up 6 and 4.

If you wish, you can make the cards come 7 and 3. This is done by drawing two cards from the top of the lower heap to the bottom of the upper as you make the cut. Now, if you prefer to have 8 and 2 as the final numbers, you can achieve that result by drawing three cards from the lower heap to the upper when you cut after the removal of the joker.

Of course you make up your mind what you are going to do

before you start the trick. Then write the two numbers that you intend to use—each on a separate slip of paper. It is not wise to use 5 and 5, because the numbers are identical. 6 and 4 are better. But sometimes you may have to show the trick to people who have seen you do it before. So use 7 and 3 instead of 6 and 4.

Try this trick, using two conspicuous cards like red aces—one on each side of the joker. Go through the entire routine and you will then understand it. It is one of the best of all impromptu card tricks.

7. VANISHED CARD

Take a pack of cards and riffle the ends. Ask a person to think of any card that he sees. This is done. Again you riffle the pack.

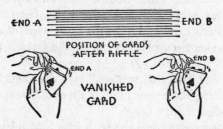

Note the projecting ends of cards and the method of riffling opposite ends of the pack.

To the person's amazement, the card is gone—even though you riffle the pack slowly, he cannot see it.

The Secret: Divide the pack beforehand and carefully dovetail shuffle the two heaps together so that they alternate. In pressing the two sections together, do not shove them all the way. One group projects at one end—the other group at the other end.

When you riffle one end of the pack, only the projecting cards will show. Thus the spectator can select only from that group. To make his card disappear, simply turn the pack around and riffle the other end. His card will not come into view.

To make the trick doubly effective, riffle end A before a spectator and let him select a card. Riffle end B before another spectator and let him think of a card. Then riffle end B for spectator A. His card has vanished. Riffle end A for spectator B. His card is gone.

Ask the names of the cards. Press the projecting ends together, turn the pack over and run through the cards face up. Both vanished cards have returned.

8. THE MYSTIC DISCOVERY

This is an unusual idea in card magic—a trick that is very puzzling, yet which offers no great difficulties in presentation. It is a trick that must be thoroughly understood and which should be practiced to give it the neat precision which it requires. For the trick is most effective when done in an easy, efficient style.

The magician takes any pack after it has been shuffled. He holds it in his left hand and riffles the cards with his right, doing this slowly so that the spectators can see the faces of the cards as they fall.

"Think of any card that you see," says the magician. "If you note two or three, settle your mind upon one. You have it? Very well, I shall deal Bridge hands."

He then proceeds to deal the pack into four piles of thirteen each, which he designates as South, West, North and East. Picking up a hand, he spreads it and studies the cards for a moment. He turns the faces toward the person who chose the card.

"Is your card in this hand?" he asks.

If the reply is affirmative, the magician uses that heap; if negative, he shows the next hand—and so on, until he learns which pack contains the mentally selected card.

"That makes my chances a little better," says the magician. "I'm pretty sure I have your card. Our thoughts are working well."

He lays the heap face down upon the table and asks the spectator to name his card. The card is named. The magician calmly turns up the top card of the pile and reveals the card that was mentally selected.

Now for the explanation. In riffling the cards, the magician begins while he is telling what he wants done. He does not turn the faces so they can be seen until he has run through about twenty cards rather rapidly—roughly, he has just about reached the center of the pack before the spectator has a real opportunity to glimpse the face of a card.

As the magician urges the person to think of a card, he lets the cards riffle slowly, one by one, allowing plenty of opportunity for the person to take any one of the cards that he sees. Approximately twelve cards are allowed to fall in this fashion; then, assuming that a card has been taken, the magician lets the rest of the cards riffle rapidly.

In brief, the wizard, despite the opportunity he seems to have given has actually limited the choice to one of a dozen cards, all located more than twenty from the bottom. When the heaps are dealt, there will be thirteen in each. They are dealt carefully; thus the bottom cards of the pack fall on top of the heaps.

Considering each heap individually, we can eliminate the top five cards and the bottom four. The selected card is sure to be either 6, 7, 8 and 9 from the top of its particular group. This is allowing sixteen cards—plenty of margin. But the magician wants an even better percentage. When he picks up one of the hands and spreads it, he is careful to keep the sixth and seventh cards out of sight behind the eighth. He allows a brief glance at the fan and asks if the spectator sees his card.

If the spectator sees his card in one of the heaps, the wizard knows that the card is either number eight or number nine from the top of the heap. Should the spectator fail to see his card in any hand, the explanation is obvious—to the magician only. He knows that the chosen card must be six or seven in its particular heap. So he chides the spectator for not looking closely enough and goes through the hands again. This time he spreads all of the cards—so the spectator naturally sees the chosen one. Thus the magician learns its heap.

Now for the finish. By the elimination process just described, the magician limits the chosen card to one of two—either six or seven in a certain heap; or eight or nine in that heap. He switches the cards around a bit and in the action puts one of the possible cards on top of the heap; the other on the bottom. In a positive manner he lays the heap face down and calls for the name of the card. When it is given, the magician either turns up the top card or turns over the entire heap to show the bottom card—according to which one is named. Either revelation is surprising to the audience. Knowing the proper card, the magician simply uses the correct discovery.

9. THE SAME NUMBER

A very neat card trick. Offer a pack to a person and ask him to shuffle it. Then tell him to count off any number of cards, while you are watching—at least ten cards—and to give you the remainder.

The person counts, say, sixteen. When you receive the balance of the pack, you ask him to lift his sixteen cards and drop them on. You hold the pack squared and show that all cards are even. Then, to demonstrate ease in counting, you lift off a bunch of cards and throw them on the table, announcing that you have taken sixteen. Counted, the statement proves correct.

It's all done when you receive the pack. Take the cards in the left hand, with the thumb across the back of the pack. Catch the ends of the pack with the right hand—thumb at one end and fingers at the other. Bend the ends up.

When the sixteen cards are put on the pack, square it and hold the cards tightly pressed. There is a space between the sixteen cards and the rest of the pack, but by pressing with the left thumb, you hide this fact.

Release pressure and the straight sixteen cards will raise, leaving the break below them. Simply lift off all cards above the break and throw them on the table. You have taken off the sixteen.

Shuffling the pack in dovetail fashion will destroy all traces of bent-up cards.

10. THE TWENTY CARD TRICK

For years magicians have been performing a trick with twenty cards that is highly effective and will always remain so. Twenty cards are dealt in piles of two cards each. Different persons are allowed to look at pairs and memorize them.

The magician gathers the pairs, and deals the cards haphazard in four rows of five cards each, faces up. He points out the four horizontal rows and asks a spectator to indicate the row or rows in which his cards appear. As soon as this is done, the magician picks up the two chosen cards. This is repeated with the other selections.

The secret of this trick lies in the fact that the apparent haphazard dealing is actually in accordance with a system. The magician puts each card in a particular place for it. Now the time-honored system for this trick depended upon the use of four Latin words—mutus, nomen, dedit, cocis—and for years no one thought of departing from it. Somehow it seemed as though only Latin words would do—and the worst of it was that the word "cocis" is not Latin at all.

An English formula is much preferable. It is more easy to remember; it has some meaning; and it will confuse those who know the old trick and who think that the antiquated system is the only one that can possibly work. Several English formulas have been devised for this trick, and now we present one that is entirely new. Note the four words in this table:

RIDER
HOODS
CINCH
TENTS

There are ten letters used in the four words and each letter appears twice. Every combination of letters is different. For instance, O appears twice in row 2; N appears in rows 3 and 4;

E appears in rows 1 and 4—and so on. Observe these combinations.

Now in dealing out the twenty cards to make four rows of five each, the performer visualizes his code as though it were inscribed in large letters upon the table. He puts the first card face up at the spot where he pictures the first R; the second card is set where the second R should be. Next he places a card for I; another card for I; then proceeds with D and D—and continues thus.

When a spectator indicates that his chosen cards are in rows 2 and 3, the magician simply repeats his formula mentally and he finds that the letter H appears in both "hoods" and "cinch"; therefore the two cards are on the spots where the letter H should be.

So much for the bare outline of this very effective trick. Let us consider presentation. To do the trick properly, the magician should allow the pack to be shuffled; then deal his ten piles of two—*faces down*. While the magician's back is turned, spectators are allowed to look at pairs. All the pairs are then gathered in haphazard form. The magician has not seen the face of a single card.

He makes his deal in careless fashion, creating the idea that he is endeavoring to mix things even more. Then, when he begins to pick out the chosen cards as the rows are mentioned to him, he will be rewarded by a perplexed group of spectators and he will realize just how effective this twenty card trick can be.

II. IMPROVED TWENTY CARDS

Not content with giving the reader an entirely new formula for the twenty cards, we shall now explain a method of distribution which requires no words whatever. In this system, the trick appears the same to the onlookers. But the magician can begin his deal anywhere, with no danger of forgetting or becoming mixed with imaginary words.

This new system depends simply upon a numerical arrangement which will be entirely clear at the first reading. It enables the magician to deal the cards in a most careless fashion.

Picture the four rows of five cards each, considered thus:

$$1 - 2 - 3 - 4 - 1$$
$$1 - 2 - 3 - 4 - 2$$
$$1 - 2 - 3 - 4 - 3$$
$$1 - 2 - 3 - 4 - 4$$

The cards in each row are simply numbered 1 to 4 from left to right. The last card in each row is the key card, giving the number of the row—hence here the numbers run 1, 2, 3, 4 from top to bottom.

This is the simple chart which the performer visualizes on the table in place of the cabalistic words. He gathers his twenty cards and begins to place them on the table, starting at any point. Suppose he sets down the middle card of row 2. That is card 3 in row 2. Very well: the next card is placed as card 2 in row 3. When the magician places a card at position 2 in row 1, he simply follows with a card at position 1 in row 2.

The purpose of the key cards or positions at the right should now be apparent. In each row, its own number appears twice. Thus when the magician puts a card at position 2 in row 2, he follows by putting a card at the right end of row 2—where the duplicate number 2 is present.

Let us suppose that twenty cards have been dealt by this formula. Using different letters to indicate each pair of cards, we will have a layout in this fashion:

DBCGD
BJAHJ
CAEFE
GHFII

The pointing out of the cards is a matter of extreme simplicity with this system. A spectator mentions that his cards appear in rows 2 and 3. The magician simply picks up the third card in the second row and the second card in the third row. If both cards

are in row 3, pick up the third card and the key (fifth) card.
If cards are in rows 1 and 4, the fourth card of the first and the
first card of the fourth are the ones the magician wants.

12. MATHEMATICAL DISCOVERY

This is an idea used by Paul Noffke, the clever card wizard.
Its purpose is to enable the performer to tell the name of a card
which he does not know.

A spectator has chosen a card. Tell him to remember its numerical value (ace, one; jack, eleven; queen, twelve; king, thirteen)—also the suit of the card.

Tell him to double the value of the card.

Then tell him to add three to the total.

Tell him to multiply the complete total by five.

This done, ask him to concentrate on the suit.

If the card is a diamond, he must add one.

If it is a club, he must add two.

If it is a heart, he must add three.

If it is a spade, he must add four.

He must then tell you the final total.

From it, you immediately divine the name of the selected card.

The secret is to subtract fifteen from the final total. You will
have a number of two figures—possibly three. The last figure
gives you the suit (diamonds 1, clubs 2, hearts 3, spades 4) while
the first figure or figures give you the value.

Examples: Jack of clubs.

11 doubled is 22. Add 3—25. Multiply by 5—125. Add 2 (for
clubs) making 127. You are told that number.

Subtract 15 mentally. Result, 112. Last figure (2) means clubs.
First figures (11) mean jack.

With the five of hearts.

5 doubled is 10. Add 3—13. Multiply by 5—65. Add 3 (for
hearts) making 68. You are told that number.

Subtract 15 mentally. Result, 53. Last figure (3) means hearts.
First figure (5) means five spot.

This is a very effective routine and it is particularly valuable when a troublesome spectator takes a card and makes it impossible for you to go ahead with the trick as you have intended it.

Remember that the spectator performs all his calculation without telling you a word about the card itself. He can do it mentally or on paper. All you ask is the total. The total does not appear to give you any clue to the card, because no one knows your secret system of deducting 15.

13. THREE HEAPS

A spectator deals three cards faces up. He counts the value of one card and turns it down. He adds enough cards to it to make

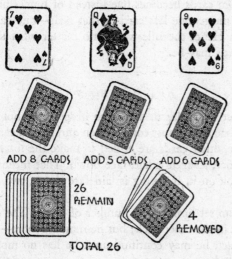

ADD 8 CARDS   ADD 5 CARDS   ADD 6 CARDS

26 REMAIN

4 REMOVED

TOTAL 26

Typical layout of three heaps, with additional cards added to make totals of fifteen.

fifteen. For example, if the card is a seven, he deals eight cards on it.

He repeats this process with the other two cards. Then the magician comes in and takes the cards that remain. He quickly tells the total value of the three cards on the bottoms.

The system is this: Count the cards that remain. Disregard four of them. The rest will be the same as the total of the hidden cards.

Face cards are usually counted as ten in this trick. If desired, jack can be eleven; queen, twelve; king, thirteen. It makes no difference.

While the trick is very bewildering to those who do not understand it, it is readily understood if we consider it with three aces as the bottom cards. That means fifteen cards in each heap. The total is forty-five. That leaves seven cards over. The total of the aces is three. So four cards must be disregarded.

Now, if a two spot is put in place of one of the aces, the total of the bottom cards becomes five instead of four. But the use of a two spot means one less card in that heap—one card more in the surplus. Hence the rule works, no matter what the value of the base cards may be.

14. MANY HEAPS

This effect is similar to the three heap trick; but in this instance the face cards must count as ten and after a card is placed on the table, other cards are added to make the total twelve.

For instance, a seven is laid face down. That means five cards must be dealt on it. If a king is laid face down, two cards must be added.

There is no set limit to the number of heaps. The dealer may use three as in the other trick; but he may use more—five, six, or seven—in fact, he may continue until he has no more cards to make up totals.

The performer recommends that at least five heaps be used—if possible. When he returns, he takes the extra cards, looks at the heaps, and names the total of the bottom cards.

To understand this, let us consider it with four heaps. Four aces on the bottoms mean forty-eight cards used. There will be four cards left over. That is the total. In other words, with four heaps in use, the extra cards tell the total exactly.

Now when the performer returns, he counts the extra cards and disregards four of the heaps. For each additional heap, he

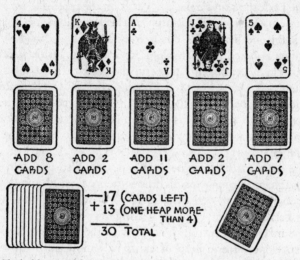

Typical layout of five heaps, indicating additional cards making totals of twelve.

simply adds thirteen. Why? Because if we had four kings as bottom cards, with two cards on each, there would be a total of forty extra cards. Now the formation of a fifth heap with an ace on the bottom would require twelve of those forty cards. It would also add one to the total of the under cards. That means thirteen.

Thus if we have six heaps and twelve cards left over the total of the under cards will be 13 plus 13 plus 6—32. With seven heaps and nine cards over, the total will be 13 plus 13 plus 13 plus 9—48.

If a spectator decides to use only three heaps, simply subtract thirteen from the total number of cards left over. If he uses only two heaps, subtract twenty-six from the remaining cards.

Four heaps is the basis of the formula and there is no difficulty whatever in determining the totals. The trick is a good one to repeat, because the spectators will try varied numbers of heaps and will find this experiment more perplexing as it continues.

15. NAME IN ENVELOPE

The performer lays a pack of cards on the table. He asks some-one to cut the pack. Picking up a sealed envelope, the magician lays it on one heap. The cut is completed. The card below the envelope is noted. The envelope is torn open. Inside is found a slip of paper bearing the name of the card.

There are two ways of doing this trick. First, by using the method described under the title "An Easy Force." The magician knows the top card of the pack and lays the envelope upon it when the cut is made, having someone put the rest of the cards on the envelope.

The other method can be used with a shuffled pack—in which the magician cannot possibly know the location of any card. He has previously removed the desired card from the pack and it is lying beneath the envelope, projecting over the edge of the table.

The magician picks up the card with the envelope. In placing the envelope on one heap of cards he simply adds the hidden card to the heap. Since that card corresponds with the name written on the paper in the envelope, the trick is sure to work.

CHAPTER VI

ADVANCED CARD TRICKS

TRICKS partially dependent upon sleights form the contents of this section. In certain cases, optional methods are given so that skill is eliminated. In most of the tricks, a very small element of skill is all that is required.

The reader will find various references to the sleights listed in Chapter One. Most of the problems in the following pages are complete tricks in themselves. The "Card in the Pocket" is one—and we present five methods of performing this ever-popular trick. We feel sure that the adaptations utilized in it will be of special interest to the reader.

Effort has been made to reduce skill to the minimum. These tricks are within the range of any reader who tries them. Some performers will choose to show them with all the elaborations possible, thus adding to the effect. That is purely a matter of individual choice.

I. CARD IN THE POCKET

The effect of this trick is that the spectator takes the pack and counts down any number of cards, noting the name of any card and its number from the top of the pack.

The magician returns and receives the pack. Glancing through it, he removes and pockets a card. He asks the spectator's number —not the card. The number being given, the magician counts down that far. The spectator's card is not there, so the magician obligingly removes it from his pocket.

There are several methods of performing this trick. They are given herewith, so that the performer can vary them and thus repeat the trick effectively.

First Method: The performer takes a card from near the bottom of the pack and pockets it. He palms it in his pocket and adds it to the pack when he brings his hand from the pocket.

When the location of the card is given, the wizard counts to it and naturally he stops one short, due to the secretly added card. Suppose the chosen card to be ninth from the top. When he reaches nine, the performer deals the card face down on the table, with the others. It is really the eighth card. Looking at it, the spectator finds that it is not his card.

Meanwhile the performer, just as attention is on the card on the table, palms the real ninth card. Going to his pocket he brings it forth—apparently the card that he put there beforehand.

Second Method: In this variation of the trick, the performer puts the top card in his pocket and leaves it there. Suppose the number is nine. He counts off nine cards with his right hand, each card on the one before, so that their order is reversed. He pushes the next card (really the tenth) from the pack and replaces the right hand cards on the pack.

The spectators look at the card on the table and see that it is not the chosen one. Meanwhile the performer palms the card now on top of the pack, reaches in his pocket and brings it out showing it to be the chosen card. He leaves the odd card in his pocket, later replacing it in the pack.

Third Method: In this version, the performer secretly notes the top card of the pack.* He tells the spectator to deal off any number, one by one; to look at the next card and put the dealt cards on top.

For instance, the spectator deals off eight, looks at the ninth and puts the eighth back on again. The magician returns and looks through the pack for the top card. It is now at number eight, due to the reversal. He takes the card below it (the ninth) and pockets it.

He asks the number. He is told nine. He deals off nine and

*By means of the "glimpse"—third method.

shows the last one. Not the chosen card. Out it comes from the pocket. This method eliminates the palming.

Fourth Method: Here the performer gives a spectator a slip of paper and tells him to write down any three figures—all different —forming a number. He is then to reverse the number and subtract the smaller from the larger.

This being done, add the figures in the result and look at the card that number from the top of the pack. The pack is first shuffled by the spectator.

The secret is the fact that the result will alway be 18.

Examples:

451	603	812	594
—154	—306	—218	—495
297	297	594	99

In each case the figures of the result (297, 594, 99) total 18. Knowing this, the magician simply runs down to the eighteenth card and puts it in his pocket, performing the rest of the trick in the accustomed fashion of asking for the number, counting down to it and showing that the chosen card is gone.

Fifth Method: In this version, the magician introduces a pair of dice. He tells someone to roll them and note the total; to pick up one of the dice, add the bottom side and roll it again, adding the new number that turns up. The dice are left on the table. The total is remembered and the card at that number in the pack is the one noted.

The magician, on returning, rolls the dice a few times as though that had some important value. He looks through the pack and puts a card in his pocket. On counting down, the chosen card is missing. It is the one he took.

Simply add seven to the dice as they lie. Thus three and two are rolled—five. The two is turned over; its under side is a five— adding makes ten. The die is rolled again and turns up four. Total, fourteen. The fourteenth card is noted.

When the magician views the dice, he notes four and three.

He adds seven to that total, arriving at fourteen. This gives him the position of the card—fourteenth.

The trick with the dice depends on the fact that opposite sides of a single die always total seven. Yet even people who know it will be fooled by the peculiar way in which the dice are rolled.

Summary: By employing the various methods of performing the card in the pocket, the magician can repeat the trick a number of times or exhibit it differently each time he is requested to perform it.

2. FOUR ACE CHANGE

This is where the laugh is turned on the audience. The magician holds the pack between his hands and shows the ace of clubs on the bottom. He deals the ace face downward. He then puts the next card on top of the pack.

He shows the ace of hearts, the ace of diamonds and the ace of spades, dealing each one and putting the alternate cards on top.

But by this time the spectators know that he is bluffing. For the magician has been showing three spots instead of aces, covering the end spots with his fingers. He has not only done it crudely; he has given it away with the ace of spades. For instead of appearing with a large, ornamental ace, that ace has been shown as only a small spot.

When the magician states that he will transform the aces into threes, everyone demands to see the aces. So the magician obligingly turns them faces up and shows that they are actually aces after all.

That turns the laugh. When the magician decides to go on with the trick, he pushes the cards around a bit, turns them faces up and shows that they are now threes.

Here is the method. The bottom card is really a three; then comes an ace, a three, an ace, a three, an ace, a three (spades) and an ace.

Showing the first three with the fingers covering the end spots, the magician announces that he will deal it on the table. Actually, he uses the "glide"* drawing back the card and dealing an ace in its stead. He transfers the three spot to the top of the pack without showing its face.

He continues thus, showing each three in turn, but really dealing aces. So at last, he has four aces on the table while the threes have been transferred to the top of the pack, each in its proper turn.

The magician then turns up the aces after a long protest has been registered by the audience. At this point he acts as though the trick is ended, with the joke being turned on the spectators.

But he really takes advantage of the situation to exchange the aces for the threes. This is done by the "bottom change"—a sleight fully described in Blackstone's "Secrets of Magic." It is given briefly here, as in this case the sleight can be done very slowly, for the audience does not know that anything else is coming.

The left thumb, on top of the pack, has pushed the four top cards well to the left. The right hand picks up the aces and holds them faces down, between the first and second fingers. The right hand approaches the left. The lower fingers of the left hand open to receive the aces. The right hand removes the threes between the thumb and forefinger. These cards are immediately dropped on the table.

The magician can then show the cards as threes when he wishes. There is an interesting bit of by-play, however, that adds to the effect of the trick. Moving the cards around, the magician peeks at the faces and selects the three of diamonds. He uses it as an indicator to point at the others—without revealing the face of the card.

"It's a funny thing," he remarks. "You thought these aces were other cards, didn't you? What's that? You thought they were the threes! Take this ace of diamonds, for instance. Look at it—you thought it was a three—"

So saying, he skims the ace upward in the air, by holding it between his two first fingers, and twirling it edgewise. As the

*A sleight explained elsewhere in this book.

spectators look upward at the spinning card, it actually appears to be an ace, for the end spots merge with the center one.

When the card strikes the floor, it proves to be a three spot after all. The magician then invites an inspection of the other three cards that are on the table. They, like the diamond, are threes instead of aces.

The success of this trick depends largely upon showmanship and the performer who practices it to gain effect will find that it is a most excellent deception.

3. THREE CARD MONTE

This is a very clever version of the three card monte trick, which can be acquired with little practice and is quite deceptive.

The magician holds three cards in a fan—faces toward the

THREE CARD MONTE

How the center ace is shifted secretly to the right. The right thumb performs the action.

audience. One card is behind the other two—that is the center card of the fan, which we will assume to be the ace of spades.

The magician calls attention to the position of the ace of spades, which is flanked by the ace of hearts and the ace of clubs. He turns the cards faces downward and asks someone to remove the ace of spades. Naturally, the person takes the center card. Imagine his surprise when he discovers that he is holding the ace of hearts instead of the ace of spades!

There is a little sleight used in this trick. Note the position of the cards. The ace of hearts is the front one; the ace of clubs next; the ace of spades behind the other two, peering from between them.

When the cards are turned face down, the right thumb, which is behind the three cards, moves to the right, swinging the ace of spades to the right position. The center card is now the ace of hearts. A person naturally takes it as the ace of spades. The swing of the arm completely covers the sliding of the ace of spades to the right and the spectator has no idea that a change has been made.

4. THE TRAVELING ACE

This follows the "three card monte" that was just explained. It is an old trick, utilized to a new purpose. The reader will recall that the three cards used in the "monte" were the aces of clubs, spades and hearts. There was a reason.

After demonstrating that the ace of hearts mysteriously takes the place of the ace of spades, the performer kindly consents to do the trick again. He turns his back for a moment, while he arranges the cards. He says that he will use the ace of diamonds. Actually, he has the ace of diamonds in his pocket. He uses the ace of hearts to appear as the ace of diamonds.

This time, the red ace is the back card. In setting it behind the angle formed by the other two aces, the wizard fixes matters so that only the point of the heart is visible—thus the card appears as the ace of diamonds.

The reader will remember than in the "monte" trick, the spectators got the ace of hearts instead of the ace of spades. The performer, now showing the three cards, tells them he will make it easy for them to get the ace of diamonds—for it is in the center.

Showing the fanned cards, he turns them faces down, making his slide and letting a spectator get the center card—one of the black aces.

"You didn't get the ace of diamonds?" comes the magician's question, as he drops the other two cards faces down on the table. "I'll tell you why. It's here!"

And he draws the missing ace of diamonds from his pocket!

5. THE HOAX WITH ACES

This is an old trick, but it is always a good one. It is performed with two aces—the red ones—and a confederate helps the magician.

The pack is divided into two packets. Upon one heap, the magician places the ace of hearts. He shows the ace of diamonds and puts it on the other heap. Lifting this heap he puts it on the ace of hearts, but as he does so, he quickly pulls the ace of diamonds from the top and drops it on the ace of hearts ahead of the descending packet.

The magician blandly states that the two aces will be found together. He deals cards from the bottom of the pack, turning them faces up, one by one. At last he comes to the first red ace. He states that the next card he draws off will be the other ace. Sure enough, it is.

Everyone laughs at the crudity of this trick and the confederate, with a wink at the audience, asks the magician to "do it again." The magician consents. But while he is showing the ace of diamonds to everyone, the confederate slyly takes a few cards from the upper heap and drops them on the ace of hearts.

Now, when the magician goes through his crude feat of slipping the ace of diamonds on to the lower heap, the laugh appears to be on him—for the aces will not be together.

The magician proceeds unwittingly, declaring that the two red aces will come together as he deals cards from the bottom. A red ace comes into view and the magician is emphatic that the next card will be the other ace. Everyone else laughs. So the magician brings forth the card and it actually is the missing ace!

Here is the method: The magician knows the card directly under the ace of hearts—say, the five of clubs. He knows what the confederate has done—that the aces will really be apart. But he deals away, pulling each card from the bottom and turning it face up until he sees the five of clubs. That tells him that the ace of hearts is next.

He does not deal the ace of hearts. Instead, he draws it back by means of the "glide"* and continues dealing other cards. The ace of diamonds comes up. To bring the ace of hearts next, the magician simply draws it forth, for it is on the bottom, waiting for him.

6. THE ACE HOAX
(With Improvements)

The effect of this trick is similar to the "Hoax with Aces." The magician shows how he can make the red aces come together even though placed apart—but the crudity of his method fools no one.

Offering to do the trick again, he places the ace of hearts on one heap and shows the ace of diamonds. The confederate quickly seizes the ace of hearts and pockets it. The magician does not see the action.

The magician puts the ace of diamonds on top of the pack and makes the crude transfer, slipping it to the lower heap. When he says that the cards will come together—two red aces—no one believes him. But the magician has the last laugh, for the red aces come together and the confederate expresses surprise at finding a different card in his pocket.

In this case, the deception begins with the exhibition of the ace of hearts, before it is placed upon the lower half of the pack. The magician picks up the ace of hearts with another card on top of it. He shows these two cards as one; by bending the cards slightly outward, they hold firmly together and appear as one card.

Thus two cards go on the lower heap. While the magician is showing the ace of diamonds, the confederate quickly steals the top card of the lower heap. He does not have time to show its face. Everyone takes for granted that it is the ace of hearts. But the ace of hearts still remains on the lower heap.

So when the magician employs his crude maneuver, he actu-

*Described in Chapter One.

ally brings the two aces together and he can deal the cards one by one from the bottom, arriving at the united aces.

In doing the trick in this form, the deal from the bottom is not essential. All through the trick, the magician can simply spread the pack face up and show the two aces side by side.

7. TRAVELING CARD TRICK

The magician uses two envelopes and a pack of cards. He asks a spectator to count off twelve cards. The spectator does this. The magician then counts off twelve cards.

He verifies the spectator's count, counting the twelve cards again. He puts these twelve cards in one envelope. He seals the envelope. A spectator holds it.

The magician verifies the count of his own twelve cards. He puts his twelve in the other envelope. A spectator holds it—the envelope being sealed.

"Pass!" Three cards go from one envelope to the other. Nine in one envelope, fifteen in the other. Spectators open the envelopes themselves and do the counting!

Here's the method: Between the two envelopes the performer puts three cards, faces down. The envelopes are face to face. They are shown casually together. No one realizes that three cards are hidden between them.

A spectator counts off twelve cards and places them on the table. The performer counts off twelve—apparently—but actually he uses the "false count"* and only counts off nine, making them appear as twelve.

When he verifies the spectator's count, he counts the cards upon the envelopes. He picks up the envelopes and lets the cards slide into his right hand. Needless to state, the hidden cards go with them. One envelope is dropped; the fifteen cards are sealed in the other.

The magician quickly verifies the count of his own cards, but he uses the elusive "false count" once more—so the packet which

*Explained in the first chapter of this book.

presumably contains twelve actually consists of nine cards. These are placed in the second envelope which is sealed. The rest is merely a matter of showmanship.

This trick is not at all difficult, but it should be presented convincingly. Afterward, spectators will believe that they did all the counting themselves. Great importance should be attached to the fact that the sealed envelopes are held by the spectators.

Also, the magician should see to it that the envelopes look the same. He can ask for the spectators to select one. The magician then offers to make cards pass from it or into it—as the case may be. This should be done in a casual manner.

He can also ask for a number of cards—say between one and four—the response usually being "three." This makes it look as though the spectators decided upon the number that was to be used in the passing.

Should "two" be stated—the only other choice—the magician gets out of it by turning to another person and saying—"I wanted you to decide the number—but since two has been mentioned, we can use two—and one for you, which makes three altogether."

8. IMPROVED POCKET TO POCKET

Have a person cut a pack of cards. Let him count the cards in his heap. Suppose there are twenty-four. That leaves twenty-eight with you, as you verify by counting. For there are fifty-two cards in a pack.

Give the person your heap and let him put it in his inside pocket. Take his heap and put it in your inside pocket. Presto! Three cards leave his pocket and come into yours. He finds that his stock of twenty-eight is reduced to twenty-five, while you now have twenty-seven instead of twenty-four.

Anyone can count the cards when they are brought from the pockets. Absolutely no deception, so it seems. Especially as a borrowed pack is used.

This is the way. Before starting the trick, smuggle three cards from the pack and put them in your pocket. Let a person take part of the pack, count it, and give it to you—twenty-four cards for example. Meanwhile you count yours as three more than are really there, using the "false count." This is not absolutely necessary as you deduct from fifty-two, but it adds to the effect and as you are merely counting as a matter of routine, no one watches you closely.

Your cards really go into his pocket—three short. His go into your pocket and there they join the three cards that are awaiting them. The trick is as good as done.

9. A FOUR ACE TRICK

This is an effective version of the four ace trick, aided by the use of four special envelopes. The magician exhibits the four aces. He deals them in a row on the table. He adds three cards to each ace. He puts each group in an envelope—each envelope having an open front, so the center of the ace is visible.

At the magician's command, all the aces gather in one envelope, leaving four indifferent cards in each of the other envelopes.

The Method: When the four aces are first shown, they are held in a fan. Behind the last ace are three cards, bunched together. When the aces are laid on the pack and redealt in a row, only one of the cards is really an ace. Note that the uppermost of the real aces should be the ace of spades. The hidden cards are the five of diamonds, five of clubs, and three of hearts.

Another system of adding the three indifferent cards is to have them lying face up beneath the envelopes. The magician starts to remove the envelopes and lays down the fan of aces at the same time, covering the three extra cards. Then the cards are closed and dropped faces down on the pack.

With a row of four cards—apparently aces—but only the ace of spades on the table, the magician deals the three genuine aces on the ace of spades. Then three indifferent cards are placed on each of the supposed aces—twelve cards in all. The packets are now inserted in the envelopes. The open-cut sides of the envelopes are underneath. So when the packets are in the envelopes, the magician can turn over the envelopes and apparently show an ace in each one. The center spots of the fives and the three look like the single spots of the aces.

The envelopes are inverted again and laid in a square—one envelope at each corner. The magician calls for a number: "one, two, three or four." Whatever is given, he counts around the square to the ace of spades. He can start his count wherever he wants, so it does not matter what number is given!

After "selecting" the ace of spades in this fashion, the magician gives that envelope into the keeping of a spectator. Removing the cards from one envelope, he shuffles them, spreads them and shows that the ace is missing. He does the same with each of the other envelopes. At the finish, all four aces are discovered in the envelope which is held by the spectator.

This routine can be performed without the envelopes, but it is not nearly so convincing. The use of the special envelopes, which are easily made, adds much to the trick. The envelopes should be slightly larger than a playing card. Envelopes that open at the end are the best.

CHAPTER VII

SPECIAL CARD TRICKS

In this section we have placed tricks which require a certain setup or arrangement of cards. With a bit of preparation, it is possible to produce effects in card magic which cannot be accomplished in a totally impromptu exhibition.

We have not, however, included tricks that need fake cards or special appliances. This section introduces a number of interesting ideas in card magic and will be of great value to the reader who is in search of novelty.

Some of the tricks require so little preparation that they can be introduced almost anywhere and will be of use to the impromptu magician as well as to the performer who has his own cards all ready in his pocket.

1. THE TEN CARD CIRCLE

This trick is simple but puzzling. It is described here in detail for two reasons: first, because it is a good impromptu trick in this form; second, because the trick which follows is a great improvement that will be more readily understood when one knows the circle method.

The cards, numbered from ace to ten, are arranged faces up like the circle of a clock dial. A spectator is invited to *think* of one card. Another person is asked to *point out* one card. Suppose, for instance, that the eight is thought of and the five is pointed out.

Noting the five, the magician adds ten, and says: "I want you—" the spectator who is thinking of the card—"to count from the five spot. Begin the count with your own number and count to fifteen, moving to the left."

The spectator does this. He places his finger on the five and says "eight"; he touches the four and says "nine"; he continues in this manner and when he reaches fifteen—the number set by the magician—he is astonished to find that his count has ended on the very card he chose—the eight spot!

This trick always works. Simply follow the system as described and the result will be the same. Remember to add ten to the number indicated.

To make the trick more perplexing, it is wise to use cards of different suits, but in numerical order, and to lay them faces down. Let a person peek at one card while your back is turned. Another person points out a card at random and turns it face up. Add ten to its value, tell the thinker to start his count at that card, and to begin with his own number. The fact that he arrives on his own card which is face down makes the experiment doubly perplexing.

2. IMPROVED CARD CIRCLE

The greatest improvement in this trick—which makes it a new effect—is the fact that the card circle is used in theory but not in practice. To the spectators, it appears to be a dealing trick.

A pack is shuffled. Ten cards are dealt off by a spectator. He notes the position of any card from the bottom of the heap—say six of clubs, four from the bottom.

The magician takes the heap. He asks someone to name a number below ten. Take eight for instance. The magician calmly removes eight cards from the bottom of the packet, saying: "Eight and ten make eighteen—we will count to eighteen beginning with your number—" pointing to the person who is thinking of the fourth card from the bottom.

The person says his number is four. The magician deals a card, counting "four." He does not drop the card to the table—he puts it under the heap from which he is dealing. He repeats this with the next cards, counting "five, six" and so on—thus he has an inexhaustible heap from which to deal. When he reaches eighteen, the number which he designated, the spectator's thought-of card is the one that he turns up. If he wishes, the performer can let the spectator do the dealing in the fashion described, counting to himself and ending on the mentally selected card. That is a good method to use as a repeat.

Keep these points in mind: the card mentally selected is noted counting from the *bottom* of the packet. The number of cards named by the second spectator are shifted in a group from *bottom to top*. The deal is made from the top, with the cards faces down, the cards going to the bottom one by one. The final card is turned up.

3. A MYSTIC PREDICTION

In this trick, the magician volunteers to make a remarkable prediction. He writes something upon a sheet of paper and folds it. He removes a pack of cards from its case and puts the folded paper therein. He arranges some cards in five heaps which lie in a row upon the table. He remarks that these heaps may be counted singly, from left to right.

A person is requested to select a heap, the magician making it plain that the heap selected will be the one used. "Take any heap," are his words, "and you will discover that I have foretold the very heap which you chance to choose!"

A heap is designated. The paper is taken from the card case. It is opened. It bears the words: "You will choose the five heap." This prediction is verified. The magician proves unmistakably that the chooser has taken the "five" heap.

The important secret of this experiment is that any one of the heaps will fill the bill. Each can be made to pass as the so-called "five" heap. This depends upon the arrangement of the cards.

One heap consists of all the five spots. Should it be chosen, the magician turns it face upward and shows that it has four fives. He shows the faces of the other cards. There are no fives among them. If this heap is taken, the magician says: "This, you see, is the 'five' heap—all five spots."

Another heap contains exactly five cards. It is the only heap which has that number—all other heaps have either more or less than five cards. Should this particular heap be selected, the wizard says:

"The 'five' heap. Your heap is the only one with five cards." He counts the cards in that heap and also the cards in the other heaps. But he turns none of the heaps face upward. This artifice is very convincing.

A third heap can also be made to appear as the "five" heap. It contains just four cards—three aces and a two spot. If this heap is selected, the magician picks it up and holds it face downward. One by one, he deals the cards face up on the table, counting the spots: "One, two, three and two make five!"

He then deals the other heaps the same way, showing that each has cards totalling more than five. When he picks up the heap with four fives, he simply deals two cards face up saying: "Five—ten—that's more than five already!"

When these heaps are laid out, the heap with the four fives should be in the center, flanked by the other two heaps just mentioned, the magician knowing the position of each individual heap. There are two more heaps to consider. These are the end heaps. Each consists of eight or nine indifferent cards.

Should one of these heaps be designated, the magician tells the chooser to leave it on the table. The paper is opened. The message is read.

"The 'five' heap," says the magician. "I told you that we count the heaps one, two, three, four, five—from left to right. That makes your heap number five—the 'five' heap."

It makes no difference which end heap is chosen. If the one selected is at the performer's right, he counts the heaps himself, running his hand from left to right. If the selected heap is at the performer's left, he orders the chooser to count to the correct heap —one, two, three, four, five—and the count ends on the selected heap.

It is advisable to call for this counting before the message is read. That makes the choice unmistakably five and the spectator picks up the heap while the paper is being unfolded. The magician then sweeps the other four heaps together and replaces them with the pack.

By having these cards set in order in the pack, the trick may be presented in a very smart fashion. It is a great improvement on old ideas of this order and can be turned into a very puzzling problem. It depends entirely upon presentation and requires no skill whatever.

4. DOUBLE DISCOVERY

A person takes a pack of cards from the performer. He cuts it in two heaps. He removes a cluster of cards from the lower half. He counts those cards and notes the bottom card of the group—say seven cards with the six of spades on the bottom. He must not take more than thirteen cards.

He is instructed to place the group with the chosen card on the other half of the pack. The performer's back is turned while this goes on. When the operation is completed, the magician turns around and picks up the pack, putting the top half on top.

Now he deals cards faces down, in a sort of circle. He does this with about twenty cards. Running his hand around, he suddenly turns a card face up. It is a seven spot. The performer announces that there were seven cards in the spectator's group. Instantly, the performer turns up another card. It is the six of spades, the card noted by the person.

In doing this trick, the magician first states that jack counts as eleven, queen as twelve and king as thirteen. On top of the pack he has thirteen cards arranged in this order, from the top: king, queen, jack, ten, nine, eight, seven, six, five, four, three, two, ace.

Note that the group taken by the spectator goes on these cards. It does not matter how many cards the group contains. The fourteenth card from the top will indicate, by its value, the number of cards put on by the spectator.

Thus the spectator takes seven cards, the bottom of his group being the six of spades, which he remembers. The performer deals from fifteen to twenty cards in a rough circle. He turns up the fourteenth card, counting around the circle and it is a seven spot.

That gives him a clue to the location of the spectator's noted card. It must be the one that was dealt seventh in the circle. Quickly going around the circle, the magician turns up the seventh card to reveal it as the selected one.

Suppose the spectator had ten cards in his group, with the five of clubs on the bottom.. The fourteenth card, when turned up by the conjuror, would be a ten spot. Counting to the tenth card in the circle, the performer would discover the five of clubs.

Immediately after revealing the selected card, the magician should mix the cards of the circle as he prepares to gather them up. This destroys any arrangement and leaves the spectators wondering, even if they do happen to see the faces of the cards.

5. THE CARD FORETOLD

There are various card tricks that involve predictions; this is one of the simplest yet most effective. It may be performed with an ordinary pack although the magician must be set beforehand.

A pack of cards is divided into two heaps which are shuffled together in dovetail fashion—a careful, legitimate shuffle. Something is written on a sheet of paper which is dropped in a glass or placed in the card-case.

Turning the pack face up, the magician states that he will carefully separate the reds from the blacks. Someone else may do this if desired—but the magician requests that it be done exactly, dealing each red or black card as it comes.

Thus two piles are obtained. A person is asked to choose either the red heap or the black heap. Suppose red is taken. The magician gives the cards value from one to thirteen—ace, one; jack, eleven; queen, twelve; king, thirteen. He asks all to note that if two cards are taken from the red heap, their value may indicate any number from one to twenty-six: two aces equaling two; two kings, twenty-six; other pairs, numbers in between. This fact is readily understood.

So the magician asks the spectator to cut the red pack at any point and to add the values of the two cards above and below the cut. These two values are to designate a card in the black heap—counting down from the top.

The cut is made. We will suppose that a five and a nine appear. They total fourteen. A spectator counts down fourteen in the black heap. The card is the ace of clubs. The folded paper is opened. It bears the name "ace of clubs"!

Now for the simple method. The magician first separates the red cards from the blacks—long before he shows the trick. He arranges the red cards thus:

King, ace, queen, two, jack, three, ten, four, nine, five, eight, six, seven, seven, eight, six, nine, five, ten, four, jack, three, queen, two, king, ace.

There is no arrangement of the black heap. The magician simply notes the fourteenth card from the bottom. That is the card upon which the choice is to fall—in this instance, the ace of clubs.

When the pack is introduced, the two heaps are segregated as described—one color being upon the other. The magician turns the faces of the cards toward himself; spreading them slightly, he separates the pack so that he has the reds in one hand and the blacks in the other. He then proceeds with the dovetail shuffle—or lets some spectator perform that action.

The result: reds and blacks are intermingled, but the reds still retain their original order and the ace of clubs is still fourteen from the bottom—among the blacks. So when the pack is turned face up and the cards are separated one by one into two heaps, the peculiar arrangement of the reds remains comparatively the same. The ace of clubs now becomes fourteen from the top in the black heap.

The arrangement of the reds is important for this reason. No matter where that heap is cut, the cards above and below the cut will add to a total of either thirteen or fourteen! If the total is thirteen, the magician asks someone to remove thirteen cards from the top of the black heap and to look at the next card. If the total is fourteen, he tells the person to look at the fourteenth card from the top of the black heap. In either instance, the action seems to abide by the magician's promise—to take the card at the number designated by the red totals. Also, in either instance, the card consulted is the ace of clubs.

The magician has, of course, written his mysterious words early in the trick—just after introducing the pack. So everyone is due for amazement when the paper is opened and seen to bear the words ace of clubs.

There is just one other point. The magician, after the cards are separated, allows the spectator to select either heap—reds or blacks. This is simply a bit of by-play. Since both heaps are to be used, the magician cannot go wrong. If reds are taken, he uses them to ascertain a number in the black heap. If blacks are taken, he states that he has predicted a black card and merely uses the red heap to pick a number at random.

6. PASSE PASSE CARDS

This wonderful effect is now explained with certain modifications that make it a most excellent mystery for performance anywhere. It can be done in the parlor or on the stage—with small cards or with giant cards.

All that is needed is two packs with different white-margined backs—preferably a red pack and a blue pack. Also two drinking glasses (stands if giant cards are used) and some rubber bands.

Taking the red pack of cards, the magician has one selected. It is replaced in a cluster of about twelve cards which the magician removes from the bottom of the deck. Encircled with rubber bands, this packet is placed in a glass.

Next a card is similarly taken from the blue pack and is replaced in a cluster of about twelve cards taken from the bottom of the pack. This group is also girded with rubber bands and it goes in the other glass.

To show the location of each heap, a card is removed from each group and set back forward in front of the glass in which the group is located. On the right, a red card shows the red packet; on the left, a blue card shows the blue packet.

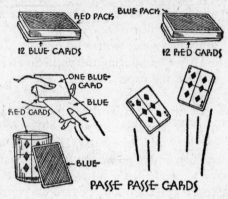

Arrangement of packs and various stages in the Passe Passe Card Trick.

The magician takes both packets, explaining that the rubber bands now make it impossible to remove a card from the group without considerable difficulty. He tosses the groups in the air. He picks them up or catches them. He puts the red group in its glass —the blue group in its glass. Now comes the baffling finish. The glasses are given to the spectators. Among the red cards is found the blue-backed card that was selected from the blue pack! Among the blue cards is discovered the red-backed card that was taken from the red pack!

A wonderful trick, yet quite simple and easy to do. Just a bit of quick preparation is necessary. Before performing, take one dozen red cards from the red pack and put them on the bottom of the blue pack. Likewise take a dozen blue cards and put them on the bottom of the red pack.

Important: The bottom card of each group should be the same —say the six of diamonds. Then the performer is ready to work. If he is using his own cards, he should have the packs in their cases.

A card is chosen from the red pack. In spreading the pack for a selection, the magician does not spread the bottom cards. Hence the blue backs do not come into view. After the card is taken, the magician spreads the faces of the pack toward the spectators. This enables him to see the backs. He draws off all the blue cards from the bottom, but keeps one red card on top of them. He squares these cards and holds them faces down for the insertion of the chosen card. The single red-backed card makes it seem as though the group consisted entirely of red-backed cards.

The procedure with the blue pack is exactly the same. The red-backed cards at the bottom are not spread when a blue card is selected. But in spreading the pack faces front, the red-backed cards are drawn off beneath a blue-backed card.

The chosen blue card goes into the little squared-up heap. It appears to be going into a packet of bona fide blue cards.

Each packet is girded with rubber bands and placed in a glass, with the bottom card facing the audience. To point out the location of red and blue, the magician takes the top card from each heap and sets it in front of the glass. This is a clever idea. It disposes of the extra card in each group.

One packet is taken in each hand—faces of the cards toward the audience. Each packet appears the same, because the facing cards are identical. Each is a six of diamonds. Now the groups are brought together and tossed. When they come down, no one knows which is which. But the magician shows the backs and calmly places the red-backed group in the glass indicated by the red card, while the blue-backed packet goes in the glass indicated by the blue card.

No one realizes the subtle change that has taken place. Yet the performer announces that the simple toss in the air has caused each selected card to leave its own group and pass into the other! Wonderful, if true.

It appears to be true when the spectators take the packets from the glasses. The blue-backed card is with the reds; the red-backed card is in the midst of the blues. Not a clue to the secret remains.

7. CARDS AND ENVELOPES

A very surprising mystery. Three selected cards apparently leave an envelope and pass into a group of cards contained in another envelope.

The magician begins by dealing sixteen cards from a pack. These sixteen cards are counted by a spectator. The magician puts them in an envelope, which is sealed and marked.

Next, sixteen more cards are counted faces down; they are spread on the table and three cards are turned up and noted by spectators. The magician shuffles these cards and puts them in the second envelope, which is also sealed.

The first surprise comes when nineteen cards are discovered in the first envelope. Opening the second envelope and counting the cards therein, only thirteen are found. Then the nineteen group is counted faces up and the chosen cards are discovered in it!

The secret depends upon two groups of sixteen cards that are exactly alike. This means that the magician must use his own pack, having his special arrangement made up with the aid of a duplicate pack. The groups of sixteen cards are on top of the pack. Thus when the magician counts off sixteen cards and then another group of sixteen, he is forming two heaps that are identical. But the cards are faces down so no one knows this fact.

Beneath one envelope—which we will call A—are three odd cards, lying faces down. The envelope and the cards overlap the edge of the table slightly. Now, the performer must secretly add those three cards to the sixteen which he intends to put into envelope A.

There are two ways of doing this. First Method: Lay the sixteen cards faces down on the envelope, drawing out the envelope at almost the same moment. Second Method: Pick up the envelope with the three cards beneath it and let it rest momentarily above the sixteen cards. The three odd cards are allowed to fall upon the sixteen, which are a trifle disarranged.

Either method works and the upshot is that nineteen cards go into envelope A, despite the fact that sixteen were carefully counted at the outset.

Three cards are now selected from the other group—the cards that are to go into envelope B. Note that these cards are turned up from among the sixteen, so no one becomes acquainted with any of the cards other than the selected ones.

Upon shuffling this bunch of sixteen, the magician holds the group in his right hand, thumb at one end, fingers at the other—the cards faces down beneath the hand. With the aid of the left hand, he forms a slight space at the bottom of the group so that three cards are detached from the others.

He picks up envelope B and holds it with the flap extended—the face of the envelope downward. He moves the envelope toward his right hand, the extended flap pointing like an arrow.

In sliding the cards into the envelope, it is a simple matter to insert the point of the flap between the bulk of thirteen cards and the three odd cards that are separated beneath. The result is that only thirteen cards actually go into envelope B. The rest go beneath. The left fingers, under the envelope, help the odd cards into position and hold them there.

This envelope is held momentarily over the pack of cards, which is lying—somewhat disarranged—on the table. The left fingers release their cards, so that the odd cards fall on the table. Envelope B is then sealed.

Now for the action, the important part of the trick being ended. The performer commands the selected cards to pass from envelope B to envelope A. Upon opening envelope A, nineteen cards are discovered, being counted faces down. Envelope B is opened. Only thirteen cards—counted faces down.

Picking up the pack, the performer holds it in his left hand, while the right holds the thirteen cards. Spectators are told to turn the nineteen cards faces up and look for the three selected cards. During this search, the magician adds the three top cards of the pack to the thirteen in his right hand and transfers all to the bottom of the pack. He quietly counts off thirteen—to be ready in case anyone asks to see the thirteen cards from envelope B.

To make this quick, those thirteen cards can be previously bent upward in the center so they can be lifted off the pack when needed. Generally the spectators are so surprised to find the chosen cards with the nineteen that the trick can be ended there. Due to the duplication of the packets, the selected cards must be in the nineteen heap.

Book Two
SECRETS OF MAGIC

CHAPTER VIII

BLACKSTONE'S SLEIGHT-OF-HAND WITH CARDS

IN A GREAT NUMBER of card tricks, a chosen card is taken from the pack, returned; and after the pack is shuffled, the card is discovered by the performer, in some mysterious fashion.

In order to do this, it is essential that the card be controlled by the magician, and it has always been customary to make use of a sleight known as the "pass" or "shift."

Now the "pass" is a difficult movement to acquire. It is nothing more than an invisible cut, executed at close range. When a card is replaced in the center of the pack, the performer invisibly cuts the pack, thus bringing the chosen card to the top or bottom as he desires.

With the majority of card performers, the "pass" is not invisible; with others, it is a suspicious movement; with all it is unnecessary. Why, when a single card is to be removed from the center of the pack and placed on the top or bottom, should anyone go to the difficulty of moving half the pack?

With some expert magicians, the "pass" works in practice; but it is wrong in theory. Furthermore, it is seldom effective unless the hands immediately move into a shuffle, which is a natural action following the return of a chosen card. The method of controlling a chosen card that is described here is direct, effective and easy of accomplishment, utilizing the shuffle as a natural follow-up. It has mystified magicians, and with it the beginner can work wonders after very little practice.

I. BLACKSTONE'S CARD CONTROL

Spread the pack between the hands, and allow someone to select a card. While this is being done, square the cards and hold them firmly in the left hand, thumb above, fingers below.

With the right hand, bend up the outer ends of the cards, and

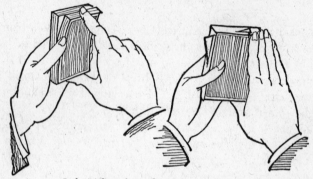

Left: Riffling the pack.
Right: Pushing the chosen card to the left.

allow them to fall in quick succession. This is known as the "riffle." Stop the "riffle," or let the cards fall slowly, so that the chosen card may be returned.

Now comes the important movement. The pressure of the left hand prevents the card from going entirely into the pack. With the right hand, push the card in, but turn it slightly to the left, so that it goes in at an angle. The outer left end of the card will project slightly when the outer right is flush with the pack.

This is the cue for the left thumb to gently slide the top cards of the pack to the left, so that they hide the projecting corner. The pack appears quite normal.

The shuffle follows immediately. The right hand comes from beneath, and the fingers grip the outer end of the pack, while the thumb presses against the inner end.

The left thumb draws off one or more of the top cards; and

the left forefinger, hidden beneath them, catches the projecting corner of the chosen card, and carries it along.

Thus the chosen card becomes the bottom one of those which have been drawn off. The shuffle is continued by drawing off more cards with the left thumb, and letting them fall on those first removed. Proceed thus until the entire pack has been drawn off in shuffles, and the bottom card will be the one that was chosen.

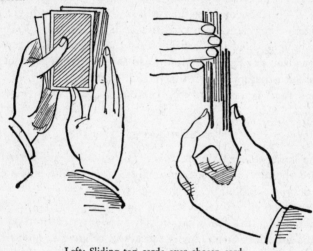

Left: Sliding top cards over chosen card.
Right: Drawing out chosen card in shuffle.

This movement is simple and natural—and for that reason it is effective. Yet there are certain errors which must be avoided.

First: some difficulty may be experienced in drawing out the chosen card easily. This can be overcome by moistening the forefinger slightly; also by lifting up with the forefinger so as to relieve any pressure on the card.

Second: there will be a tendency to draw off all the cards above the chosen one in a single group. This ruins the effectiveness of the movement. To counteract this tendency, press the upper half of the pack very firmly between the right thumb and fingers. This makes it necessary to draw out the chosen card.

The beauty of this sleight lies in the fact that the chosen card actually goes in the center of the pack; and the shuffle follows in a natural manner. The passage of the selected card is absolutely invisible, being completely covered by the cards above; and sharp-eyed observers begin to look for some action *after* the essential part of the maneuver has been accomplished.

Speed is not necessary; but smoothness should be acquired. Hesitancy will cause suspicion, even though the sleight is indetectible. The movement of the cards to the left should begin immediately after the chosen card has been inserted.

In shuffling, hold the cards close to the horizontal, or turn so that the backs of the cards are toward the spectators. A slight tilt to the left is natural; but if the vertical position is preferred, precaution must be taken to keep the bottom card from showing.

2. FALSE SHUFFLE SYSTEM

The false shuffle is the movement whereby the performer apparently shuffles the pack thoroughly, yet keeps the chosen card in a desired position.

In connection with the system of card control, the best method is a shuffle that constantly transfers the chosen card from bottom to top, and vice versa. This is actually a genuine shuffle; hence cannot excite suspicion.

To bring the card to the top, utilize the same method of shuffling, peeling off a few cards from the top with the left thumb. But when the bottom of the pack is reached, draw off cards one by one. Result: the chosen card will end on top.

To bring it to the bottom again, merely draw off the top card alone, and shuffle the others on it. Moistening the thumb often helps in this action.

Several cards are controlled as follows: Bring the first selected card to the bottom, and either leave it there, or shuffle it to the top and back to the bottom.

Then the second selected card is returned to the pack.

Bring it to the bottom by the card control; but as the shuffle is concluded, run the cards one by one so that the first selected card remains on top.

Then place the left thumb on top of the pack and the fingers beneath, and draw off the top and bottom cards together. Shuffle the rest of the pack on them. The two selected cards will be at the bottom. They can be brought to the top in the usual fashion, for they are treated singly at the finish of the shuffle.

If a third selected card is used—or a fourth—have the cards previously selected at the bottom, and proceed exactly as with the second card. With three cards under control, one will come on the bottom and two on top.

To bring all to the bottom, draw off the top and bottom cards as one; draw the next top card on to them; and continue the shuffle. With four under control, there will be three on top; so bring two off singly.

Experiment with the cards will show that any number of cards can be controlled in this manner. The performer must keep his mind on the cards, and practice the various movements; but throughout the actions will always be natural.

It will be observed that the card control and the shuffle system work together. One is virtually a part of the other. All awkward movements are avoided, and in the apparent action of mixing the cards, the performer can keep them on the top or bottom of the pack as he prefers.

With a group of chosen cards on the bottom, shuffle naturally until the group is reached; then finish by single runs, a card at a time. The same group can be brought to the bottom by running the top cards one at a time and then shuffling the rest of the pack on them.

3. THE END SHUFFLE

In addition to the usual shuffle, described above, the "end shuffle" should be cultivated. The pack is held in the left hand, which is palm upward, fingers at the left of the pack and the thumb at the right. The pack is in a horizontal position.

With the thumb and second finger of the right hand, pull a

clump of cards from the center of the pack, drawing the cards toward the body. Drop them on the pack, and immediately

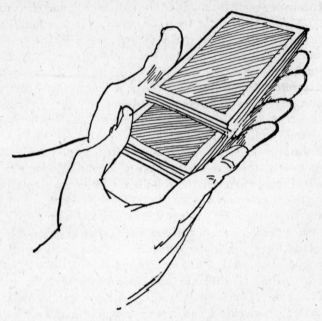

draw out a smaller cluster of cards, placing them on top; and continue this operation several times, the group of cards dwindling with each withdrawal.

This can be done quite rapidly, and makes a very convincing shuffle. It also serves as a false shuffle when the chosen cards are on the bottom, for the lower cards of the pack are not disturbed, no matter how often the shuffle may be repeated.

This shuffle also serves another important purpose. The "pass" was not employed merely to bring chosen cards to the top of the pack; it was sometimes used to bring a desired card back to the center, from either the top or the bottom.

Now with the "end shuffle," this is very easily done. The shuffle is virtually continuous, done time and again; and in concluding the shuffle, the right hand merely draws out the bottom half of the pack, and drops it on top, thus bringing the bottom card of the pack to the center. By dropping the section at an angle, a slight step is formed, so that the pack may be separated at that point.

4. TO FORCE A CARD

Making a person take a certain card from the pack is called the "force," and it is a useful accomplishment. It has been described in many works on magic, and the instructions invariably say to note the bottom card, bring it to the center by the "pass" and proceed.

The author's plan is to sight the bottom card by turning the bottom of the pack toward himself. Then he begins the "end shuffle," apparently mixing the cards, and finishes by a cut that brings the known card to the center of the pack.

At this point, the section placed on top of the pack should be set well to the right, so that it rests on the third and fourth fingers

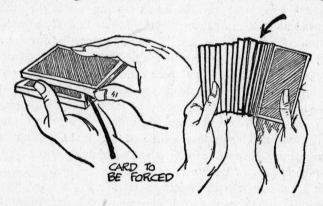

CARD TO
BE FORCED

of the left hand. The pack drops flat on the left palm, and the thumbs of both hands begin a spreading process so that a person may select a card.

The theory of the "force" is to spread the cards in such a manner that the chooser will naturally take the desired card. This is accomplished by timing the speed of the cards as they go from left to right, so that the particular card reaches the person's hand just at the instant he is ready to draw a card.

The most important element in the "force" is that of surprise. If the spectator does not suspect the performer's purpose, the chance of success is very great.

Most magicians time the "force" according to the spectator. In some instances they are very leisurely. As it is a bad plan to slow down or speed up to a noticeable extent, once the cards are being spread, the spectator not infrequently takes a card very close to the desired one, and the "force" fails. This is not alarming, because the card can be "forced" on another person; nevertheless, a sure-fire "force" is something to be desired, and I shall explain just such a method.

Do not start to spread the cards until the spectator is virtually ready to take one. Inject a spirit of action into the procedure. Then begin to spread the cards, quite rapidly—so rapidly indeed that the person cannot easily take one.

At the same time, keep the hands moving so that the pack is always going away from him, moving here and there, and making it impossible for him to get the card. Just as the chosen card arrives, reverse the process, suddenly stopping the retreating policy and letting the pack come suddenly toward the person. At the instant he grasps, the chosen card is ready for him—the spreading has ceased; and he gets the card you want him to have.

The card to be "forced" should be quite a bit below the center of the pack; and if this plan is followed, the "force" will not only be sure, but will be quite as effective as a leisurely system.

In brief, the spectator is ready to take the card all along, but he can't get it until the performer wishes. Yet the movement must be natural. The spectator, in his eagerness, will not realize that the performer is keeping the cards just out of his reach, and he will snatch the proper card with pleasure.

In actuality, the performer spreads the cards until he reaches the proper one and then thrusts it into the spectator's hand; but in performing, this should be done artfully. The magician must seem indifferent about the matter; his speed must seem his natural method; he must not apparently draw the pack away nor thrust it forward.

Whenever a "force" fails through any cause, the card should be "forced" on another person. Then the first card taken may be used in another trick, by means of the card control.

Summary of Preceding Sleights

The various movements just described constitute a new variety of card work that is in opposition to most accepted systems. The "pass" is avoided. A chosen card is preferably kept on the bottom instead of on the top. The constant transfer from bottom to top eliminates tricky shuffles.

The "pass" whenever necessary is replaced by an open cut in the course of the "end shuffle." The "force" is rapid instead of leisurely. By conforming with these methods, effective results will be obtained.

5. THE SECOND DEAL

The "second deal" is a sleight neglected by magicians; yet it is extremely useful. It consists in apparently dealing the cards in a regular manner from the top of the pack; but actually retaining the top card all the while.

To accomplish this, lay the pack across the left palm, so that the left thumb may rest lightly along one edge. Hold the hand toward the body, so that the left thumb extends directly outward.

Now practice dealing the cards one by one; drawing the top card directly to the right with the right thumb, which touches the card at the outer right corner. As each card clears the pack, the right fingers grip it from beneath, and carry it away.

This is the natural, simple method of dealing that is to be simulated with the "second deal."

Press the tip of the left thumb lightly on the top card and move the thumb slowly toward the body. You will observe that the top card will move inward, as though pivoted in the form of the left thumb—the outer left corner of the card will retain its position.

By advancing the thumb, the card will resume its former place. This must be done very lightly, in order to move the top card independently.

When the outer right corner of the top card has been drawn inward about half an inch, you will find it an easy matter to pull

The position of the hands in the "Second Deal."

out the second card with the aid of the right thumb—exactly as you would normally draw off the top card.

As the right hand draws the card clear, advance the left thumb again so that the top card resumes its normal position. This is the basis of the second deal.

But in actual practice, the left thumb should draw in the top card as little as possible—not much more than one-eighth of an inch. This is because the left thumb serves to hide the top card, and no clue should be given to movement of the top card.

If both thumbs are slightly dampened, the sleight will become much less difficult; for less pressure will be necessary on the part of the left; and the right will be able to pull away the second card even though it touches only the edge of the card at the corner.

The position of the left thumb is important. It should rest at the extreme edge of the top card, so that the end of the card will not be in view beneath the thumb. The left fingers also assist by curling up against the side of the pack, thus holding the deck square. Each card that the right hand deals slides over the tips of the left fingers.

This sleight is quite easy to learn; but it is one that requires considerable practice to perfect. The performer must learn to execute it with constant precision, and he must also learn to deal the cards with the rapidity that is customary in dealing cards normally from the top of the pack.

A natural motion of the hands also serves to facilitate the sleight as well as making it more deceptive. The left hand should approach the right while the left thumb is drawing back the top card. The moment that the hands meet, the deal of the second card begins, the left hand going away as the right hand removes the card. The hands should perform their functions automatically, the eyes of the performer being on the cards that have been dealt, or gazing toward the spectators. Ordinary dealing is a very easy process; and the magician should endeavor to make the "second deal" appear just as easy.

6. THE CHANGES

The sleights just given are new, and little-known. I shall explain two old sleights for the sake of completeness. These are the "changes."

(A) The "Bottom Change"

Hold a card between the first and second fingers of the right hand. The pack lies in the left, as though ready for a deal—the left thumb on top.

As the right hand approaches the left, all the left fingers except the forefinger are lowered, so the single card may be placed between them and the forefinger.

At the same instant, the left thumb pushes the top card of the pack to the right, so that it may be taken between the thumb and forefinger of the right hand. These two motions, the deposit of one card on the bottom of the pack and the removal of the top card take place simultaneously.

Left: Beginning the "Bottom Change."
Right: The exchange of the cards.

(B) The "Top Change"

This is the reverse of the "bottom change." The single card is held between the right thumb and forefinger. The left hand

Left: The beginning of the "Top Change."
Right: The exchange of the cards.

pushes the top card to the right. As the right hand lays its card on the pack, the forefinger and second finger simultaneously grip the top card of the pack and carry it away.

The "changes" when executed, require a good misdirection.

The right hand holds a card and thrusts it toward a spectator while the performer inquires "Your card?" As he awaits an answer, and the person's eyes meet his, he brings the card back to the pack and makes the change, the left hand withdrawing while the right comes slowly forward.

Or the performer may show a card to a person on his right; and as he turns to his left, the hands meet in front of the body long enough for the "change" to be made—a fraction of a second. Never look at the hands while executing one of these sleights.

7. CARD TRICKS WITH SLEIGHTS

With the various sleights at his disposal, the magician can perform many excellent tricks. A few are enumerated here.

(A) The Self-Turning Card

Bring a chosen card to the top of the pack. Lay the pack on the palm of the right hand, crosswise; with the thumb over the center. Push the top card slightly forward with the thumb and tilt it up a bit with the tip of the second finger.

Then slide the cards along the table. The top card will be turned over by the pressure of the air, and will appear face up in the midst of the spread out pack.

(B) A Double Mistake

Have two cards selected and bring them both to the top. Show one card to the person on your right—the card that he did not choose. He will state that it is not his card. Turn to the left, making the "top change." Show the card you now have to the person on your left—he will not recognize it either.

Turn slowly to the first person, and let him see the card again. To his surprise it has become the card he chose. While he is admitting that he was mistaken before, turn to the second person, executing the "bottom change" (or the "top change") and let him see the card again. He will have to admit that it is also his card!

(C) Any Number

This is one of the most effective of card tricks. Bring a chosen card to the top; and ask for any small number. Suppose "eight" is given. Deal off seven cards with the "second deal"; then turn up the top card at number eight. It will be the chosen one, appearing at the number desired.

This can be done without the second deal, by simply counting off eight cards one by one, drawing each one on the card before, thus reversing their order. The eighth card will not be the chosen one. In replacing the eight on the pack, the chosen card naturally becomes the eighth; so you ripple the pack and let the chooser count eight for himself. He will find the card there.

An improvement on this version is to count off the eight, and drop the eighth face down on the table. While people are looking at it, return the other seven to the pack; but let the bottom card of the group rest for a moment on the tips of the left fingers, while the right fingers flip it face up beneath the other cards of the group. The card on the table is put back on the pack. When a spectator counts off eight, he finds the chosen card there—face up.

(D) All Alike

Let a person select a card. Bring it to the bottom of the pack. Force the same card on a second person; bring it to the bottom and force on a third person. Then bring the card to the top. You lay this card on the table and state that it is one of the three cards chosen; that any one of the three who really believes it is his card will find that it is.

Turn the card up, and all persons will recognize their card. This can be varied by first showing a card from the center of the pack. None will acknowledge it. Make a change, and lay the card on the table. This time all will be forced to acknowledge it.

(E) Self-Revealing Card

This is a nice little finish to a card trick. A chosen card is brought to the top and the pack is laid on the right hand. Draw the top card slightly inward so that one corner presses into the base of the thumb; and the other corner comes beneath the tip of the little finger. Press downward with the little finger and the card will mysteriously rise to an upright position.

8. THE KNIFE IN THE PACK

This is a new trick—a very clever effect. Holding a pack horizontally between the tips of his left thumb and forefinger, the magician inserts a knife into the center of the pack.

He immediately announces the name of the card above the knife. He places his right forefinger on top of the pack and lifts up all the cards above the knife, showing the card he named.

The trick may be repeated; and spectators may insert the knife. But the performer, before he lifts the cards will always name the card correctly.

The Method: Use a table-knife with a bright blade. When the

knife has been inserted, tilt the pack very slightly to the right. At the same instant, tilt the knife blade slightly to the left, moving it so that it comes directly under the inner left corner of the

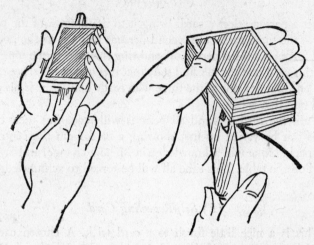

pack. You will immediately catch a reflection of the index corner of the card above the knife. That is the card you name, before you lift up the upper half of the pack.

If the pack is held high, so that it is almost on a level with the eyes, the tilting motions are virtually unnecessary. The weight of the knife will bend down the lower half of the cards a bit, and you will catch the reflection easily.

With practice, this trick can be accomplished easily, and with regular precision.

9. THE SPECTATORS' TRICK

The ambition of every magician is to allow a spectator to shuffle a pack, and have another person take a card from it and replace it, shuffling the pack for himself—after which the magician finds the chosen card.

This seeming miracle of card magic is quite possible, with the use of a "one way" pack—or "single enders" as they are sometimes termed. Such a pack consists of cards which have a design on the back that is different at one end from the other. Obviously, if the cards are arranged with the patterns all one way, a card that is turned around can be easily discovered by looking through the pack.

Armed with such a pack, with the cards all pointing in one direction, the trick may be undertaken. Let a spectator shuffle the cards—taking care that he does not "riffle" the ends together, but merely uses the ordinary overhand shuffle. Then tell him to spread the cards and let a person take one.

While the pack is still held, tell him to turn his back so that the chooser may insert his card without anyone seeing where it goes. This automatically turns the ends of the cards the other way; so when the chosen card is inserted, the pack may be shuffled normally; yet the magician can immediately find the card by looking through the pack for the one that is reversed.

Most expensive cards are "single enders"; but the patterns are too obvious. There are two styles of "Bicycle" cards—the "Emblem Back" and the "Wheel Back" that are excellent one-way cards, as the pattern does not reveal this peculiarity to the average person.

10. THE TRAVELING DEUCE

This is an old trick with a surprising finish that is quite new. A deuce of diamonds is inserted at various positions near the center of the pack, but it always appears on the top or the bottom.

Place the deuce on top of the pack to begin; and see that the trey or three-spot of the same suit is located fourth.

Show the deuce; execute the "top change," and insert the card which people believe to be the deuce in the center of the pack. Naturally, it passes to the top.

Then make the "bottom change" and push the card into the center; this time the deuce turns up at the bottom.

Turn away for an instant to pick up a table-knife. In so doing, slide the deuce under the trey which is on top of the pack.

Insert the knife beneath the top card, so that it runs diagonally across the center of the card from right to left. Press the forefinger on top of the card, and raise it so all can see the face.

The knife blade, passing across both index corners and the center spot of the trey, make it appear to be the deuce. There is no

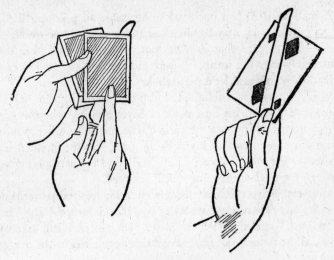

Lifting the three spot to make it appear as a deuce.

mistake this time; everyone sees the card pushed into the center of the pack with the aid of the knife; and all are convinced it is the deuce. Remove the knife and insert it diagonally under the top card from right to left, this time. Turn up the card on the knife and reveal the deuce—the index corners being unconcealed.

This is a very convincing procedure, that is sure to prove mystifying.

11. THE TEN CARD TRICK

Two heaps of ten cards—from one heap, three cards pass invisibly, one at a time. They appear in the other heap. Both heaps are held by spectators. This is always a good trick; and the author's favorite sleight is absolutely indetectible.

This trick is one of the specialties of Nate Leipzig, the famous card manipulator.

Let someone count ten cards on your left hand—one by one. This person stands on your left. Then you place a borrowed

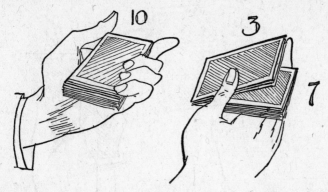

handkerchief over your extended left arm, and allow someone to count ten cards on to your right hand, the counter standing on your right.

While this is taking place, slide the three top cards of the left hand on to the tips of the left fingers.

Turn your left side toward the man on the right, and request him to remove the handkerchief from the arm. This brings the left hand close to the right, and slightly above it, as the left arm is raised a bit. The three loose cards are immediately slid on to the cards in the right hand.

Face the audience the instant the handkerchief is removed, swinging the hands wide apart. Tell the man on your right to "find the center of the handkerchief—which is in the middle." Then give him the cards from your right hand and see that he wraps them tightly in the cloth.

Flip the cards in your left hand, and state that one has passed from that group, into the handkerchief. To prove this, you count the cards.

Here you must utilize a simple sleight known as the "false count." Draw the top card of the heap away in the right hand, counting "one." Place it on the second card of the heap and count "two," drawing both cards away. Do the same on "three";

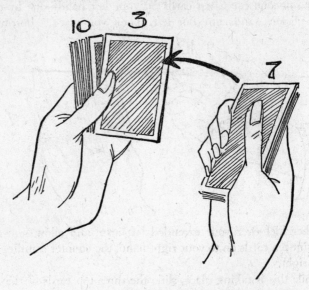

but on the counts of "four," and "five," do not remove any cards from the heap. Then proceed "six, seven, eight, nine," in normal fashion.

State that another card will pass into the handkerchief. Flip the cards, and count them again, this time making the "false count" on but one occasion, thus counting eight.

Place the cards in the hands of the man on your left, and give them another flip. Tell him to count them. He finds only seven. The man with the handkerchief finds that he has thirteen cards!

Note: If difficulty is experienced with the three cards to be transferred, stop the first man when he has counted to seven, and bend the sides of the cards downward, as they lie in the left hand. Then let him resume the count, with three more cards. This will let the three cards rest separately on top of the heap, ready for the toss.

Be sure that the man who is to receive the handkerchief is on your extreme right. Thrust your elbow close to his face, so that he cannot see the transfer. The other spectators will not see it, as your arm and body are turned away.

Be sure that the cards are clearly counted before and after the trick, so that the effectiveness of the mystery will not be lost.

Variation: In this method, the man on the left uses red backed cards; the man on the right uses blue backed cards. Yet the trick takes place, and three red cards are found among the blue!

The right hand has a more difficult task in this form of the trick. The cards are rested on the fingers; and as you turn to the right, the right thumb must lift a few of the cards, making an opening into which the cards from the left hand slide. The right hand instantly squares its cards, showing a blue back still on top. The trick then proceeds in the usual manner. The three red cards are found among the blue.

By way of increasing the effectiveness, you may lay the right hand cards face up in the handkerchief, after displaying the blue back on top. When the handkerchief is opened, tell the man on your right to shuffle them face up, to see if they feel like thirteen. This mixes the reds among the blue, and when he finally turns them over and counts them on your hand, the red cards make their appearance at different places.

The actions of the hands may be reversed, if desired, the right hand making the throw instead of the left.

12. BLACKSTONE'S KING AND QUEEN

Three cards, queen, king and deuce are shown, and this little story is unfolded:

"Many years ago there lived a king and queen on the Isle of Bong. She was very fond of him, but one day she became rather peeved, and gave him the deuce (1) for no other reason than that he came home with his hair dyed red (2) and her thoughts were of another queen who had told him to do this. So the king in turn became peeved, and leaving her with the deuce, went away —never to return."

At this point, the king becomes a blank card.

There are three cards used in the trick; a deuce, a blank, and a queen. But the queen is a faked card; for on the right half of it, you paste the face of a king.

When the three cards are exhibited, the blank card is placed in back of the deuce, and the two are placed over the side of the faked card, so that the cards appear to be fanned—queen, king and deuce. (1) Point to the deuce.

When the backs of the cards are shown, the thumb of the hand slides the deuce aside, showing the back of the blank card, which is taken to be the back of the king. It should be red backed, and the others should preferably be another color.

This draws attention from the spreading action, and naturally explains why the backs are shown (2).

Draw out the blank and lay it face down on the table. Slide the deuce under the face of the faked card so that it hides the portion of the king pasted thereon. Show the two cards back and front and pocket them. The "king" on the table proves to be a blank.

13. THE TURNING CARD

A very clever feat with prepared cards is performed with three cards—two spots and a face card.

DRAW OUT
TURN OVER

CLOSE AND REVERSE   REOPENED

The picture card is shown between the other two. Then the fan is closed, and the cards are turned over. When they are spread again, the picture card is face up, while the others are back up! Yet all three cards are shown separately back and front.

Preparation: Cut a good-sized corner from a duplicate picture card, and paste it to the upper left corner of the back of the genuine card.

This enables you to show three cards in a fan—the face card between the others—but with the face card actually back up. The backs of the cards are not shown.

The fan is closed. The cards are turned over, and also turned around, so that the fan is formed from the other end. The genuine face of the picture card shows between the backs of other cards. Turning the fan over, the back of the picture card is seen between the faces of the spot cards—the fake corner still being hidden in the fan, under one of the spot cards.

Now comes the clever maneuver. Seize the end of the picture card, and draw the card quickly from the fan, at the same instant turning it face upward. Slap it down on the table. This action makes it appear that you have shown the card back and front— apart from the other two cards, whereas you have not shown the back completely.

Then turn the spot cards over, one at a time, and drop them faces down on the table. You have shown three separate and distinct cards—back and front.

14. BLACKSTONE'S MASTERPIECE PACK

Some years ago, this pack of cards was planned, and it has still retained its value of general utility to the average magician.

The pack utilizes two "key" cards—one shorter than the other cards in the pack; the other narrower. These can be prepared with a pair of scissors; but it is best to trim them with a photographic cutter, and have the corners carefully rounded afterward. About $\frac{1}{32}$ of an inch is cut off.

This pack will stand inspection; it can be used in ordinary card games; yet when tricks are in order, it will be very easy to perform them.

The pack may be shuffled and a card selected. When the pack is laid on the table, the magician takes it by the sides and lifts off some of the cards. His fingers finding the break at the narrow card naturally lift all cards above that point, and the chosen card goes on the narrow one.

The pack may be cut frequently; but the performer has merely to cut at the narrow card again, and he will show the chosen card on the bottom of the portion he has lifted.

A second card may also be controlled with the aid of the short card; in this instance the performer cuts at the end instead of the sides.

An effective trick is to have a card taken from the pack. Then riffle the ends of the cards, inviting return of the selected card. As the riffle reaches the short card, it will suddenly stop, and the selected card will go back on top of the short one. After the pack has been cut several times, remove any card, and push it face upward into the pack. Do this at the end, and make sure that it goes in just above the short card. Thus when you run through the pack, the chosen card will be face to face with the upturned card.

To "force" the short card, get it to the middle of the pack. Riffle the ends of the pack very rapidly, inviting a person to thrust his finger in the cards as they fall. Start the riffle as his finger approaches. He will have difficulty inserting his finger until the short card brings the riffle to a sudden stop. Advance the pack at that instant and catch his finger.

This movement is bold but effective, and he will be sure his choice was free. Tell him to look at the card below his finger. Naturally he sees the short card. He may then shuffle the pack to his heart's content. As soon as you cut at the end of the pack, you will bring the chosen (and "forced") card to the top.

Worked in combination, the short and narrow cards produce some amazing results. Here is the feature trick with this pack.

Have the short card on top; the narrow card on the bottom. Let a spectator count off any number of cards—say sixteen— face down on the table, while your back is turned. This action reverses the cards counted; so when he replaces them, the short card will be the sixteenth from the top.

The pack may then be cut several times. When you take the pack, find the narrow card and cut at that point, so that it is on the bottom again. Then riffle the ends to find the short card. Lift off the short card and all above it. Count the cards and you will have sixteen—the exact number he counted! They are actually the spectator's cards.

15. CORNER BENDING

One of the neatest—and easiest—principles of modern card conjuring is that of the "bent corner."

When a card is chosen from an ordinary pack, the performer secretly bends the inner corner with the fingers of his right hand. This may be done while a spectator is pointing to the card he desires to select; or it may be performed after the card has been returned to the spread out pack. The fingers of the right hand, under the pack, accomplish the action with very little difficulty.

No matter how much the pack is shuffled, the chosen card can always be discovered by looking at the corners; and it can be brought to top or bottom by cutting the pack there.

The cleverest trick dependent on this principle is to insert a card face up under the bent corner, and to lift the cards there, showing the one selected. This may be varied by showing two cards face up, and thrusting one in below the bent corner; and the other above. When the cards are withdrawn, the chosen card comes between them.

Or it may be done thus: Show a card and ask: "Is that your card?" When "No" is answered, say: "Remember this card." Put it in the pack face down, under the bent corner. Do the same with another card, and put it over the bent corner.

Then turn the pack face up, and spread the cards, asking everyone to watch for the two cards just shown. When they are observed, the chosen card will be seen between them.

16. THE MYSTIC REVERSO

This trick is quite new in principle, and has never been described in print. It requires practice, but can be easily acquired.

In effect, a card is chosen from a fan and is replaced in the pack. A card is withdrawn, but it is not the chosen one; so the pack is cut, and the chosen card is found face up among the others.

First obtain a pack with white margins on the backs. This is essential. Now reverse one of the spot cards and insert it about sixteen from the top.

Fan the pack from right to left—opposite to the usual direction. The cards are fanned very slightly at the top of the pack—just enough so that you can detect the reversed card by its slightly wider margin.

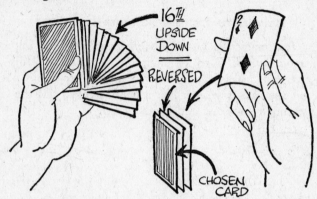

After a card is chosen from below, where the cards are spread more widely, take the card from the chooser and push it face down in the pack—directly above the turned-up card.

Square the pack, and state that you will find the chosen card. Riffle the cards slightly until you see the reversed card. Cut the pack one card below it.

Thus on the bottom of the pack you will have first an indifferent card (say the two of clubs); next the turned-up card; and then the chosen card.

Hold the bottom of the pack toward yourself, and carefully remove the three bottom cards as one. Do this by sliding them off slightly, and squaring them. Show this card—which appears to be the deuce of clubs—back and front, keeping the hand in motion as you do so, so that no one will detect the unusual thickness of the card.

Lay this "card" face up on top of the pack, and remark that it should be the chosen card. The reply is made that it is not.

Remove the deuce of clubs alone, and push it into the center of the pack, face down. This leaves the card that was formerly the turned-up card face down on top of the pack. The second card will be the chosen one—face up. Allow the pack to be cut, and when you spread the cards, you will reveal the chosen card —face up.

17. CARD THROUGH HANDKERCHIEF—AND CASE

Very few magicians know this excellent trick—an improvement upon the old "Card Through Handkerchief." In this version, a chosen card is shuffled into the pack; the pack is put in the case; the case is wrapped in a handkerchief, and the card comes through both case and handkerchief.

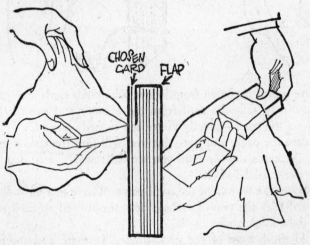

Illustrating the removal of the chosen card from the case; also how the flap is set under the chosen card.

The procedure is as follows: First bring the chosen card to the top of the pack, and put the pack in the case, which should be of the usual variety—with a flap—not a fancy box.

Put the pack in the case so that the top card is away from the flap. Then close the flap, and in so doing, insert it between the top card and the rest of the pack—a natural easy action. Then you show the case on all sides, keeping your thumb over the semi-circular cut that is in front of the flap, and which might reveal a portion of the back of the chosen card.

Take the case in the right hand, holding the back of the case toward the spectators. The case is at the finger tips, and the second finger touches the projecting back of the chosen card.

Throw the handkerchief over the case, and as you do so, draw the chosen card out an inch, so that it may be firmly clipped between the side of the thumb and the hand.

With the left hand, reach beneath the cloth and bring out the case, leaving the chosen card in the right hand. Put the case on the handkerchief, so that it lays directly over the card hidden beneath.

Fold up the lower portion of the handkerchief, over the case. Then grip the case and the card beneath, with the thumb and second finger of the left hand. This lets the right hand fold one side of the handkerchief underneath the chosen card; then the pack lays on the right hand. The left hand takes the other side of the cloth, including the portion just folded under by the right, and folds it back the other way.

This simple procedure of winding the handkerchief about the pack forms a pocket which conceals the chosen card and the handkerchief may be shown from both sides, while the loose corners are held at the top.

When the handkerchief is shaken, the chosen card will gradually come loose and will make its appearance through the cloth, dropping to the floor. Then case—handkerchief—cards—everything may be thoroughly examined by the audience.

18. THE HUNG CARD

The principle of this trick is so simple, that it can be performed with nothing but a piece of string. But in its elaborate form, the string is attached to a miniature gallows.

A card is selected and returned to the pack. The pack is in-

serted in a loop in the end of the string. One card in the pack—
namely, the chosen card—is the culprit; and it must be executed.

With a simple piece of string, the pack is shaken loose and all
the cards fall except the chosen one, which hangs there. With
the gallows, a trap is pulled and all the pack falls through—
except the chosen card.

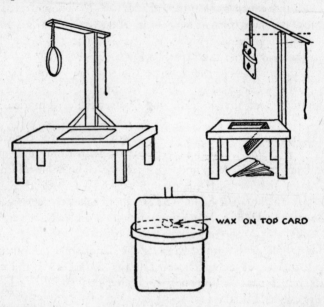

WAX ON TOP CARD

In the improved gallows, the release of the trap raises the top
portion of the gallows, so that the card comes upward as the
pack falls, making the appearance more effective.

Yet the simplicity of method is used in each instance. The loop
is of fairly heavy string; and a dab of wax (or lead plaster) is
attached to it. The chosen card is brought to the top of the pack.
The pack is slipped into the loop, and under pretense of tighten-
ing the loop, the portion of the string that bears the wax is
pressed firmly against the back of the chosen card.

The pack hangs in the string, but the loop is not tight. A slight
shake will release the pack, leaving the chosen card hanging in

the loop. With the gallows arrangement, the loop is quite loose so that the pack will surely drop when the trap is released.

19. DIVINATION CARD TRICKS

There are three clever ways of divining a chosen card apparently hidden from view. These may be worked separately or in combination. I shall describe each one in brief.

(A) X-Ray Pack.

Half of the cards of a pack are prepared by having the index corners punched out. This is concealed with the thumb. Any card is inserted among the fake cards, which are held face down. When the performer turns the faces of the cards toward himself, he lifts his thumb and sees the index corner of the chosen card.

(B) X-Ray Case.

This is merely a card case with the proper corner cut out, and hidden by the thumb. A card is dropped into the case. By turning the faked side toward him and lifting his thumb the performer will see the chosen card.

CARD CASE
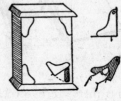

(C) X-Ray Box.

This is an excellent piece of apparatus—a wooden box with a loose lid, large enough to hold a playing card. The corners are ornamental raised pieces. All appear tight, so the box may pass examination. But when he turns the box toward himself, the performer pushes upward on the lower right corner piece. This raises a pin from a small hole in the bottom of the box, and the corner pivots inward, giving a glimpse of the concealed card— a glimpse of the tell-tale index corner.

The ornamental piece is swung back and pressed down into place. Then the performer names the chosen card.

Two of these methods may be worked together—or all three may be combined to make a more remarkable illusion.

20. THE LATEST CARD BOX

The card box is an apparatus of utility for causing the appearance, disappearance, or change of a card. The old wooden box has a flap in the top that falls into the bottom, and it has become generally known. The nickeled card box is a piece of apparatus that can be examined; but its size and weight are suspicious. The "Latest Card Box" is very thin.

It consists of a single piece of metal with a molding all around it—slightly larger than a playing card. It has two thin hinged doors, which open on opposite sides, each opening to the right.

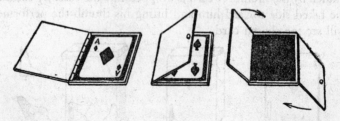

Thus there are two compartments, one on either side of the box. One of the doors fits loosely, and has a knob on it; the other is tight fitting, and cannot be opened except by striking the box forcibly against the hand. This door has no knob.

We will presume that the magician intends to transform a card with the aid of this box. He puts a red card in the side of the box that opens easily. Then he opens the other side, and lets the box lay in this condition.

He carries the opened box to a spectator and lets him place a black card in the box. He closes the door quickly, and transfers the box to his other hand. This enables him to exert sufficient pressure to lock the black card firmly in one side of the box.

When the spectator receives the box, and is told to open it, he naturally employs the door with the knob—the only door that he can see. There he finds the red card, and no trace of the black one. The original door has become the solid back of the box, and no one suspects its presence.

"El Barto," the well-known magician, utilizes the "Card Box" in combination with the "Card Through Handkerchief." He has a duplicate card in the pack—and "forces" one of these. This is the card that he shakes through the handkerchief. He places the card in a card box, from which it disappears. When the handkerchief is unwrapped, the card is discovered back in the pack.

The judicious combination of existing tricks is an excellent practice that leads to originality and effectiveness.

21. THE IMPROVED FALSE COUNT

This is a very effective form of the "False Count," executed slowly and deliberately.

The cards are held upright in the left hand, the faces of the cards toward the performer. The left thumb, touching the face of the card nearest the performer, pushes it to the right, where it is removed by the right hand.

This is repeated with the second card; the third card; and so on, but the cards retain their same relative position; that is, the cards in the right hand are placed upon each succeeding card as it is drawn off.

Now in the course of slowly removing one of the cards from the left hand, the right hand pushes the nearest card of its group back to the left, where it is gripped by the left thumb. This takes place while the hands are momentarily together; the slide back of the card is completely masked by the other cards, which are unevenly spread in the hands.

This secretly adds one card to the left hand group; and by

repeating the maneuver more cards may be added, one by one, to the group in the left hand.

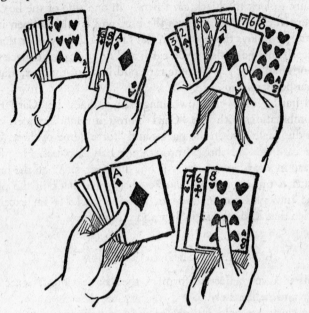

The "False Count." Note how the first card is transferred from right to left during the count. Spectators see the backs of the cards.

Thus with seven cards in his left hand, the magician may count ten, thus: one, two, three (slide back), four, five (slide back), six, seven (slide back), eight, nine, ten.

Nine, or eight may also be counted by merely sliding back one or two cards less.

While this sleight may be done very slowly, it should be practiced to do at a moderately rapid speed, in which case it will be quite indetectible.

CHAPTER IX

EFFECTIVE POCKET TRICKS

POCKET MAGIC HAS BECOME an art in itself. Years ago they had no place in the magician's repertoire. There were only a few worthwhile tricks that could be shown in an impromptu manner.

But the demand for this style of entertainment has greatly increased; and quite as much attention has been given to the devising of clever little mysteries as has been devoted to the invention of stage effects.

There are some very clever tricks of this nature that require no apparatus whatever; but others need special appliances of a miniature nature—articles which can be carried in the pocket and given for inspection whenever required.

In this section I have made no division between the two types. My whole purpose has been to explain the most effective pocket tricks, giving exact instructions as to their working. Most of the special appliances may be obtained from reliable dealers in magical apparatus; others can be easily prepared. But it should be remembered that all magical apparatus should be carefully constructed, and this is particularly true of special pocket tricks which may be subjected to close inspection.

I. TORN AND RESTORED PAPER

The trick of tearing a piece of paper and restoring it to its original condition is one that has been performed for many years, and which has been presented in a variety of ways. In most instances, two sheets of paper are used, one being substituted for the other during the course of the trick.

147

The method which I shall explain here is not a new one; but it has come into recent popularity, because it disposes of the extra piece of paper in a most ingenious manner.

The effect of the trick is as follows: The magician shows a strip of thin paper, and tears it into pieces. He has shown his hands absolutely empty; and when he folds up the torn pieces, he keeps them constantly in sight.

But when the papers are unfolded, they are restored into a single strip!

The trick must be performed with a special crepe paper, which may be purchased in narrow rolls at stationery stores. This paper can be stretched to twice its length.

The magician begins with a single sheet of paper, about twelve inches long—only about an inch in width. He tears it deliberately in half; then he tears it some more; but he only tears one section of the paper. The result is that he has a six inch strip remaining when he folds the torn pieces.

He hold this in his left hand, calling attention to the fact that the end of the paper is always in view. With his right hand he draws the paper slowly between his left thumb and forefinger, exerting pressure so that the paper stretches as it emerges.

The result is that he draws forth a twelve inch strip of paper —presumably the piece with which he began—but in reality, half of the original strip!

The "getaway" or disposal of the torn pieces is an important item. Inasmuch as only one strip is used, there is little suspicion of remaining pieces. If the performer is near a table or a chair, he can easily drop them (folded tightly) on the floor.

In the open, the best plan is to show the right hand empty, and to moisten the fingers every now and then while drawing out the restored strip. While doing this, the right thumb and fingers take hold of the extra pieces and leave them in the mouth during the second or third moistening process. The tongue pushes the paper up in the cheek.

Another plan is to tear off a corner of the original strip, and to keep that corner in view all the time. After the paper is folded, it is transferred from the right hand to the left; but the extra pieces are kept in the right.

As the left hand shows the complete piece folded up, with the corner still in view, the right hand has plenty of opportunity to pocket the extra pieces without suspicion.

A clever plan is to use a ruler to show the approximate length of the paper. Put the ruler in the pocket. Show the hands empty and proceed. As the paper is drawn out in one hand, the other reaches in the pocket for the ruler, leaving the extra pieces there.

Both measurements should be made quickly, as it is likely that the paper will vary slightly before and after the restoration.

2. ANOTHER PAPER TEARING

This is a variation of the trick just described.

The effect is exactly the same; and the method is quite similar; but instead of crepe paper, very thin tissue is used.

A strip of this paper is folded in half at the center, and a few light dabs of paste are applied to make it appear as a single strip of ordinary thickness. Pressed flat, this strip will pass as a single layer.

It is torn in half. The portion with the fold at the end is kept intact, but the other half is torn several times. The doubled piece is then separated by pressure of the fingers, and is drawn out as a single strip—the exact length of the original double strip.

The torn pieces are disposed of by any of the methods previously described.

In tearing the paper in either one of these tricks, it is not difficult to make the spectators believe that the paper is being torn indiscriminately. The magician should make a great show of the torn ends, and the smaller fragments.

3. THE BALL AND TUBE

The magician exhibits a tiny tube of brass, slightly over an inch in height and about five-eighths of an inch in diameter. In addition, he has a solid steel ball, which may be set upon the tube.

He holds the tube upright in his left hand, with the ball on top, and mentions that both objects are made of solid metal; nevertheless the steel will show its power over brass.

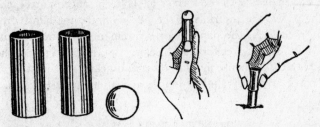

The "Ball and Tube" showing the secret removal of the outer tube.

"You can imagine," he remarks, "that the ball is growing smaller—or that the tube is unable to withstand its weight. See— it is gradually sinking into the tube."

The spectators are doubtful at first; but as they watch, they see the ball sink bit by bit until its top alone is visible.

"A little squeeze on the side of the tube," says the magician; "and the ball will emerge."

He squeezes the tube with his right thumb and forefinger, and little by little the ball comes out. It hesitates at the finish, but another squeeze and it rests on top of the tube. Both the ball and the tube are immediately given for examination.

Two tubes are used in the trick. One fits easily over the other. Both are made of thin brass, and they can be exhibited as a single tube, before the trick.

The inside diameter of the outer tube is virtually the same as the outside diameter of the inner tube. The ball has the same diameter—five-eighths of an inch—and it is just large enough to rest on top of the inner tube, and just small enough to drop through the outer tube.

The tubes are held as one at the finger tips of the left hand, and the ball is placed on top. The four fingers and the thumb form a cluster about the bottom of the tubes. When pressure is slightly released, the ball will sink, pushing the inner tube down with it. The fingers prevent the tube from sinking too rapidly.

To make the ball emerge, the fingers must support the bottom of the inner tube, while the thumb draws down the outer tube. The right thumb and forefinger squeeze the tube as though to help the process. This is done with a purpose.

When the ball has reached the top, the right hand covers the tube for an instant to give it another squeeze. The fingers come in front, but the top of the ball is visible above the temporary screen. The right thumb and forefinger grip the outer tube, and draw it straight upward, over the ball. This leaves the inner tube alone with the ball on top, while the extra tube is secretly held in the right hand.

Some performers make the final squeeze at the base of the thumb and forefinger. This is particularly good if the performer is smoking while performing the trick, as his fingers will be free to handle his cigar or cigarette; and this action of the right hand seems so natural that no one will suspect it of holding anything concealed.

In the simplest and newest "getaway," the right hand sets both tubes upon the table—the ball upon them. In moving away the right fingers deliberately draw off the outer tube. Fingers should be pointing directly downward.

In causing the ball to sink and rise, an excellent plan is to insert the tip of the thumb in the bottom of the tube. The lowering and raising of the thumb does the trick, while the fingers support the outer tube.

4. IMPROVED BALL AND TUBE

In this version of the "Ball and Tube" a much larger ball and tube are used. The effect of the trick is precisely the same. The outer tube, however, is of different mechanical construction. It is shorter than the inner tube—a fact which is not noticed as only the upper portion of the tube is in view, the lower part being hidden in the hand.

A loop of strong thread passes through a hole in the lower part of the outer tube, and this is fastened to a piece of cord-elastic that goes under the coat, and through the belt loops of the trousers. A device such as this is known as a "pull."

The trick is done at a slight distance. When the ball has risen, the right hand approaches to take the tube. It pushes the outer tube down and lifts out the inner tube with the ball on top.

The outer tube is momentarily concealed in the left hand, but as all attention is centered on the right, the extra tube is released, and it flies unseen, beneath the coat.

5. BALL AND GLASS TUBE

This is an ingenious variation of the "Ball and Tube." It cannot be done quite as close as the other method—yet the spectators will see more action.

The whole procedure is exactly the same as the first method of the "Ball and Tube," but the tubes are made of glass instead of brass. As a result it is possible to see the ball when it has sunk into the tube.

As the glass is thicker than metal, a little distance is required to make the trick effective, especially as the upper edge of the inner tube is visible. Yet a few feet away, this rim cannot be detected, against the silvery surface of the ball, and the trick is very mysterious in appearance. An amber-tinted glass is best to use.

6. GIANT MATCH PRODUCTION

A very surprising trick.

The magician takes a match-box from his pocket, opens it and extracts a match. But the match is nine inches in length and of proportionate thickness!

The box must be prepared beforehand. It is an ordinary safety-match box; but the inner end of the drawer is cut away, and a

V shaped space is made in the bottom of the cover, running from the end toward the center.

The giant match is up the left sleeve.

The right hand places the box in the left, and moving toward the wrist, grasps the end of the match and draws it forward. The drawer of the box is opened, and the right hand slides the box back into the left hand so that the end of the giant match comes inside. Then reaching into the box, he draws the match directly through.

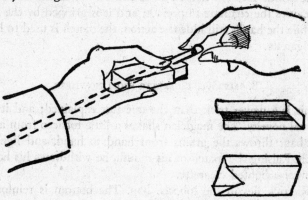

Instead of a dummy match, a match with a metal head may be used. A hole in the metal head enables the performer to insert the head of a small match, and to strike it on the box, after the production of the large match. Whenever the trick is to be done, the head is prepared.

It is also possible to obtain giant safety matches by the box. One of these can be used for the production instead of an imitation.

7. THE CIGARETTE FROM NOWHERE

The magician pretends to roll an imaginary cigarette, going through all the motions of using tobacco, and paper. He places the invisible cigarette in his mouth; strikes a match, and to the surprise of everyone he is smoking a real cigarette.

The whole secret lies in a specially constructed match-box. The drawer of the box is faked by running a metal tube through it, lengthwise at one side. The box is filled with matches and is partly opened; then a cigarette is concealed in the tube.

Everything is pantomime until the performer needs a match. Then he picks up the half opened box, removes a match, and strikes it. As he holds it in his right hand, the left retains the box. Both hands are raised to the mouth, as though lighting a cigarette in the wind. The left hand pushes the drawer of the box shut; this causes the cigarette to project; and it is gripped by the lips.

While the hands still hide the action, the match is used to light the cigarette.

8. IMPROVED CIGARETTE FROM NOWHERE

This is a newer trick than the one just explained; and it has unusual novelty. The magician shakes a little tobacco from a ten cent bag; throws the grains from hand to hand, and lights a match. Raising the match to his mouth, he withdraws his hands to reveal a lighted cigarette.

The trick lies in the tobacco bag. The bottom is reinforced with metal, and a metal tube extends upward. It holds the cigarette. But when one thumb is kept over the hole in the bottom of the bag, it appears quite normal.

A little tobacco is shaken from the bag, the right hand doing the work, and the thumb keeping the cigarette in place. Then the bag is transferred to the left hand, which has its fingers pointing directly up. The cigarette slides down into the left hand.

The right hand and teeth are used to pull the strings of the bag, which is placed in the pocket by the right hand. The tobacco is poured from the left to the right hand and back again; very little is used, and most of this is dropped during the pouring. The left hand retains the cigarette.

The right strikes a match; the hands are raised, and the lips take the cigarette from the left hand, while the match is used to light it.

9. THE FOUR COLORS

There are many divination tricks, and this one belongs to the list. But it involves a new principle, which has been employed in several similar tricks.

A small circular mirror is used. The back is painted white, and is covered with glass; and on its surface appear four spots of different colors.

The device is laid on the table, and a person is told to cover any one of the spots with a dime. The magician turns his back while this takes place.

When the dime has been removed, the magician picks up the mirror, and turns aside a moment. He finally looks into the reflecting side, and immediately names the color of the spot that was covered.

The method is very ingenious. The surface on which the spots appear has been coated with luminous paint. The paint absorbs light, and when a coin is placed over one of the spots and allowed to remain there about a minute, it leaves a shadow.

When the magician takes the mirror, he slips it under his coat as he turns away from the light, and detects the shadow in the darkness—for the rest of the surface will glow. Thus he knows which spot was covered.

The magician may stay out of the room during the trick and ask that the mirror be passed to him. This proves that he is not in collusion with anyone in the room, and it gives him an opportunity to hold the mirror in darkness.

10. THE DIVINING DIE

This appliance is very simple and inexpensive. A single die about an inch in diameter, and a cubical celluloid box with tight fitting cover.

Someone drops the die in the box; notes the number on top and puts on the cover. The magician takes the box, holds it to his forehead, and names the top number.

The bottom of the box is quite thin. The sides and top are ornamental; but the smooth bottom is transparent when the die rests against it. Thus if someone turns the box upside down and looks at the bottom, he cannot see through. But when the magician holds the box upright and tilts it slowly forward, he will see the number on the bottom while the die still rests there.

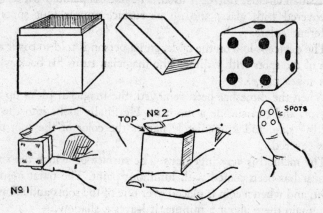

The bottom number tells him the top; for the opposite sides of a die always total seven, and a simple subtraction tells him the top side.

By way of variation the magician may hold the box behind his back. In this case he lifts the cover and presses his thumb firmly against the top of the die, replacing the cover immediately.

He hands the box back to someone, and turns his back for an instant. On the ball of his thumb he will see a clear imprint of the upper side of the die with the correct number of spots.

In this form, the trick can be worked with any box, or a die may be placed upright on the palm of the left hand, held behind the back.

II. KNIFE THROUGH THE HANDKERCHIEF

This is another trick with an improvement; both methods will be described under one heading.

The magician borrows a pen-knife and a handkerchief. The handkerchief is spread out and the corners are held by spectators. A square sheet of paper—smaller than the handkerchief—is placed upon the cloth. Then the magician lowers the knife under

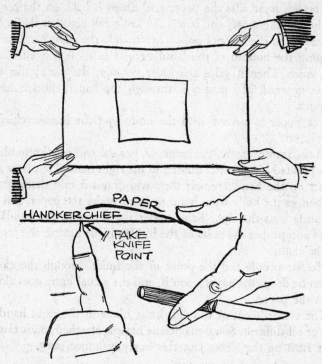

the handkerchief, and states that he will try to cut the paper without injuring the handkerchief—something that appears impossible.

He taps the handkerchief several times, causing the paper to bob up and down. Suddenly he pulls the knife right through the paper—yet the handkerchief is uninjured!

This is all done during the preliminary part of the trick. As he taps the paper through the handkerchief, the magician holds the knife in his right hand. As if by accident, he knocks the paper to the edge of the handkerchief. There the left hand takes the side of the paper—thumb above and fingers beneath. The right hand has moved over also and the left fingers grip the handle of the knife.

The left hand lifts the paper and drops it back on the center of the handkerchief; and it lets the knife fall between the handkerchief and the sheet of paper. Meanwhile the right hand keeps tapping the bottom of the handkerchief as though it still held the knife. Then it grips the knife through the cloth; tilts the blade upward, and pushes it through the paper, the left hand helping.

The paper is pierced with the knife—yet the handkerchief is uninjured.

In the improvement, the magician has the end of a knife blade or a pointed bit of metal hidden in his right hand. He places the paper on the handkerchief; then withdraws it and deliberately exchanges the knife from hand to hand under the paper. But he instantly puts the right hand under the center of the handkerchief and pushes the point of the hidden blade against the center of the cloth.

He lets people feel the point of the knife through the cloth. Then he drops the paper upon it, and the actual knife goes along with the paper.

The concealment of the dull knife blade in the right hand is not at all difficult. Some magicians have it attached to an elastic that runs up the sleeve, but this is really unnecessary.

12. THROUGH THE COAT

This is an effective variation of the previous trick. The magician removes his coat and lays it over the back of an open-backed chair, the back of the coat being toward the audience.

His right hand holds a knife and lowers it behind the coat, while the left hand holds a sheet of paper in front of the coat.

Suddenly the sheet of paper is pierced by the knife, which makes its appearance through the uninjured coat.

The magician simply drops the knife in the collar of the coat as he lowers his right hand. While the right forefinger taps against the center of the coat to indicate the presence of the knife, the left hand raises the paper to show the center of the coat. The left thumb and forefinger are behind the sheet of paper and they pick up the knife, carrying it under the paper to the center of the coat in front. Then the right hand grips the knife through the coat and the left hand pulls the knife through the paper.

With an extra knife blade, the right hand can show the actual point of the knife at the center of the coat, when the left hand lifts the paper. The extra blade may be easily dropped in the inside coat pocket.

13. SELF RISING MATCH-BOX

The match-box that rises and falls on the back of the hand is a rather crude and simple trick. But this method, which the

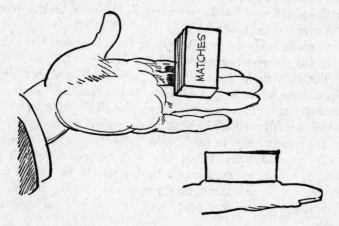

author has found effective, while involving nothing but the box, makes a new trick.

The match-box is laid *across* the fingers of the left hand. Suddenly it rises—very slowly; then it sinks again. It is finally handed for examination.

The Method: Open the box very slightly in an inward direction. Set that end of the box upon the third finger of the left hand. Close the box with the right hand, catching a very tiny bit of flesh on the left finger.

Now the slightest tipping of the hand will control the box. Even the natural shaking of the fingers is sufficient. With a little practice the performer can make the box rise and fall at will, with no unnatural motion of the left hand.

The right hand in taking the box opens it slightly so it can be removed from the left fingers. People may watch as closely as they desire; yet the magician makes the box obey every command without detection.

14. THE CIGARETTE TUBE

This is one of the finest pocket tricks ever made. The magician is smoking a cigarette. He places it, lighted end downward, in a nickel-plated tube just large enough to receive it; and he places the cover on the tube.

Someone holds the tube. When the cover is removed, the cigarette has completely disappeared.

The cigarette is made of metal, painted white, with a slight tip of brass which is kept between the lips. The tube is open at the inner end; but the outer end has a pierced disc of brass against which a small portion of a genuine cigarette is inserted.

The cigarette may be smoked, for a short while, and it appears to be quite ordinary. When it is pushed into the tube, it fits snugly, and its presence cannot be detected. In fact, if the tube is correctly manufactured, the cigarette can only be removed by jamming a pointed lead pencil into the tube, and pulling it out again.

A special rod is also made that screws into the metal disc and brings out the cigarette.

Some performers vanish a match and cause it to appear in the tube in place of the cigarette. This is simple enough, because a duplicate match is kept inside the fake cigarette. But this part of the trick is hardly worth while. The reproduction of the lighted cigarette is a good effect, however. It is accomplished by the aid of the apparatus shown below.

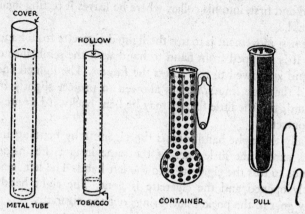

COVER

HOLLOW

METAL TUBE   TOBACCO   CONTAINER   PULL

15. THE CIGARETTE HOLDER

The "Cigarette Holder" is a device of metal with airholes all around. It holds a lighted cigarette, and may be carried in the pocket with no fear of burning.

After disappearing the cigarette with the "Cigarette Tube," the magician merely reaches in his pocket and brings out the lighted cigarette.

The best holders are fairly large; they are made of a heavy wire screen, with two clips at the top to hold the cigarette in position, so the lighted end does not touch the bottom of the tube. Some holders have safety pins attached to fasten them in the pocket; but with the larger holder, the size and weight is sufficient.

16. THE MYSTERIOUS CIGARETTE

This combination of cigarette effects is highly effective; following the "Cigarette Tube and Holder" it is unusually good, as the preliminary trick leads up to it.

The magician vanishes a cigarette and reproduces it lighted from his pocket. Again it vanishes and is brought from another pocket. The magician smokes the cigarette; then pushes it, lighted end first, into his collar, where he leaves it resting against his neck!

The first movement is to toss the lighted cigarette from hand to hand. It is dropped from hand to hand with the semblance of a toss, and is allowed to rest across the fingers. The lighted end is toward the little finger, and is allowed to project slightly from the hand; but the little fingers may be bent backward to prevent any contact.

Finally the right hand retains the cigarette by bending in all fingers except the little one. At the same instant the magician pretends to toss the cigarette into the left hand. The left hand is quickly opened and the cigarette is gone. The right hand instantly goes to the pocket and brings out the cigarette.

This bit of by-play leads up to the final effect.

Under his coat the magician has a "Cigarette Pull," a tube of metal with cord elastic attached, which runs through the belt loops of the trousers. In his right coat pocket he has an imitation lighted cigarette—of the type sold very cheaply at novelty stores.

He puffs on the cigarette and takes it in his right hand, while his left gets hold of the "pull." The magician retains a large quantity of smoke in his mouth. He deliberately inserts the lighted end of the cigarette into his left fist, where it goes into the "pull." He releases the "pull" and shows his left hand empty.

His right hand then goes to the pocket and produces the imitation cigarette. He puts it in his mouth and exhales the smoke that is there. By short puffs he appears to smoke the cigarette. Everyone is sure it is a genuine cigarette—and when the magician inserts the supposedly lighted end beneath his collar, everyone will be amazed.

As a follow-up, the "cigarette" can be pushed completely out of sight beneath the collar, and a real lighted cigarette be reproduced from a holder under the cuff of the trousers. A holder located there must be pinned in place.

17. THE DIVINING DIAL

This little device is about the same size as the mirror used in the "Four Color" trick. It consists of a dial with an arrow in the center; and anyone may point the arrow to any spot he wishes. Instead of clock numbers, the dial has eight colored spots as illustrated.

A cover is placed on the little box that contains the dial; and the magician merely sets the whole affair on the table; yet he instantly names the color to which the arrow is pointing.

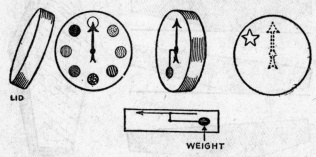

LID

WEIGHT

Between the dial and the bottom of the shallow box is a small weight that moves with the pointer. On the bottom of the box (outside) is an ornamental star that seems to have no special purpose; but it indicates the position of one of the colors.

The magician stands the box on its side, and being circular it rolls as he moves his hand along. It stops when the weight is at the bottom. The position of the star on the box then indicates the color to which the arrow is pointing, as the magician has familiarized himself with the dial.

18. THE MUMMY CASE

Various divinations can be performed through the use of weights. One of the adaptions of that principle is the "Mummy Case."

This case is only a few inches long; and it is painted to represent the coffin of an Egyptian mummy. The lid pivots, and spectators are invited to place one of three mummies in the case —hiding the other two.

Each mummy is different in color and appearance; and the performer can instantly name the one that occupies the case, without even touching the little box.

One mummy is weighted in the feet; another in the head. The weight of the third is evenly distributed. The bottom of the box is curved, so the ends do not touch the table.

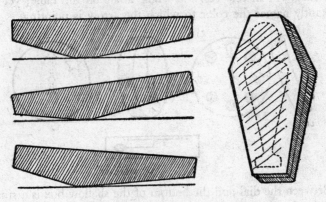

Thus the box will tilt in one direction or the other—or will remain level, according to the particular mummy which is within. This is not noticeable to the average person; but the magician looks for the tilt.

The case should be so constructed that the mummies will fit only one way—thus preventing anyone from reversing one of them.

19. THE FOUR COLOR BLOCKS

Among the newest divination tricks, the "Four Color Blocks" is a novelty. These blocks fit in a shallow box about six inches in length.

Each block has a different color on its opposite sides—the blocks being quite thin, an inch square but only a quarter-inch in thickness. Thus there are eight possible colors; and spectators are requested to arrange the blocks in a row so that any four colors may be in view. Then the box is closed and fastened.

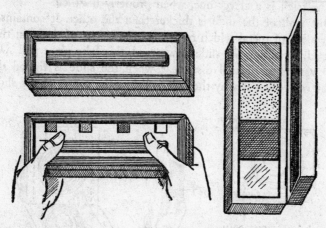

The magician holds the box to his forehead, and immediately names the colors on the tops of the blocks, in their proper order.

The top of the box is paneled, having a raised surface in the center. The magician places his thumbs upon this and presses toward the front of the box. The panel slides and four small openings come into view—one for each block. He notes the colors in an instant, and when he releases pressure, a spring forces the panel back into position.

The box will stand considerable examination, as the panel must be pressed quite firmly to operate. The mechanism is so ingenious that no one will suspect it, especially as the operation cannot be noticed.

20. PENCIL THROUGH COIN

This trick requires a special slide made to hold a coin of half-dollar size. For a reason which will be explained, a "palming coin" of odd design is used instead of a half-dollar.

The coin is put in the slide and it can be seen through a hole below the center of the slide. Then a silk handkerchief is put over the slide and a pencil is used to push the handkerchief down through the hole—and completely through the coin!

The trick is a clever one, when properly handled.

One wall of the slide is thicker than the other. It contains a thin piece of metal which represents the center of the coin that is used. By tilting the slide downward, this fake piece will slide into view; but it will disappear when the slide is tipped the other way. That is why the hole is below the center of the slide.

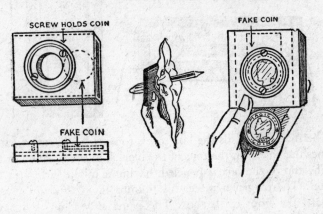

The brass molding which surrounds the round hole may be turned by pressing the fingernail against one of the screws. It shifts less than an inch; but the upper screw may thus be shifted so as to hold the fake metal disc in concealment.

In performing, the slide is set with the fake hidden and locked in place. While the coin is being examined, the magician releases the fake but holds the slide level so that the fake does not appear.

He inserts the coin in the slide, and shows both sides. This lets him drop the fake behind the coin; so when he turns the slide around again, the fake is seen instead of the coin; and he permits the coin to drop out the bottom of the slide, into his hand.

The process of penetration is the easiest part of the trick. By tilting the slide, the magician can push the handkerchief through with the pencil. Just as the handkerchief finishes its journey, he tilts the slide the other way and the fake slides into view.

The important part of the trick is getting the real coin back into the slide at the finish.

The magician removes the handkerchief and boldly shows the slide with the fake in view. Then he lays it on the fingers of his right hand—the exact spot where he has retained the real coin.

Thus the slide covers the real coin. The hand is flat—palm upward. The top of the slide is toward the performer.

He tilts his hand toward himself. The fake slides back into its hiding place. He releases the coin at the same instant, and it drops from his right hand to his left. But the keenest observer will be positive it dropped from the slide.

The right hand now has the slide out of view; and the right thumb secretly pushes the screw that holds the fake in place. The slide itself may then be given for inspection, along with the coin.

21. THE COLORED BARS

This is another divination trick. Three cylindrical bars, each one inch in length are used. The bars are painted different colors.

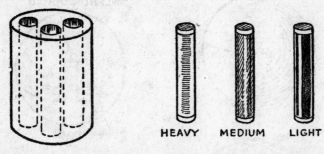

HEAVY   MEDIUM   LIGHT

The magician shows a cylindrical box slightly deeper than the length of the bars. It has three holes in the top, and they are numbered 1, 2, and 3.

He holds the box behind his back and lets some person drop

the bars in—the first bar in hole 1; next in hole 2; the third in hole 3.

Then the magician immediately names the color of the bar in each hole. And he is always correct, no matter how often the trick may be repeated.

Why? Because each bar is of different weight. One, for example may be made of lead; another of copper; the third of aluminum. Such great difference of weight is not, however, essential; and all the bars may be made of the same material, but hollowed in different proportions.

The bottom of the box is just a thin disc of metal; and the performer's finger, resting there, can feel the difference in the weight of each bar as it drops.

22. THE RED HOT BALL

While hardly a pocket trick, this is an unusual mystery for the parlor—or for any close-up performance. A brass ball some two and a half inches in diameter is used. It rests on a little stand; and taking it from there, the magician passes it for inspection, stating that he will perform a trick with it.

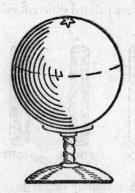
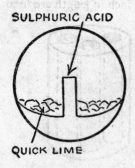

SULPHURIC ACID

QUICK LIME

A spectator holds the ball, and it seems warm to him. Then it becomes hot; and finally he is forced to drop it on the floor. Anyone who tries to pick it up will give up the attempt.

The ball is hollow; and it screws apart in the center. On one hemisphere is a little cylinder. This is filled beforehand with sulphuric acid; while quicklime is placed around it. Then the top is screwed on the ball.

A star on top indicates how the ball should be set, to prevent its contents from mixing. That is why a little stand is used.

When the spectators begin to examine the ball, they naturally turn it over, causing the sulphuric acid to join the quicklime. The ball will become hot very quickly.

23. CIGARETTE TO CIGAR

This is a good trick for the smoker. He lights a cigarette; then pushes it into his left fist; and it turns to a cigar, which he continues to smoke as though nothing had occurred.

The cigarette is a real one; but the cigar is an imitation made of wood. It is hollow, and of just sufficient length to receive a cigarette. It is held in the left hand; and the cigarette is pushed in—lighted end last.

The cigar has an air passage going to the stem; so the magician can continue to smoke for a minute or so, just as though he had a real cigar.

24. COLORED CRAYONS

Reverting to divination tricks, there is one that requires only a few colored crayons; yet which is quite effective.

The magician receives a colored crayon behind his back, and, still holding it there, faces his audience and points to the person who gave him the crayon.

"You gave me a green crayon," he says; and the spectator admits that the magician is correct.

As he turns to face his audience, the magician marks his right thumbnail with the crayon. In pointing to the person, he sees the color on his nail and immediately names it. The color is quickly removed by the forefinger.

25. BLACKSTONE'S PAPER BALL TRICK

This trick has been performed by the author for many years, and it has come to be recognized as one of the best of impromptu tricks. I shall explain it with its many variations.

Three little paper pellets. They are thrown on the table, and two of them are dropped in the left hand. The third is thrown away—but when the left hand is opened, out roll the three paper balls.

Time and again the trick is repeated. Yet the three paper balls constantly appear in the left hand. Every movement is natural and convincing; and when the trick is finished with some of the variations that will be given, the spectators are unanimous in declaring it one of the most perplexing mysteries they have ever witnessed.

While the trick is not difficult, it is one that improves with practice, and the magician who uses it should seek to show it effectively.

A fourth paper ball is used, and it is concealed between the tips of the first and second fingers of the right hand. It is placed there with the aid of the thumb, which holds it against the second finger until the forefinger is ready to take its place.

With the extra ball in position, pick up the first paper ball between the thumb and the tip of the forefinger. You can show the inside of your hand as you do so; for the thumb hides the extra ball. Drop the first paper ball in the left hand.

Repeat the movement with the second ball; but in dropping it in the hand, let the extra ball go with it, immediately closing the left hand.

Spread the fingers of the right hand, and pick up the third ball between the thumb and second finger. Pretend to throw it away, but clip it between your finger tips. Roll the three paper balls from the left hand, and you are ready to start again.

By way of variation, reach under the table and pretend to knock the third paper ball up through. Whenever a glass-topped table is available, this makes a remarkable illusion; the left hand, dropping three balls at the same instant, gives the effect that one ball came up through the glass.

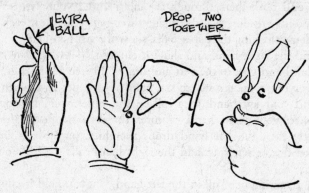

Another scheme is to drop the third ball in the pocket—apparently. Always retain it in the right hand.

By way of variation, cup the left hand, and in dropping in the first paper ball, let the extra ball go in. This gives you unusual freedom with the second ball, which follows. Then throw the third away—the three will be in the left hand.

Another surprise is the introduction of some other object, such as a coin or a lump of sugar. Drop the third ball in the pocket, and while rolling out three from the left hand, obtain the other article. Then place two balls in the left hand, without showing the right empty; and let the large object drop in also. Pretend to throw the third ball away, and the coin or lump of sugar will roll from the left hand instead.

Place the two balls in the left hand, and let the extra one fall with them. Put the large object in your pocket, and the three balls again appear in the left hand.

Now comes a vanish of the three paper balls. Put them one by one into the left hand—apparently; but retain each in the right hand, between the fingers. When you pocket the third ball, drop all three in your pocket; and show your left hand empty.

Or place all three apparently in the left hand; then show the left hand empty, at the same time dropping the three from right hand onto the floor. This is specially suited when seated at a table.

Some previous preparation helps the trick. Take some ordinary pins and push them through the cloth under your vest, so that the points are downward. Impale three paper balls on each pin.

After vanishing the paper balls, show the left hand empty; then extend the right hand and show it empty too. At the same time, the left hand goes to the vest and draw off three paper balls.

Everyone wonders where the balls have gone; and when you extend your left hand, they roll on the table again. During the surprise, your right hand captures three from one of the pin points; then the left hand drops the three paper balls in the pocket on the left side, and the right hand rolls the balls on the table.

By retaining one ball in the left hand, you can hold it cupped; then the right hand drops two in the left and throws the third away; the three appear in the left. You are back at the beginning again; and at a later period you can get three more from your vest to conclude the trick.

Of course the routine should not be overdone. At the same time it is one of those tricks that gets better as it progresses; and it should be adapted to the occasion. When to do a trick and how long to do it is something that must be learned by experience.

26. THE UNCANNY DIE

This is a trick with a die that is somewhat different from others. The die is placed upon the magician's palm and is covered with a little metal box of five sides—large enough to fit over the die but with no cover.

One person has noted the upper side of the die—which we will suppose is six. The magician extends his hand to another spectator and asks him to lift the cover and note the side. He sees a three.

A third person sees another number. In fact, no one is sure which side of the die is up after all!

Skill and boldness accomplish the trick, yet it is not overly-difficult. The die is set on the fingers of the left hand. The cover is placed over it and the thumb steadies the cover. As the hand is moved the fingers spread slightly; the die settles between them, and in pressing it up into the cover, the performer gives it a quarter turn.

With a little practice this can be done with no apparent motion. It is indetectible under the very eyes of the observers.

27. THE ADHESIVE CIGARETTE PACK

This is an interesting stunt. The performer attaches an empty cigarette package to the wall by merely pressing a match against it. Then he puts several pencils, a fountain pen and some matches into the pack. Still it stays there and supports them all.

A package of twenty cigarettes is used—and it must be a pack which is enclosed in wax paper. The wax paper is torn off. The empty pack is set against the wood-work of the doorway. A match is lighted, and the burning end is pressed against the side of the package, pressing it firmly against the wood-work. The magician blows out the light before it can ignite the cigarette pack.

The surface of the pack is waxy because of the wax-paper covering. The heat causes the wax to become sticky—instantly—and the pack adheres to the wood-work.

It will stay there quite firmly, and it is surprising how many different articles such as cigars, pencils, etc. can be placed in it without their weight causing it to fall.

28. THE IMPROVED COIN BOX

The box consists of two parts, the bottom (with a flange), and the top. There is no trick to the box.

There are four important phases of this trick.

(A) Balance the bottom of the box on the tip of your left second finger, with the first and third fingers pressing against the sides. A marked half dollar is dropped in the box. Take the cover in the right hand between the thumb and fingers. Hold the cover vertically.

As the right hand reaches the left, tilt up the bottom of the box slightly with your left thumb. Press the inside of the cover against the outer edge of the bottom, and press with the cover. The bot-

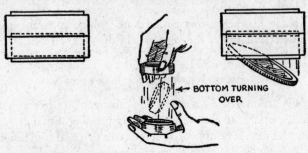

Left and right: Action of the coin when bottom of box is inverted.
Center: Turning the bottom right side up.

tom will swing up to a vertical position, and the cover will lock in the flange that is on the bottom of the box (underneath). Instantly you let the box fall horizontal on your fingers and place the left thumb on top. The bottom of the box is now UPSIDE DOWN. The fine construction of the box makes this move exceptionally easy; the box does not move from its position on the left hand, and the turnover cannot be detected. You can fool yourself with it! The top of the box covers it.

(B) Shake the box, pressing down on the cover with the left thumb. The coin will rattle inside the inverted bottom. Now toss the box easily towards the right hand, and swing the right hand up catching the box with the right fingers beneath and the right thumb above. With a little practice you can execute this move without fail, and the box may be tossed from hand to hand two or three times if you wish, but it should end in the right hand.

(C) Hold a playing card in the left hand, fingers beneath, thumb above, the card tilted slightly forward. Swing the right hand towards the left; at the same time tilt up the outer side of the box by pressing on the inner side with the right thumb. The coin will be lying on the right fingers, and as you slide the box on to the card, the coin will go beneath, where it is held by the left fingers. The sweeping move of the right hand, with the back of the hand toward spectators, prevents a "flash" of the coin.

Command the coin to fall through the box and the card. Simply release the coin with the left fingers and it drops on the table.

(D) After penetrating coin, hold box between index finger and thumb. Relax fingers slightly, and at same time touch extreme bottom of box with middle finger and the bottom will drop right side up, into the other hand, which is held beneath.

Then drop the cover and give both sections for examination.

Note: In place of the first movement, this action is effective: set the box on the palm of the left hand. Hold the cover between the thumb and forefinger of the right. The coin is in the box.

As the right hand is lowered so the cover is over the box, the second finger of the right hand presses the front edge of the box. The pressure causes the box to turn over, and the cover is immediately placed upon it.

29. COIN CHANGING SLIDE

A clever mechanical device for exchanging one coin for another or causing the disappearance or appearance of a coin.

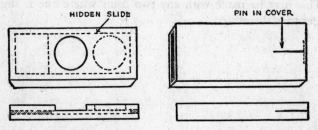

HIDDEN SLIDE   PIN IN COVER

The slide is a flat strip of wood, with a circular depression in the center—large enough to receive a small coin. The slide is pushed into a long cover, open at one end; when the slide is removed, a coin has appeared in the center.

Both the slide and the cover will stand close examination, as the secret is virtually indetectible.

The slide is hollow, with a shorter slide within it. There are two depressions in the inner slide, which may be pushed back or forth so that either comes beneath the outside opening.

The only way to operate the inner slide is by inserting a pin through one of two small holes (one at each end of the slide), according to the direction in which the inner slide is to be pushed.

The inner end of the outer cover is provided with such a pin. It is permanently in place, projecting outward. When the slide is pushed in, the pin enters the hole and shifts the inner slide. The operation is automatic, and the magician may use the ingenious apparatus in whatever manner he may choose.

It is particularly suited for the reproduction of a coin that has disappeared, as in

30. PENNY AND DIME TRICK

The most ingenious of coin tricks. A penny is placed overlapping a dime. When the dime is covered with the penny, it disappears.

The penny is a hollowed-shell. The underside of the dime is faced with the tail side of a penny. The shell penny picks up the dime, and the two form what appears to be an ordinary penny.

This may be made with any two coins where one is slightly larger than the other.

CHAPTER X

MAGIC WITH APPARATUS

A GREAT PERCENTAGE of magicians are interested in magic with apparatus, as distinguished from pocket tricks and stage illusions. A great many amateurs would rather give regular magical shows than do impromptu magic; and the great bulk of the semi-professional magicians are necessarily limited to apparatus of small size because they more frequently appear upon the platform than upon the stage.

As for the beginners in magic; most of them look forward to performing before groups rather than individuals, and by choosing the proper tricks with apparatus they can make progress very rapidly.

The tricks which are explained here have been chosen because of their effectiveness, novelty, and reliability; and they will prove useful to all classes of magicians.

1. THE REPEATING HANDKERCHIEF VANISH

Magicians vanish handkerchiefs so frequently that such a demonstration is not unusual. But when a magician makes the same handkerchief vanish again and again, his audience will sit up and take notice.

Yet the repeating handkerchief vanish is merely an adaptation of an old piece of apparatus—the "Handkerchief Pull." This is a cup-shaped appliance attached to a piece of cord elastic. The elastic runs through a safety pin below the arm-hole of the vest, and through the belt loops of the trousers.

When the "pull" is held in the left hand, and a handkerchief is pushed into the fist, the "pull" when released will fly under the coat, so that the hand may be shown empty.

In the repeating vanish, the "pull" has a hole punched in its outer edge. A piece of black thread one foot long is tied through the hole; and the other end is attached to the corner of the handkerchief.

The handkerchief is pushed into the "pull" and the apparatus is left under the coat, ready for use.

In performing, the magician reaches beneath his coat and pulls out the handkerchief, as though taking it from his pocket. He spreads it in front of him, the corner with the thread being at the left.

Then the right hand takes the left corner of the handkerchief and moves it slowly to the right. The left hand rests idly against the coat lapel. The thread becomes taut as the right hand progresses, and then draws the pull outward, so that it may be gripped by the left hand as it reaches the lapel.

The left hand is advanced a trifle, drawing the elastic to its full length. Beginning with the threaded corner, the right hand pokes the handkerchief into the "pull," and the piece of silk disappears.

It is immediately ready for a repetition of the trick.

With the proper "patter" this becomes a very entertaining bit of magic.

"The first trick I ever learned," says the magician, "was with this silk handkerchief that I always carry in my pocket. I found that when I pushed it into my left fist, in this manner, something unexpected would happen. The handkerchief would disappear!

"I learned this trick in school. The teacher asked me what I was doing. I told her that I had merely taken a silk handkerchief from my pocket—like this; had pushed it into my fist—like this; and had made it disappear.

"She sent me home with a note to my father. When he asked me what I had been doing, I told him that I had only taken a silk handkerchief from my pocket in this manner; had held it in my right hand, and pushed it into my left fist, and made it disappear.

"My father called up the neighbors. When they came in, he told me to go ahead, so I took a silk handkerchief from my pocket; held it up for all to see; poked it into my left fist and made it disappear!

"So that's how I became a magician. The first show I ever gave, I began by taking a silk handkerchief from my pocket, holding it in my right hand, and pushing it into my left fist—from which it disappeared.

"And now I will show you my favorite trick. I take a silk handkerchief from my pocket; hold it in my right hand and slowly place it in my left fist—and you see the handkerchief has disappeared."

2. THE DRUM PRODUCTION

This is a very simple yet effective production of a group of silk handkerchiefs. The apparatus consists of a cylinder six or eight inches in diameter, and four or five inches in depth, mounted on a slender rod one-half an inch thick. The cylinder is set on its side, and the rod, which is about a foot in height, is mounted on a large nickel-plated base.

The magician places a piece of tissue paper in front of the cylinder, and fastens it in position with a band of metal. Then he breaks the paper and proceeds to extract a dozen or more silk handkerchiefs from the empty tube.

Paper may be placed over both sides of the cylinder, and some handkerchiefs taken from each side.

The spectators do not suspect where the handkerchiefs come from, because they do not believe that a silk handkerchief one foot square can be passed through a tube only a half-inch thick.

The handkerchiefs are concealed in the base; and they come up the slender rod, which is hollow. The end of each handkerchief is twisted around the one next in line, forming a chain. The first handkerchief should be black—the color of the inside of the cylinder. After the front paper has been fastened on, the magician gets hold of the end of this silk, which is at the top of the rod, and draws it upward. This begins the chain, and the handkerchiefs are produced in quick succession.

A solid base with a hole through the center may be used; in this event the handkerchiefs are compressed in the hollow leg of an undraped table, which has a hole in the top to correspond with the tube above.

3. THE NEW CONFETTI BOWLS

The magician uses two bowls of metal, each six inches in diameter, and four inches in height.

He fills the first bowl with confetti, and places the other mouth to mouth with it. Upon removing the upper bowl, the confetti has doubled in quantity, now filling both bowls.

The confetti is leveled; and the empty bowl is placed upon it. Again the confetti doubles in quantity.

For the third time it is leveled, and the empty bowl placed upon it. Upon removal of the upper bowl, the confetti has doubled again.

The bowls are constructed as follows:

(A) An empty bowl that has a loose lining which fits snugly. The lining is shallower than the bowl; and its inner surface is covered with confetti, which is glued or cemented in place.

(B) A bowl filled with confetti. Near the mouth are four bits of metal that project about a half an inch inward. They are equidistant apart.

A celluloid disc also fits in the bowl. It has a small knob in the center; and four cut-out portions on the rim to correspond with the arms that project from the side of the bowl. Both sides of the disc are coated with confetti.

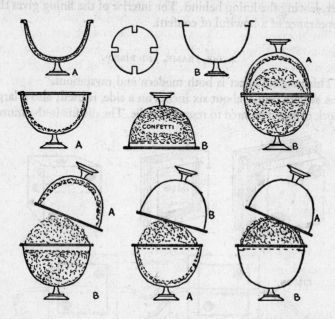

Bowl B is filled with confetti beforehand. Then the celluloid disc is placed in it; the cut-outs are slid over the projecting arms. The knob on the disc is upward, and by turning it, the disc is locked below the arms. Then the bowl may be inverted.

In performing, Bowl A is shown empty. It is filled with confetti. Bowl B is picked up in a careless manner—apparently empty because it is upside down—and is placed on Bowl A.

The bowls are inverted. Bowl A is lifted off (the loose lining with it) and the confetti appears to have doubled.

The confetti is leveled off, and the knob is turned so that the celluloid disc of Bowl B is free.

Bowl A is set on Bowl B; they are inverted. The disc sinks into

Bowl A, and the confetti from Bowl B is piled upon it, when Bowl B is lifted.

Now the confetti is leveled off to the disc. Bowl B is placed upon Bowl A. The bowls are inverted. This time Bowl A is lifted free, leaving the lining behind. The interior of the lining gives the appearance of a bowlful of confetti.

4. DIE, FRAME, AND RIBBON

This magical effect is both modern and mysterious.

A square frame, about six inches on a side, is used; also a large block of wood painted to resemble a die. The die fits in the frame.

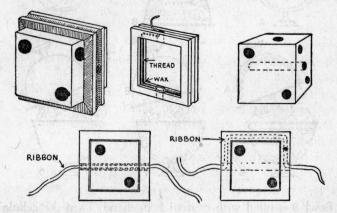

A hole runs through the die and there are corresponding holes in opposite sides of the frame.

The die is placed in the frame, and a ribbon is run through the holes, penetrating both the die and the frame. The ends of the ribbon are held by spectators. There is no possible way to remove the die.

The magician seizes the die and takes it right out of the frame, *leaving the ribbon through the frame*. The die is solid, and everything may be examined!

The inside of the frame is beveled. Therein lies the secret; but there is nothing suspicious about the construction of the frame.

Around one of the holes of the frame, on the inside, is a slight coating of wax. A slip-knot of black thread surrounds the hole, being pressed against the wax. The free end of the thread runs around inside the frame, being waxed at the corners, and out the other hole, where it is attached to the outside of the frame by the dab of wax. The thread is not seen.

The die is placed in position, and the ribbon is pushed through the holes. But when the magician pulls the ribbon through, his hand, which is hidden by the die, pulls the thread instead. This yanks the ribbon *around the die* through the beveled depression. As soon as the end of the ribbon emerges, the magician seizes it. In handing the ends to the spectators, he pulls the slip-knot off the end of the ribbon and drops the thread onto the floor. This is easily done.

The die fits rather tightly in the frame, so it does not need the ribbon to support it. It sticks firmly in place. Nothing could appear fairer.

All the magician has to do is to pull out the die or knock it from the frame. The spectators are told to pull on the ribbon, so it immediately runs straight through the frame, the instant that the die is released.

The secret of this excellent trick is known to comparatively few magicians. The apparatus will stand close inspection; and the frame is painted solid black so that the black thread will not show. The author considers it to be one of the best effects of recent years, especially suited to the requirements of the platform entertainer.

5. THE ELASTIC STICKS

The magician uses two curved sticks—each more than a foot in length. One is painted black; the other is white. He compares the sticks and shows that the black one is larger than the white. He places them together, and presses on the ends until the condition is reversed—the white stick is larger than the black. Then he presses them until they both become the same size.

This trick is simply an adaption of an old optical illusion. The sticks are the same size—but one held below the other appears to be larger.

The clever part of the trick lies in the pretense of changing the sizes of the sticks. In placing them together, the white is set so that its end is further in than the black, but this is covered by the hands. By pushing forward on the white and drawing inward on the black, the condition appears to be reversed as is demonstrated by holding the black above the white. (The black was originally below the white.)

Again the sticks are brought together, the end of the black being further in, and they are apparently made the same size, as is shown by setting one on the other.

6. CHINESE WANDS

This is a method of restoring a cut string with the aid of a pair of Chinese wands, through which the string runs.

The wands are held side by side, and the string is drawn back and forth through them. Then the string is cut at the center; but is quickly restored, and drawn through the wands again.

Ever since the original "Pillars of Solomon" trick which is probably a hundred years old, magicians have sought to improve this idea so that the wands could be separated. With the "Chinese Wands," the string is actually cut; it is restored to its original length; it may be drawn from the wands and given for examination.

The wands are prepared thus:

Wand A has a projecting knob at the bottom. The wand is hollow, and the string passes through a hole in the top, down over the projecting knob, up in the wand again and out a hole on the other side. The wand is open at the bottom.

Wand B has a slit through which the string passes at the top, and the string also passes through a lead weight which is free inside the hollow wand. The wand is closed at the bottom. The slit at the top is not noticeable, as it is kept toward the performer and is camouflaged with painted lines.

The string is pulled back and forth through the wands. To all appearances it passes through holes in the upper ends of the wands and goes straight through. The magician creates this impression as he draws the string back and forth.

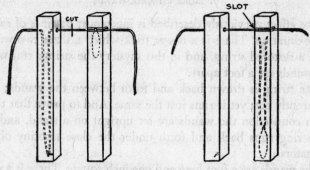

Left: The wands before the trick.
Right: The wands after the trick.

He also calls attention to the exact length of the string. Then he invites some person to cut the string between the wands. This is done when the string is just about centered.

Now it will be observed that the string is actually much longer than it appears to be, due to the double length inside of Wand A. When the string has been cut, the magician brings the wands together and in so doing, he slips the string from the knob in the bottom of Wand A, releasing the extra length.

As he turns away, he seizes the center of the string, taking the cut end that protrudes from Wand A. He draws the string through the slit in Wand B, at the same instant raising the wands from the horizontal to the vertical. The sliding weight drops and carries with it the length of string that is projecting from either side of Wand B.

Thanks to the extra portion of string hidden in Wand A, the magician is now drawing a string back and forth—through the upper ends of the wands—and the string is quite as long as it was in the beginning!

The string may then be drawn clear of the wands and taken out for examination proving that it was restored. The wands, however, are laid aside.

7. MORE CHINESE WANDS

The effect previously described is ingenious; but it is of rather short duration. There is a newer trick which utilizes two wands with a restored string, and in this mystery the strings run while the wands are a foot apart.

The string is drawn back and forth between the wands; it is apparently cut; yet it runs just the same. And to prove that there is no connection the wands are set upright on a stand, and yet the string runs back and forth under the close scrutiny of the spectators.

The wands are a foot long and one inch square. There is a cord in each wand, and it runs down through to the bottom. These cords are connected by a black thread, two feet in length, which emerges from a hole in the bottom of each wand. Each string is just one foot long, and the free end has a tassel attached.

Half way up the side of one wand—on the outside—is a tiny hook. There is a depression in the other wand, so the two may be flush together. The thread runs over this hook and down to the bottom of the other wand.

At the outset, the string of one wand is pulled out to its full length. There is a foot of thread inside that wand; a foot of thread between the wands; and a string one foot long in the second wand.

By pulling on the short tassel, the string is apparently drawn through the wands at the tops—back and forth. This is done several times; then the string is apparently centered, and the wands are separated very slightly.

This reveals a dummy inch of string that is set between the wands at the top, to make it appear that the string actually runs through the top. The little length of string is cut.

The wands are then separated by raising the left wand (the one

with the depression in the side). It can be carried six inches from
the wand on the right.

When the wands are put together, the string can be drawn
back and forth again. This is repeated several times.

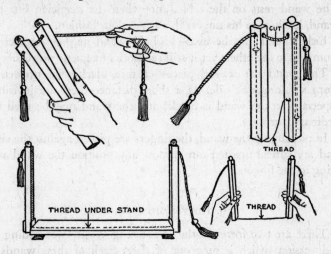

Now comes the perplexing part—the finish of the trick. The
thread is slipped from the hook on the side of the right wand.
The magician carries the wands to the stand, which is a flat
pedestal one foot long, mounted on small feet.

A clamp is provided for each wand. The magician holds the
wands upright, stretches them a full foot apart, and brings the
lower end below the bottom of the stand. As he sets the wands
in the clamps, which are at the extreme ends, the thread goes
under the stand.

When he pulls the string on one wand, the other string short-
ens, and vice versa. The stand may be placed directly before the
spectators, but they will detect nothing; for the thread is completely out of sight beneath the stand, where it runs under the
bottom.

This final demonstration is the conclusion of the trick. The
wands are left on the stand at the finish.

8. THE CLINGING WAND

A magician's wand of the usual pattern is utilized in this effect. The wand rests on the table, and when the magician lifts the wand, it clings to his fingers in a mysterious fashion.

Either hand may be used—and the wand may be transferred from one to the other; yet it still retains its magnetic powers.

The wand has several pieces of thin black wire projecting from it, along one side. At a short distance these are invisible, especially as the wand is black; and the wand may be used for ordinary purposes.

In picking up the wand, the fingers are placed against the side, and are spread apart. From almost any position the wand will cling to the fingers.

9. THE VANISHING WAND

There are two forms of the "Vanishing Wand"—excluding an old version which is now out of date. Each of these wands is demonstrated to be quite solid, but when the wand is rolled in a piece of paper, it disappears.

The first type of wand is made of glazed paper, but the tips are genuine metal. The end of the wand may be wrapped on the table. When the wand is rolled in paper, the tube thus formed is torn to pieces, leaving no trace of the wand. The ends are tossed carelessly aside with the other bits of paper, the greatest amount of tearing taking place near the center.

The second type is a much heavier wand that may be dropped on the floor. It consists of a series of jointed parts, which are held together by a length of heavy cord elastic. Over these are sections of metal tubing, painted black. These sections slide about a half inch along the wand. So they keep the jointed parts from collapsing.

Thus the wand is used as a regular wand. When it is to be vanished, it is wrapped in a sheet of paper; the end section is shifted, pushing the others along, and the wand is ready to collapse. The paper tube is crumpled with the wand inside.

10. DOUBLE PRODUCTION WAND

The purpose of this wand is to enable the magician to produce two silk handkerchiefs from his empty hands.

The wand is hollow, and the tip of one end is loose. Inside it is a loop of wire. A handkerchief is thrust into the loop, and is pushed into the wand. When the tip is replaced, the wand appears quite ordinary.

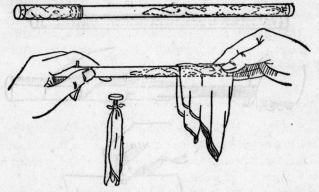

The first handkerchief is in the left end of the wand. The drawings show the removal of the second silk with the fake cap.

There is also an extra piece that fits on the other end of the wand—a piece of tubing less than three inches long which accommodates a twelve-inch silk handkerchief. This tube appears to be part of the wand.

The magician shows his hands empty and picks up the wand in his left hand, holding it by the extra piece. He puts the wand under his right arm, retaining the piece in his left hand. Bringing his hands together he produces the handkerchief.

In reaching for the wand, he attaches the extra piece of metal to the wand. He shows each hand empty, and lays the handkerchief over the other end of the wand. He seizes the center of the handkerchief with his right hand, holding the wand with his left; and as he draws the handkerchief away, he brings the tiny tip with it. He lays the wand on the table, and uses his right hand to draw the second silk from beneath the first. The little tip is laid on the table under the handkerchiefs.

II. FRANCISCUS HANDKERCHIEF WAND

In contrast to the clumsy and slow-working wands that have been devised to vanish a handkerchief, the wand invented by Franciscus stands out as a remarkable piece of apparatus.

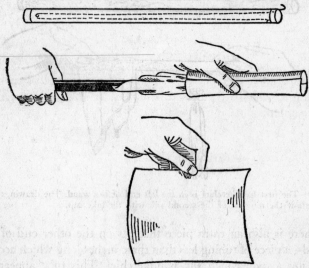

Top: Construction of the fake wand.
Center and Bottom: How the trick appears.

The effect of the trick is as follows: A piece of paper is rolled into a tube, and a handkerchief is pushed into the tube. To aid the progress of the silk, the magician picks up his wand and forces the handkerchief completely into the paper. Then he lays the wand aside. When the paper is unrolled, the silk has vanished.

The wand is hollow and is open at one end. A piece of cord

elastic runs down into the wand, through a pulley at the solid bottom, and up the other side to the top where it is attached.

On the free end is a small nickel-plated tip, slightly smaller than the diameter of the wand. A groove underneath enables it to be fastened to the edge of the open end of the wand, where it holds the elastic taut. This metal tip has a hook soldered to it, the hook pointing downward.

When the handkerchief is in the paper, the magician pushes it further in with the wand. The hook catches the silk near the center. Then the end of the wand is tapped against the inner wall of the paper tube, and the tip is released. It is drawn rapidly to the bottom of the wand, taking the handkerchief with it.

12. THE HANDKERCHIEF PEDESTAL

The handkerchief pedestal is a well-known piece of magical apparatus, which is explained here because of its use in certain new combinations.

The pedestal stands nearly one foot high. A glass is placed upon it, and a cloth is thrown over the glass. When the cloth is removed a handkerchief (previously vanished) is seen in the glass. The handkerchief comes from the pedestal. The glass is bottomless, and the handkerchief is pushed up by a mechanical action.

One type of pedestal has a spring to eject the handkerchief which is just below the top of the pedestal. There are various models of this type.

The other type is operated by pressing down on the glass, thus lowering the top of the pedestal a little more than an inch, and forcing the handkerchief up with the rod of the pedestal. The change in height of the pedestal is not noticeable.

In both types the operation is quick and effective, and this piece of apparatus is usually very satisfactory.

13. HANDKERCHIEF AND GLASS PRODUCTION

The following trick utilizes the handkerchief pedestal. An empty tube is set on the pedestal. A handkerchief is vanished; and when the tube is lifted, the handkerchief is seen inside a glass on the pedestal. Both the glass and the handkerchief have appeared simultaneously.

The tube is of double thickness, with a space between the walls. The space is closed at the top of the tube, but not at the bottom. Hence the tube can be shown empty from one end, although a bottomless glass is concealed between its walls.

The bottomless glass in this case is virtually a cylinder of glass.

When the tube has been shown empty and placed upon the pedestal (which is of the spring type), the handkerchief is released, and it arrives in the tube. The tube is lifted leaving the glass with the handkerchief inside.

14. VANISHING GLASS AND HANDKERCHIEF

In connection with the preceding trick, the disappearance of a glass containing a handkerchief is an effective combination. A handkerchief is placed in a solid glass. Both are wrapped in a sheet of paper which is then crushed, showing that glass and handkerchief have vanished.

The glass has a celluloid lining. It is set on the table directly in front of a well or a servante. The handkerchief is inserted in the glass, and as the right hand takes the glass, the left hand holds the sheet of paper in front of it.

The right hand lets the glass slide into the well but retains the celluloid lining and the handkerchief.

These are shown and wrapped in the paper. The lining will pass as the glass at a very short distance. Then the paper is crumpled. Obviously the tumbler must have disappeared as it would be impossible to treat glass in such a manner.

The immediate reappearance of the glass and handkerchief heightens the effect.

Special celluloid linings can be obtained very cheaply as they are very thin and inexpensive to make.

15. EGG CLING CLANG
(*With Handkerchief Pedestal*)

This is a combination of several effects. An egg is set in a glass; the glass is placed on a pedestal and covered with a cloth.

A handkerchief is rolled in the hands, and becomes an egg. When the glass is uncovered, the handkerchief has taken the place of the egg.

Requirements: One handkerchief pedestal.
One hollow egg, with hole in the side.
Two silk handkerchiefs of the same color.
One bottomless glass.

The fake egg is dropped in the bottomless glass. The glass is covered with a cloth, and is lifted from the right hand, upon which it is resting.

The egg remains in the hand, which closes over it and palms it. When the glass is placed on the pedestal, the handkerchief in the pedestal is released.

The duplicate handkerchief is taken in the hands, and is worked into the hollow egg. Then the egg is shown and is laid on the table. The cloth is lifted from the glass to reveal the silk handkerchief.

16. MYSTERIOUS PENETRATION

The effect of this trick is unusual. A glass is filled with ink and is placed on the table. Two empty cylinders are exhibited, and one is placed over the glass.

A sheet of glass is set on the cylinder, and the other cylinder is placed on top. When the upper cylinder is lifted, the glass of ink is seen there, while the lower cylinder is empty.

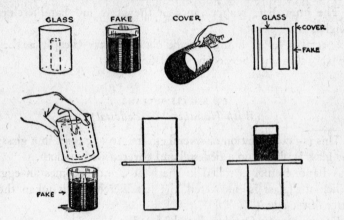

The glass used is of a special type, called the "Demon Glass." It is cylindrical, and it has a small cylinder in the center. The center portion being of glass also, it cannot be seen.

One of the two cylinders contains a tube of celluloid, painted black nearly to the top. The cylinders may be shown empty, as they are black inside, and the celluloid fake cannot be seen.

The cylinder containing the fake is placed over the glass—after the glass has been filled with ink. When the cylinder is lifted, the first two fingers enter the top and engage the center of the glass —one finger within; the other without. Thus the glass is lifted with the cylinder. But the celluloid fake remains, as it is larger than the glass, and everyone thinks it is the tumbler.

The other cylinder is placed over the celluloid fake. The sheet

of glass is placed on the cylinder. The cylinder with the tumbler-
ful of ink is immediately set upon the sheet of glass.

The upper cylinder is lifted showing the glass of ink. In showing the bottom cylinder, the celluloid fake is lifted with it and
the tube may be shown quite empty.

17. THE CHINESE WONDER BLOCKS

Two black blocks, threaded on a piece of tape, with a tassel
at the bottom to prevent them from falling. A bandana handkerchief is slipped over the tape, and a spectator is invited to hold
the upper end of the tape.

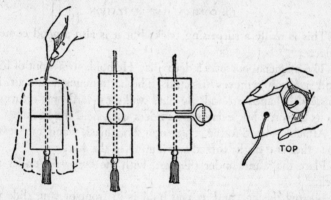

The magician shows a small gold ball. He puts it under the
handkerchief, and immediately places it on the tape between
the two blocks. Both the blocks and the ball have a hole in the
center; and the entire apparatus is left in the hands of the audience, while they wonder how the ball managed to get between
the blocks!

The ball is on the tape at the beginning. But it is pulled up
behind the blocks. The blocks are three inches square; while the
ball is only an inch and a half in diameter.

The left hand supports the blocks, holding them together, and
keeping the ball hidden in the palm, while the right hand draws
the ribbon back and forth through the blocks.

Then the handkerchief, which has a hole in the center, is slipped over the tape. The blocks are released, and the ball slides between them—the click being the natural noise of the blocks themselves.

The magician takes a duplicate ball and reaches beneath the handkerchief. He holds the ball palmed in his right hand, and lifts the handkerchief with that hand, showing the ball between the blocks.

As the spectators are not aware that a duplicate ball is used, this becomes a real problem.

18. COMEDY HAT LEVITATION

This is really a surprising trick; but it is also a good comedy effect.

The magician borrows a derby hat. He holds it in front of him, and suddenly removes his hands. The hat remains in the air. He passes his hands around the hat; walks forward and returns it to its owner, while everyone wonders what held the hat up.

Attach a thread to the center of a short black wand, and fasten the other end of the thread to a button of the vest.

Place the wand under the vest, with the lower tip under the belt.

Borrow the hat, and as you hold it in front of you, slide the wand down from under the vest, and swing the upper end forward. The tip of the wand presses against the body, and the belt acts as the fulcrum of a lever. The mouth of the hat should be toward you, and you merely hang the hat on the projecting end of the wand.

The hands may then be removed and passed around the hat, which seems to float in mid-air. To conclude the trick, push inward with the hat, and the wand will slide down the trousers leg; but the thread will stop it as soon as it is out of sight. The hat may then be returned to the owner and not a trace of the trick will remain.

19. THE BILLIARD BALL BOX
(*Improved by El Barto*)

This is the newest version of the "Billiard Ball Box" in which a billiard ball disappears from a box with two compartments. It is an improvement by El Barto, over his original box.

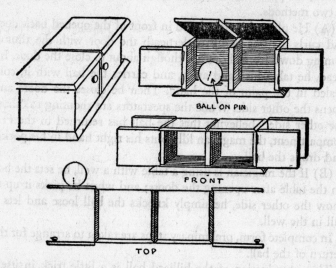

BALL ON PIN

FRONT

TOP

The box has four doors, and is divided into two compartments. Two of the doors are in front; two in back. The magician places the ball in one side of the box. Then he opens the doors and shows that the ball has gone. But it has been heard to slide to the other side. So he opens the doors there, after closing those of the first compartment. This process is repeated for some time. Finally all the doors are opened to show that the ball is not in the box.

The ball used is made of rubber—an imitation golf ball of the ten cent store variety is suitable. One back door of the box has a needle point projecting inward—and therein lies the secret.

The ball is put in that compartment; and when the doors are closed it is impaled on the needle. The box is tilted, and thanks to a sliding weight in the thin double bottom of the box, everyone thinks the ball has gone to the other side.

The first compartment is now shown. The back door is opened first, and the ball goes with it—out of sight in back of the box. Then the front door is opened.

While everyone is demanding that the other side of the box be shown, the performer makes away with the billiard ball, by one of two methods.

(A) He places his right hand in front of the opened back door and curls his fingers up underneath the door with the thumb coming down from above—as though about to close the door. Instead, he takes his hand away, and carries the ball with it, concealed in the palm of the hand. Then he closes the doors and opens the other side. While the spectators are shouting to "show the other side," believing that the ball has returned to the first compartment, the magician idly puts his right hand in his pocket and drops the ball.

(B) If the magician is using a table with a well, he sets the box on the table after opening the doors; and when he picks it up to show the other side, he simply knocks the ball loose and lets it fall in the well.

In complete form, preliminary steps are taken to arrange for the return of the ball.

The reproduction of the billiard ball is a little trick in itself. The magician uses a cardboard horn, of the New Year's variety. He shows this empty and drops the ball inside to prove it. He has a duplicate ball concealed in his hand, and when he turns the horn over, the first ball remains inside; but he places his hand beneath the horn and brings the palmed ball into view.

Then he sets the inverted horn on the table; lifts it, and sets it down again, this time with a slight thump which lets the ball drop to the table.

The ball in his hand is the one he vanishes from the box. The horn is then lifted to show the ball beneath.

20. PRODUCTION OF FOUR BOUQUETS

A cardboard flower pot is inverted upon a tray. It is lifted to show a bouquet of flowers. The flowers are removed; the trick is repeated, not once, but three times, four clusters of flowers being produced.

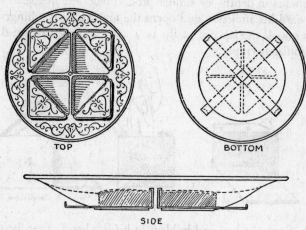

TOP   BOTTOM

SIDE

Upper left shows the containers open.
Upper right and lower drawings illustrate the releases.

The flowers come from the tray. The center is divided into four sections, and each one operates on a spring. Thus there are four compartments, shallow, but large enough to contain fifty "spring flowers" each.

The flowers of each bouquet are joined by light cords. The magician inverts the bowl on the tray—which is about twelve inches in diameter—and releases one section by a rod beneath the tray. The lid springs back automatically, releasing the flowers. The action is repeated with the other containers. The tray may be turned toward the audience at any time, for the pattern is designed to conceal the mechanism.

Each bouquet as withdrawn should be laid upon an ordinary

tray. If an assistant holds the tray, and releases the flowers, a handkerchief can be used instead of the flower pot; the assistant making each release just as the tray is covered.

21. NOVEL PRODUCTION BOX

This is a box about ten inches long by five inches in width and five inches in depth—or similar proportions. The magician holds it toward his audience, and opens the top, which is a hinged lid. This reveals the interior of the box, and everyone can see that it is completely empty.

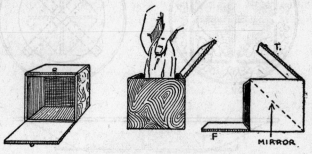

He closes the box and holds it in his left hand. Then he opens the lid and proceeds to extract many silk handkerchiefs and flags from the interior.

The box has two lids—one on top; the other on the bottom. Extending from side to side, and set diagonally across the interior of the box is a mirror—preferably of metal. The inside of the box is papered with fancy material.

The space behind the mirror is "loaded" with the handkerchiefs and flags. Both lids are closed, and the side containing the silks is set downward.

Picking up the box, the magician opens the lid, and reveals the interior. The mirror creates the illusion of an empty box. Upon closing the lid, the magician immediately shows all sides of the box to the audience; and this simple procedure enables him to turn it upside down. So when he opens the lid again, he has the compartment containing the handkerchiefs. He keeps the opening upward and produces the silks one by one.

If the audience is above the performer, he should set the box on the table, and open the lid part way—toward the spectators. This will conceal the interior of the box as he produces the handkerchiefs. By using a double-faced mirror, the handkerchiefs can be brought out in groups and the box be shown empty at the finish.

22. TWO NEW COIN STANDS

The "coin stand" is a little easel used by manipulators on which to rest coins. By a simple mechanical arrangement, the stand itself is used to effect the disappearance of several coins.

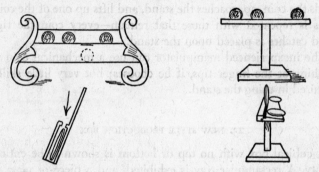

The first type of stand is a flat board set at an angle, with ornaments at the ends. The surface is covered with velvet, and a ledge runs along the center.

Four coins rest upon the ledge, setting in slight depressions. To the right of each coin is a slot, invisible in the velvet. If the coin is pushed to the slot, it will drop in and fall into the lower section of the easel; for the ledge is formed by an additional half-board superimposed on the front of the easel.

With four coins on display, the magician places his fingers upon the first one, and as he covers the coin, slides it to the slot. As the coin drops he pretends to take it in his hand, and to place it in the other hand—from which it disappears. The move-

ment is repeated with the remaining coins. With virtually no
skill, the magician can make coins vanish in a manner that rivals
the best sleight-of-hand.

The second type of stand may be used for the production of
coins as well as for their disappearance. It is simply a flat bar,
cross-wise on an upright post. The coins stand on edge, in a ledge
at the front of the bar. In covering a coin with his fingers, the
magician lets it fall back on the bar, where it lies level, and cannot
be seen because of the ledge.

With a single coin palmed in his right hand, the magician can
have a row of coins out of sight on the stand. He lets the coin
appear at his finger tips; apparently transfers it to the left hand,
but retains it palmed in the right. The left hand, pretending it
holds the coin, approaches the stand, and lifts up one of the coins.
This is repeated with those that remain—every coin the right
hand catches is placed upon the stand.

The inexperienced manipulator can use a mechanical coin for
catching at the finger tips, if he chooses; but very little skill is
required in using the stand.

23. NEW STYLE PRODUCTION BOX

A cubical box with no top or bottom is shown to be entirely
empty. A rectangular tray is exhibited, and a piece of glass the
size of the bottom of the box is placed upon the tray. Then the
box is put on the glass.

Reaching in the box, the magician produces a quantity of silk
handkerchiefs.

The handkerchiefs come from the tray. The tray is double, with
a space between, and it has four tiny triangular traps near the
center—these corresponding to the corners of the box when it is
set on the tray.

When the glass is placed on the tray, it is turned so that it takes
the position of a diamond instead of a square. When the box is
placed upon it, the corners have access to the traps in the tray.

Several silks can be drawn from each trap, the ends of the silk being linked together so that one will draw the next from its hiding place.

The trick is specially effective when an assistant holds the tray.

24. THE BOGART TUBE

This is a stage trick which is suitable for platform performances, as it can be done with spectators on all sides. It is a trick that is not often seen, and one that has not been explained in any book on magic.

A nickel-plated tube, nine inches long, open at one end, is passed for examination. Then water is poured into it, and a piece of tissue paper is placed over the opening and is clamped there with a ring.

On the platform is a stand with a projection at the top; the projection holds a band about four inches in height, of larger diameter than the tube.

The magician inserts the tube in the band, and tilts the stand forward to show the unbroken tissue paper. Then he breaks the paper and produces an array of silk handkerchiefs ending with large flags. At the conclusion he removes the tube from the stand and pours out the water!

The "load" containing the handkerchiefs is in the metal band on the stand. It consists of an acorn-shaped metal tube, with holes in the sides; and a piece of tissue paper is over the opening, at the top, held there by a metal band.

The original tube is only half-filled with water. In inserting it in the band, it is pushed upward. The point of the acorn-loader pierces the tissue paper; but as the loader is slightly smaller than the tube, the tube picks it up, and the paper on the loader takes the place of the torn paper on the tube.

A flange on the tube catches in place and holds the tube in position in the band.

The magician breaks the paper and produces all the silks from the loader. Then he removes the tube—upward—and pours out the water which comes through the holes in the loader.

The loader is only about four inches deep; hence the water does not reach it before the production of the silks, as there is less than five inches of water in the tube.

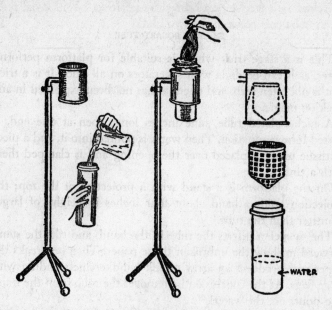

The movement of putting the tube in position is natural and effective and the fact that the paper is not broken during the tube's passage through the band seems to preclude the possibility of anything having been secretly placed within the tube.

25. THE PASSING KNOTS

This is one of the most popular of handkerchief tricks—a clever effect that has been considerably improved since its invention some fifteen years ago.

The magician has two sets of handkerchiefs—three in each set. Red, white and blue were the original colors. Then all whites came into common use. The best combination is to have two reds and a blue in one set; two blues and a red in the other.

The magician picks up the two blues and a red; and places
them in a tumbler or on a stand. Then he ties the blue between
the two reds. Shaking these three handkerchiefs, the blue handkerchief falls free. Upon lifting the other set of silks, the red is
seen to be tied between the two blues!

There are two phases to the trick: first the vanishing of the
knots from the first set; second the appearance of the knots in
the second set.

The first is accomplished by tying a trick knot. If an ordinary
square knot is tied with the corners of two handkerchiefs, it will

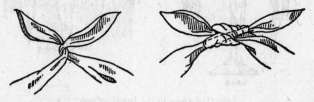

become a slip-knot if one corner is tied around the other. Tie the
red around the blue; then pull the blue handkerchief straight,
and it can be drawn free from the red.

But the quick vanishing knot is tied thus:

Simply cross the corners of the blue and red like a letter X.
Bend the red under the blue and the blue over the red. Hold each
handkerchief with the third and fourth fingers of the hands,
while the thumbs and first two fingers tie a single knot with the
corners.

This knot can be drawn very tightly; it will not pass the twist
originally formed. Yet a mere shake of the handkerchiefs will
cause the separation. In making the twist, the hands should be
kept in motion, imitating the tying of a single knot.

The appearance of the knots in the other group of silks is
simple: the knots are already there; but the side tips of the silks
are tied, and not the upper and lower corners. The knots are concealed in the folds of the silks. The handkerchiefs are rolled together; when they are unrolled, grasp the side corner of one of
the blue handkerchiefs, and shake them into a string of three.

This may be done without apparatus; but with the use of apparatus, the effect of the trick is increased. It is possible to show the handkerchiefs well apart before the trick begins.

The first method utilizes the table drape. Lay the three silks side by side on the table; then tuck the knotted corners down under the ribbon of the table drape. The silks will appear to be separate.

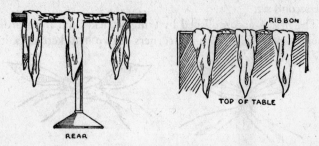

Left: The twist in the handkerchiefs.
Right: The fake knot.

The second method is to drape the silks over a crossbar on an upright stand. The knotted corners are hidden behind the bar, and from in front the silks appear to be apart.

A special stand may be used; hollow at the back, into which the corners are introduced.

In picking up the silks from either of these positions, the magician must spread them out sufficiently to cover up the knots when the handkerchiefs are raised.

26. COIN ACT FINALE

A flashy trick is always effective at the end of a routine with coins. The old-fashioned "Coin Ladder" is an expensive apparatus that may be easily broken; and this newer variation, combining a table with the ladder effect is far more practical.

The magician sets a derby hat upon the table; places half a dozen coins in a glass; covers the glass with a handkerchief and sets it upon the hat.

As a center leg, the table has an upright plank with a molding; the plank is studded with nails and is fronted with a sheet of glass.

The magician taps the glass with his wand; the coins apparently pass through the hat, and appear one by one in the center leg, running down among the nails. They drop out the bottom into a bowl. Then the glass is shown empty.

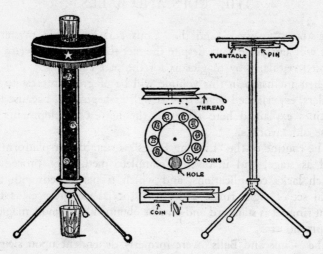

Duplicate coins are used. The originals are dropped in a bottomless glass, ornamented at the lower edge. They fall into the performer's hand and he palms them away, dropping them in a pocket of his coat or the pocket of another table when he obtains the handkerchief.

The duplicates come from beneath the table top. Two wooden discs are located there. The lower is firm and is grooved to hold the coins. It has a hole the size of a coin just above the opening of the upright plank. The upper disc revolves, being controlled by a cord passing out the back of the table. The magician draws this cord as he moves away. The upper disc revolves, and a nail in the disc pushes the coins so that they are forced into the frame, one by one.

CHAPTER XI

THE "LINKING RINGS"
AND
THE "CUPS AND BALLS"

THE "LINKING RINGS" and the "Cups and Balls" are mysteries that will always be new, despite the fact that they have been performed regularly by magicians for the past century.

Their inclusion in this volume will be of great interest to all readers, experienced magicians as well as beginners, because the routines explained here represent the newest developments of these old favorites.

The routine of the "Linking Rings" is suitable for platform as well as stage, and involves a complete method of procedure which lacks complications, and which is performed with the usual set of eight rings. This is of special importance, as the eight ring set is standard and may be obtained from most magical supply houses.

The "Cups and Balls" were formerly dependent upon sleight of hand; but years ago a new method of presentation was evolved, and it has come into prominence because it eliminates all the difficult sleights and unnatural movements. With it, anyone may learn the trick; but the new method has never before appeared in a book on magic. With this volume as reference, the magician can learn the improved "Cups and Balls" and he will have one of the finest tricks of magic in his repertoire.

The descriptions of these tricks are easily understood when followed with the actual apparatus.

I. THE CHINESE LINKING RINGS

The "Linking Ring" mystery is more than a century old; but it still stands as the greatest trick in existence. The magical penetration of supposedly solid rings has all the semblance of real magic. Despite the fact that the trick has been exposed frequently, very few people can explain how it is done; and a clever magician can mystify people who know how the rings are constructed.

Psychologically the "Linking Ring" trick is perfect. A booklet could be written dealing with the reactions of those persons who witness its performance. Every magician has his own pet methods, so two performers rarely present the effect in the same way.

A mere knowledge of how the trick is done does not suffice. Therefore, comparatively few magicians are able to perform the trick. They know the secret of the trick, but they cannot present it.

Books on magic that explain the "Linking Ring" trick generally give a variety of moves; but when the beginner tries to perform them, he becomes confused and bewildered. He cannot work the different movements into an orderly procedure.

The whole secret of success is ROUTINE. The magician must practice a regular routine and learn it so that it becomes automatic.

Before describing the routine, we must first consider the construction of the rings. There are eight rings to the set, as follows:

Two single rings.

Two rings linked together.

Three rings linked together.

One "key" ring; a single ring which has an opening, large enough to admit the passage of another ring. The "key" ring is never closed. It does not lock; and it cannot be given for examination. When it is handled, the magician always keeps his fingers over the opening.

The rings are arranged in the following manner before presenting the trick.

The three linked rings are slipped on the right arm, up to the elbow. Then the "key" ring is placed on the arm; then the two linked rings; and finally the two single rings. The break in the "key" ring is hidden in the bend of the elbow.

The magician walks forward and states that he will pass all

the rings for examination, and that as every ring is inspected, it will be placed on the left arm, so that the examined rings may be distinguished from those which have not been looked over.

He removes the two single rings with his left hand and gives one to a person on his left; the other to a person on his right.

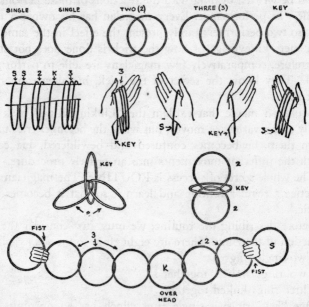

The illustrations show the entire set of linking rings; how they are placed on the left arm. The movements of exchanging the "key" for a single ring are shown also. Two designs—The "Stirrup" and the "Chain of Eight" are also illustrated.

"Now," he states, "I will demonstrate what may be done with these rings. Watch!"

He takes the two linked rings with his left hand, holding them together, keeping the hand slightly in motion. No one knows that the rings are already joined.

"Here are two separate rings," says the performer.

He rubs the rings together, draws them apart and gives them a sudden twist. Then he holds them up—joined!

"Will you take these?" asks the magician, of a spectator. "Try to take them apart like I put them together. It's very easy—when you know how!"

This illusion is so deceptive, and so bold, that everyone believes the rings were originally separated. In print, this sounds strange. In practice, the ruse has been working for a hundred years.

The magician then takes the rings that are on his right arm, and holds them for a moment in his left hand, his fist covering the opening in the "key" ring. He turns to the man on his right who has the single ring, and takes the ring in his right hand.

Now comes an important and subtle move.

In turning to the person on his left, the magician drops the single ring along with the rings in his left hand. Then he throws the single ring and the three linked rings back on his right arm, retaining the "key" ring in his left hand.

The movement is so natural that everyone supposes the left hand is holding the single ring previously examined by the spectator on the right.

The "key" ring is transferred to the right hand. The left hand takes the single ring from the spectator on the left. The magician approaches the person who is holding the two linked rings.

"Again," says the magician, "I will show you how to put two single rings together. I will use these two single rings which *have just been examined and given back to me.*"

He rubs the "key" ring and the single ring together, with plenty of easy motion. This gives him an opportunity to slip the single ring through the opening in the "key" ring. The motion is kept up so that the spectators will not observe the exact moment of linking; then the rings are twisted and are shown joined, the single ring dangling from the "key."

"To take them apart," says the magician, "we reverse the procedure." He rubs the rings and slowly separates them. He lets the single ring fall on the left arm, and holds the "key" ring in the right hand.

"Give me your two rings," says the magician.

He takes them in the left hand and pushes the opening of the "key" ring through both sides of one of the two rings. Then he lets the two rings fall and holds the "key" ring. The two rings hang from the "key," and form a figure that resembles a stirrup.

The magician lifts one of the two rings and shows that the "key" ring is between them—but not connected. He slides the opening of the "key" through one side of the two rings, and lets the two rings fall. He then has a chain of three rings. His fingers cover the opening in the "key" ring.

Then he demonstrates how a ring may be removed by simply sliding the "key" ring off the upper ring of the two linked rings.

He lets the upper ring of the two linked rings slide on his left arm; then he puts the "key" ring on his left arm also, putting the opening of the "key" in the crook of his elbow.

Now comes the boldest part of the trick. Many performers slide through the following maneuver, and do not perform it effectively. On the contrary they should emphasize it, in the manner to be described.

"I will now," announces the magician, "present the most difficult feat ever attempted with the Chinese Rings. I will cause three separate rings to link together while in mid-air."

With his left hand, the performer seizes the three linked rings from his right arm. He holds them in his left fist, and with his right hand spreads them slightly apart at the outer extremity. He swings his left hand back and forth and suddenly tosses the rings in the air. As they fall, he catches one of the rings and exhibits the chain of three linked together, the rings dangling and clanging. The right hand grasps one end of the chain, the left hand the other. This bold procedure is extremely effective, and when the magician immediately gives the three rings for examination, the audience is greatly impressed.

The magician refers to his right arm and finds that a single ring remains there.

"Here," he says, "is one ring which has not yet been inspected. Will you please examine it?"

He gives the ring to a spectator. (The ring has, however, been examined before.)

Up to this point, the routine of the "Linking Rings" has been presented at close quarters. The magician asks for the return of the single ring, and places it on his *right* arm. He takes the chain of three in his right hand and moves a short distance from the audience. (In a hall, or theater, he goes to the center of the stage.)

The magician slides the "key" ring into his left hand, and transfers it to the right, holding the chain of three in his left.

"The climbing ring," he announces.

He starts the "key" ring at the bottom of the chain of three, slides it up the chain, and links it to the top ring. This movement must be practiced to make the link without hesitation. Performed gracefully, it appears as though the ring has moved up the chain link by link. At this point the magician may form fancy designs with the four rings. The formation of the designs will be explained later.

Taking the single ring from his right arm, and holding it in his right hand, the magician tosses it in the air once or twice, and then slides it up the chain, pushing its upper side through the opening in the "key" ring. He thus has a chain of five rings; but he must retain the "key" ring in his left hand, otherwise the opening would show.

In order to display the chain of five to good advantage, the magician should transfer the "key" ring to his right hand, and take the bottom ring of the chain in his left. Holding the chain horizontally in front of his body, he states that the rings now form a "Giant Watch Chain." The odd ring hanging from the "key" ring is the charm on the end of the chain, according to the magician.

The left hand immediately takes the "key" ring; the right hand seizes the odd single ring, and slipping it out of the "key" ring draws it down the chain and off the bottom. The optical illusion again takes place; the single ring appears to go from ring to ring in its passage down the chain. The single ring may then be given for examination, but this should not be prolonged, as the trick is now working to its climax.

The single ring is thrown on the right arm. The two linked

rings are slipped off the left arm, and one of them is linked to the "key" ring, making a row of six.

While he is doing this, the magician states that he will form all eight rings in one long continuous chain. He slips the "key" ring over his head, so that the opening is behind his neck.*

Then he lets one single ring slide down each arm, catching one in each fist. The fists immediately grasp the end rings of the chain of six, and the arms are lifted, holding the row of rings in a horizontal position. The single rings are held so that they extend straight out; and they appear to be attached to the ends of the chain.

This is another bold part of the "Chinese Rings," and many magicians would hesitate to keep the long chain in position, fearing that suspicion would be attached to the end rings. On the contrary, the chain of eight is the formation most appreciated by the audience, and they become so bewildered by the previous actions of the rings that they never realize that the chain is not complete.

Bringing his hands together, the magician links the rings at random, mixing them on the "key" ring so that they form a jumbled mass.† He may conclude his performance at this point, bowing, and laying the rings aside; or, if he is on a platform or in a large room, he may finish by shaking the "key" ring violently, letting go of the opening. As a result, the rings will fall to the floor in groups, and the "key" ring may be tossed off in a corner where it will be out of sight.

Always make plenty of noise with the rings. The constant clanging is proof of their solidity, and it makes the trick more effective. The larger the rings the better.

There are dozens of possible variations with the "Linking Rings." Many of them are superfluous and weaken the effect of mystery. The preceding routine should not take more than five minutes, allowing for the examination of the rings. Performers

---

*Some sets of rings are not large enough to pass over the head. In that event, the opening of the "key" ring should be taken between the teeth.

†*Never* arrange the rings so that they will hang on the "key" ring alone. The action calls attention to the one ring.

who stretch the "Rings" to fill in fifteen minutes or more usually succeed in tiring their audiences.

Most of the variations of the "Linking Rings" are the formation of designs. A few of these are good. The best is the "Rocking Chair." The designs are formed immediately after the formation of the chain of four rings, with the "key" ring at the top.

To make the "Rocking Chair," twist the chain to the right, by means of the lowermost ring. Give the bottom ring a half turn to the left, bring it up and immediately attach it to the "key" ring.

By bringing the "key" ring and the ring opposite together, a "Base-ball Mask," may be formed.

When the fist is held with the rings upward, and pressure is slightly released, the rings will spread out and form the "Opening of the Flower."

The position into which the rings then fall may be designated the "Square of Circles."

When the rings are shaken, they will form a three link chain, the center of which is double. When the bottom ring is brought up along with the "key" ring, the performer has a "Giant Chain," formed with two double links.

At the conclusion of the designs, one ring must be loosened from the "key" ring in order to come back to the chain of four.

THE DROPPING RING
(An Additional Move)

This is a very unusual movement with the "Linking Rings," used when there are four together (three rings and "key").

In effect, a ring goes link by link from the top of the chain to the bottom.

The Method: Hold the "key" ring at the top and twist the bottom ring to the right, forcing all the rings as far as they will go in that direction.

Then swing the bottom of the chain upward, so the "key" ring becomes the lowest of the chain.

Slide the "key" ring toward you. Then bend it back, until it is nearly flat against the ring to which it is connected—just like closing a book. Raise the right hand again, still holding the other end of the chain with the left hand.

You will now have two rings supported by the right hand—the "key" ring in the fist, and the top ring of the chain of three, which rests on the knuckles of the right hand.

Shake the ring from the knuckles, and it will drop to the ring below. Let it stay there an instant; then slightly release pressure with the left hand; and the middle ring of the chain of three will drop to the bottom ring. Now let go of the bottom ring, and it will fall with a clang on the bottom of the chain.

The illusion created is that one ring has dropped link by link from top to bottom. In reality, another ring has taken up the journey at each step.

ADDING THE "KEY" RING

An effective way of presenting the Ring trick is to pass all the rings for inspection at the beginning. First, two singles; then link two and pass them out; then link three and pass them for examination.

When this is done, the "key" must be secretly added to the other rings.

Method One: Place the "key" ring under the coat, hanging it over a fountain-pen in the vest pocket. Button the coat. Gather the examined rings in the left hand. Hold the hand at the bottom of the coat.

In turning to the left to receive an odd single ring, press against the left side of the coat with the right hand, thus raising the hidden "key" ring. As the right hand reaches toward a spectator, the "key" drops from beneath the coat, and is caught by the fingers of the left hand, so that it joins the other rings.

Method Two: Lay the "key" ring on a chair. Cover it with a handkerchief and lay the other rings on top of it. Proceed with the solid rings, and as you receive them, lay them on the chair.

Pull the handkerchief up through the rings and toss it aside or put it in your pocket. This leaves the "key" at the bottom of the pile, and it is picked up with the others.

Method Three: This is with pocket sized rings—between three and four inches in diameter. Slip the "key" over the wrist and up the sleeve. Proceed with the solid rings, and as they are returned, slip them on the wrist. In removing them, the thumb goes up the sleeve and brings the "key" ring along with them.

2. THE CUPS AND BALLS

The following routine with the "Cups and Balls" serves to modernize the famous old trick; and possesses the great advantage of requiring no sleight of hand. All that is necessary is to acquire a thorough knowledge of the routine, which may then be worked at a fairly rapid speed; not too quickly to be confusing; but rapidly enough to leave the keenest spectator far behind.

The outfit consists of three nickel-plated cups, which are identical in appearance. In practicing the movements, it is wise to paste a small label to each cup, marking the cups A, B, and C. These letters are used in the directions. In actual working, of course, the labels should be removed. Besides the cups, seven small balls of sponge rubber are used. These are preferable to the old-style cork balls, as they do not "talk."

The trick should be performed on a box about 12 inches long, seven inches wide, and six inches deep. Behind the box are three pieces of tubing, about one inch in length. Each piece of tubing is set upright; and on each tube is set a rubber ball, orange (tangerine), potato, or any other spherical object which may be wedged up into one of the cups.

Preparation. Before showing the trick, drop a rubber ball in cup A, and then insert cup B, in cup A. Drop a ball in cup B, and insert cup C (of course these are the small balls of sponge rubber). The cups will nest perfectly, because their peculiar construction leaves a space between their bottoms.

Place the five remaining balls to the left of the box.

The "key" move. The success of the trick depends upon a "key" move, which is quickly learned. Hold the cups in the left hand, with the mouths up. Now with the right hand, remove the bottom cup, and with a swing of the forearm turn the cup mouth down and bring it smartly down on to the box. The ball will not fall from the cup during this operation; it will be trapped

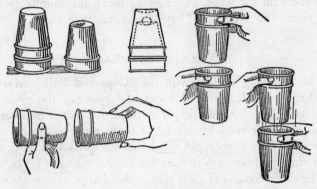

At the left the concealment of a ball between cups is shown; also the method of setting a cup on the table. At the right the illusion of dropping one cup through another is given in detail.

beneath the cup. The movement is so clean and natural that no one will suspect there is anything beneath the cup. Whenever a cup is set mouth down on the table, it is always with this movement, whether the cup is empty or not.

Setting Down Cups. The three cups, nested, are set on the table, mouth down, and in the following directions, whenever the text reads "set a cup on the table" or "set a cup on another cup," the directions mean to set the cup down, *unless otherwise stated.*

Move One. The various operations are called "moves." The cups are set mouth down, nested, in the order (top to bottom) A, B, C.

Remove cup A and set it at the right of the box. Remove cup B and set it at the left. Place cup C in the center.

Move Two. Place one of the five visible balls on cup A. Set cup C down on cup A, rather forcibly, as though to drive the ball through. Pick up the two cups together and reveal a ball beneath cup A.

Move Three. Remove cup C from cup A and set it on cup B. (There is a ball in cup C which will be trapped between the cups C and B.) Pick up the ball which appeared beneath cup A, set it on cup C and set cup A on top of cups C and B.

Move Four. Lift all three cups together, and show that the ball has "passed through."

Now remove cup A, placing it at the right; remove cup C setting it down on the ball at the left, and place cup B in the center.

Continue by taking the second of the five visible balls. Place it on cup A at the right. Set cup B on top, and lift both cups showing the ball beneath.

Move Five. Set cup B on cup C. Put the ball on cup B. Place cup A on cup B and lift all three cups, showing *two* balls beneath.

Move Six. Set cup A at the right; cup B on the two balls at the left, and cup C in the center. Pick up the third original ball; place it on cup A. Set cup C on cup A. Lift both cups, showing the ball beneath.

Move Seven. Put cup C on cup B. Put the ball on cup C. Set cup A on cup C. Lift all three cups and show *three* balls beneath.

Move Eight. Set cup A at the right; cup C on the three balls at the left, and cup B in the center. Pick up the fourth original ball. Place it on cup A. Set cup B on cup A. Lift both cups showing the ball beneath.

Move Nine. Set cup B on cup C. Put the ball on cup B. Put cup A on cup B. Lift all the cups and show four balls beneath.

Move Ten. Set cup A at the right; cup B on the four balls at the left; cup C in the center. Put the fifth visible ball on cup A. Set cup C on cup A; lift both cups and show the ball beneath.

Move Eleven. Place cup C on cup B. Put the ball on cup C; set cup A on cup C. Lift all three cups and show five balls beneath.

Note: Up to this point it will be noticed that each pair of moves repeats the previous pair, with one more ball appearing at the left each time.

Move Twelve. Set cup A at the right; cup C on the five balls; cup B in the center. Catch an imaginary ball from the air; toss it at cup A. Lift cup A and show the ball.

Move Thirteen. Set cup B aside. Put the ball on cup C. Set cup A on cup C. Lift the two cups together and reveal six balls. Immediately take cup A from cup C and set it on cup B. Exhibit cup C and then lay it aside.

Move Fourteen. Pick up cups A and B. Remove cup A and set it on the box. Take one of the balls, set it on cup A; put cup B on cup A. Lift both cups and show the ball beneath.

Move Fifteen. Set cup B on the ball; put a ball on cup B; put cup A on cup B. Lift both cups and show the *two* balls beneath.

Moves 16, 17, 18 and *19.* Move 16 is a repetition of 14; putting cup A on the two balls; but this time three balls are beneath the cup. Move 17 repeats 15, with four balls appearing beneath. Moves 18 and 19 are likewise repetitions of the preceding moves, producing five and six balls, respectively. At the end of move 19, lift both cups; remove cup A (which will be on cup B), and set cup A on cup C. Then show cup B with the six balls.

*   *   *

Penetrating Cups. At this point it is a good plan to introduce the effect of dropping one cup through another. Pick up cups A and C, and remove cup A; turn it bottom down, and let the ball contained in the cup slide into your right hand. Pass cup C for inspection, and do likewise with cup A, dropping the extra ball behind the box.

Take back the cups, and hold one, *mouth up,* between your left thumb and second finger. Drop the other cup (*mouth up*) into the cup in your left hand, and let it knock the cup out of your hand—your thumb and fingers catching the cup just dropped from the right hand. The effect is that you dropped one cup right through the other. This may be repeated and given as a pseudo explanation of why the balls went through the cups.

*   *   *   *

The Big Finish. Set three of the small rubber balls on the box, and lay a cup in back of each ball, the mouths of the cups toward the spectators. Pick up the right cup with the right hand; show it casually, pick up the ball with the left hand; as you exhibit the ball, set the cup, mouth down behind the table, on the big ball at the right. Press the cup over the ball and it will pick it up. Then put the cup mouth down on the table and set the small rubber ball on top of it.

Repeat with the other two cups.

Lift the right cup, showing nothing beneath it (the big ball being wedged). Set the cup down with a bump, and the big ball will drop and rest loose beneath the cup. Perform the "French Drop" vanishing the small rubber ball; lift the cup and reveal the big ball. Get rid of the small ball behind the box.

Repeat this procedure with the two remaining cups.

* * * *

Notes

Cups Upon Balls. If you experience trouble setting a cup over all the balls in moves 11 and 19, group four balls together and set the fifth on top, making a pyramid. As you set the cup down on the balls, if any start to escape, you can lift the cup slightly, and draw them in with the edge.

The Whirligig. When you take a cup containing a concealed ball, hold the cup mouth up in your right hand, and you can toss it in the air, letting it describe a complete revolution. Toss the cup easily, and catch it upright. Then set the cup down as previously described. This move should only be used occasionally, and it should be done several times with cups that are *actually empty,* allowing a glimpse of the interiors as you set down the empty cups.

The French Drop. This consists of holding a ball between the thumb and forefinger of the left hand. Right hand fingers encircle ball and apparently remove it; but ball is secretly allowed to drop in left hand.

New Additional Routine

The following moves may be introduced when the production of large balls is impractical, as is sometimes the case. The additional routine may also be used in connection with the regular movements.

Refer back to the Note following "move eleven." At this point, the three cups have been lifted showing five balls beneath. From bottom up the cups are B, C, and A. There is a ball beneath cup C and a ball beneath cup A.

Eliminate "moves 12 and 13." In their place do as follows: Set cup A at the right. Set cup C at the left. Pick up one of the five balls that are on the table and set it on cup A. Then execute move 14, and follow with 15, 16, 17, and 18. You will then have cup B on cup A; and when the two cups are lifted, five balls will be seen beneath.

Move Twenty. Set cup B on cup C. Pick up a ball and set it on cup B. Drive cup A down upon cup B. Lift all three cups showing ball beneath.

Move Twenty-one. Set cup A over the single ball. Set cup B on cup A. Put a ball on cup B and drive down cup C. Lift all three cups showing two balls beneath.

Move Twenty-two. Cup C on the two balls; cup B on C. Put a ball on cup B and drive it through with cup A. Lift cups showing three balls beneath.

Move Twenty-three. Cup A on three balls; B on A; ball on B; drive cup C down on B; lift three cups showing four balls.

Move Twenty-four. Cup C on four balls; cup B on C; ball on B; set A on B and lift all three cups showing five balls.

Final Moves. Set cup A on the table (a ball going beneath it). Set cup B on cup A (a ball being under cup B). Set cup C on cup B. Then lift cup C in a very matter-of-fact manner. There is no ball beneath cup C. Tap cup C with the hand or wand, calling attention to its solidity, and set it mouth up on the table, with the right hand.

The left hand slides the cups B and A over by the five balls that are lying on the table. The right hand picks up the two cups together, and at the same instant, the left hand sweeps up the five balls, taking with them the ball which was beneath cup B, and which was left on the table when the two cups were lifted. The balls are deposited in cup C.

Cups B and A are lifted together. Cup A is set on the table (a ball going beneath it). Cup B is then placed on cup A (no ball beneath).

Cup B is casually lifted and shown empty. It is tapped to show its solidity. The balls are poured from cup C into cup B and from cup B into the left hand, cups B and C being set mouths upward. The left hand, filled with balls, slides along the table to cup A, which is tilted upward as on a hinge, while the left hand shoves all the balls into cup A, along with the ball which is already there. Cup A is then set aside, mouth upward.

The magician picks up cups B and C and states that although they are solid, it is really possible to drive a solid object through them, as he has previously demonstrated with the balls. He then goes through the business of apparently dropping one cup through another (see "Penetrating Cups") and gives the two cups for immediate examination. The spectators are thoroughly mystified, and the magician thus concludes his exhibition of the "Cups and Balls," laying them all aside.

Note: A good way of secretly obtaining a ball from beneath a cup is the following: Slide the cup forward along the table, tilting it forward slightly so that the ball is pressed under the edge of the cup. Then press the cup flat on the table, and continue to push it forward. The ball will pop out the back and will come into the palm of the hand which should be flat on the table.

By drawing the cup toward oneself, and tilting it slightly forward, a ball may be introduced beneath the cup, by a reversal of the procedure just described.

These movements require skill, and they are not essential to the routine of the "Cups and Balls." They are worth practicing, however, as they sometimes help the performer out of an emergency.

Conclusion: The additional routine is a good one, because it eliminates the pretended catching of a ball from the air. Seven balls are used throughout the trick; but the spectators believe that only five are employed.

The person who practices the "Cups and Balls" will probably introduce various movements of his own origination, as the possibilities are limitless.

When the performer has mastered the routine—which depends upon memory, and not upon skill, he will soon forget all about cups A, B, and C. He will find that each move leads logically to the next, and no great memory work will be required. A smooth, finished routine should be performed leisurely, but without hesitation, with constant patter, to keep the spectators' attention on each penetration. The result will be a finished exhibition that is thoroughly bewildering and mystifying.

CHAPTER XII

STAGE MAGIC AND ILLUSIONS

THE STAGE MAGICIAN must use special care in the choice of his magical effects. The tricks he employs must be large enough to be seen at a distance; and for this reason he is forced to omit some very clever smaller effects from his program.

He does, however, have the advantage of distance. He can use certain apparatus that would not be effective at close range, without fear of detection.

Under the head of stage magic come large tricks and illusions, the last named being those effects that involve the appearance, disappearance, or transformation of human beings or large animals.

There are, of course, some stage tricks that can be done on a small platform; just as there are some close-range tricks that will work on the stage. There is no exact dividing line, but a study of each individual trick will show its limitations and its qualifications.

The stage magician usually has the advantage of one or more assistants, so in the description of the effects which follow, the presence of such helpers is understood.

I. PRODUCTION OF FLUIDS

The production of articles from beneath a cloth is customary with most magicians. In this production the performer brings forth a tray with half a dozen small glasses of vari-colored liquids.

Two trays are used—a lower and an upper. The upper tray is cushioned and covered with rubber. The glasses are put on the lower tray, and the upper tray set upon them so that the cushioned rubber side protects the liquid.

A strap passes over both trays, holding them together, and it is designed for easy release. There is a hook on the bottom of the lower tray, which enables the magician to hang it in one of three places: beneath his coat; on his back; or on an assistant's back.

This is an opening production—the magician's first trick. He shows a foulard or cloth on both sides, and drapes it over his extended left arm. Under cover of the cloth, he obtains the trays, which are hanging vertically. He raises them to the horizontal, releases the straps and lifts off the upper tray with the cloth, so that his left hand appears holding the tray with the glasses filled with fluid.

If the apparatus is concealed beneath the coat, the magician can hide any bulkiness by keeping the cloth constantly in the left hand—the side on which the apparatus is placed.

If he has the apparatus on his back, he must constantly face the audience; the cloth over the left arm will hide the right hand as it reaches under the left arm.

If the apparatus is on the assistant's back, the assistant brings in the cloth, and while the magician holds one side in his left hand, and the assistant holds the other, the magician's right hand gets the trays.

2. FLOWER BASKET PRODUCTION

This is a neat production as the apparatus is not bulky. It is a shallow circular tray about six inches in diameter. Projecting upward are several rods, which are connected by horizontal ribbons, giving the effect of a basket.

A quantity of "spring flowers" is placed in the basket; and the upright rods are folded inward. Each one has a spring to force it upward; but they are all held down by a catch on the last rod.

A hook on the bottom of the tray lets it hang beneath the coat, and it takes up very little space.

The cloth is thrown over the left arm. The right hand brings out the tray, holds it horizontal, and pulls the catch. The rods

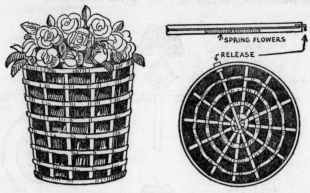

SPRING FLOWERS

RELEASE

The open basket appears at the left. The appearance of the basket when collapsed is at the right.

spring up and the compressed flowers fill the basket, making a very nice display when the cloth is removed.

3. LIGHTED LAMP PRODUCTION

This is the production of a lighted lamp on an undraped table. It is an ingenious device that must be carefully constructed. It is hidden in the table.

The lamp consists of a rod which goes down into the table leg. The top of the table is hollowed and it contains the collapsible base of the lamp and the cloth shade, which presses flat. To hide the lamp, a circular piece of black cloth is set over the top of the table.

The magician drapes a large foulard over his left arm and pretends to catch the lamp. He goes to the table, and holds the cloth above it. With his right hand he reaches through a tiny hole in the black cloth that covers the lamp, and grips a hook with his finger, drawing the lamp up from the table leg. When the lamp is fully extended it lights automatically from a flashlight battery in the center rod, and it becomes firm, so when the foulard is removed, the lamp stands on the table.

The black cloth is carried away in the foulard.

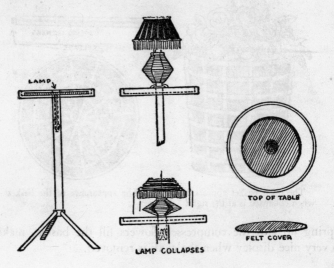

LAMP

LAMP COLLAPSES

TOP OF TABLE

FELT COVER

4. THE VANISHING LAMP

A lamp is resting on a tray. The magician places a paper about it, and carries the lamp away. It disappears from the paper.

The lamp is just half a lamp, made entirely of wood. It is at the front of a rectangular tray, which is held lengthways by an assistant.

When he covers the lamp with the piece of paper, and starts to form the tube, the magician knocks the lamp flat. It locks in position when it strikes the tray; and at the same instant the assistant tilts the tray forward.

The tray has three lengthwise panels; the center one is reversible, and the weight of the lamp makes it do a turn on its pivots which are in the ends of the panel.

So as the magician pretends to carry the lamp away, the assistant holds the tray with the top directly toward the audience

showing that there is nothing there. The assistant carries away
the tray with the imitation lamp hidden on the bottom.

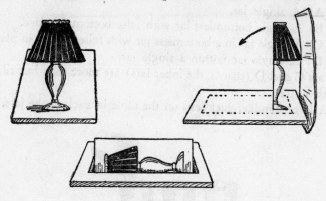

5. THE GERMAINE JARS

The "Germaine Water Jars" have enjoyed considerable fame,
but few magicians have ever used the standard sets effectively
because the trick in its usual form lacks conviction. The following method is an improvement.

The magician has four jars or vases, each eight inches high and
six in diameter. He shows each vase empty and proves that it
contains nothing.

He puts two jars side by side, and sets a single jar upside down
upon each one. When he lifts each upper jar, he pours a vaseful
of water into it, from the jar beneath.

Six jars are used. All are the same size, and they nest snugly; but
two are bottomless. When one jar is placed within another they
fit so neatly that at stage distance they appear to be a single jar.

The magician also requires two discs of metal, each with an
inner ledge. The tops of ten cent paint cans are just right as they
have a diameter of slightly less than three inches—the diameter
of the bottom of each jar. When one of these discs is set on the
table, with the ledge upward, a bottomless jar can be placed
upon it, and the disc will act as a temporary bottom, the ledge
keeping it in place.

The jars are set as follows, from left to right as the performer sees them:

(A) A single jar.

(B) A single bottomless jar with false bottom in place.

(C) A single jar in a bottomless jar with false bottom in place.

(D) A single jar within a single jar.

Jars C and D (that is, the inner jars) are more than half-filled with water.

A large handkerchief rests on the table in back of the jars.

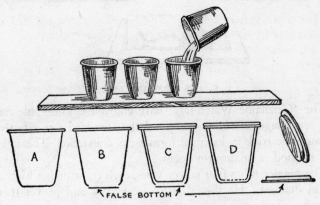

Top: The Germaine jars as they appear.
Bottom: Arrangement of the jars before the trick.

Procedure: The magician shows Jar A empty. He sets it down and shows Jar B empty, by lifting the false bottom with it. Then he replaces Jar B on the table.

To demonstrate that Jar B is really empty, he inserts Jar A in it. He shows Jar A empty again; picks up Jar B and shows it empty.

He palms the disc from the bottom of Jar B, and inserts the jar in Jar C. As soon as it is in, he drops his right hand to the handkerchief on the table and leaves the disc.

Then he apparently removes Jar B from Jar C; but he brings out the solid jar with the original Jar B inside it.

Then he picks up the single Jar C (with its false bottom), shows it empty, palms off the disc, and puts Jar C slowly into Jar D. He lifts the solid jar from Jar D, bringing the bottomless jar within it.

He then picks up Jar D and shows it empty; to complete the circuit he inserts Jar D into Jar A.

He removes Jar D and inverts it on Jar C; he inverts Jar A on Jar B. Then he is ready for the production of the water.

The "patter" shows how natural and convincing the procedure can be.

"Here," says the magician, "are four empty jars, which I shall exhibit one by one. The first jar, you see is empty.

"The second jar is also empty. Now these jars are all the same size. To prove conclusively that they contain nothing and that no optical illusion is employed, I shall place the first jar—empty —into the second empty jar.

"Obviously the second jar must be empty when it will hold a jar quite as large as itself. It is empty—as you can see.

"You will note that the second empty jar fits into the third empty jar—filling it entirely. And when I show you the third jar, your eyes see that it is empty.

"This third jar fits into the fourth—proving its emptiness; and when I remove it, I show you the fourth jar—empty as ever. To show that the first jar is empty, I complete the chain by inserting the fourth jar.

"On one jar I place another; and invert a second jar upon the jar that remains. Nothing can enter those jars. But while you are watching, something has entered them. We find that this lower jar is filled with water—and that this lower jar also contains the same fluid."

6. BLACKSTONE'S THREE CARD TRICK

"Three Card Monte"—on a giant scale.

The magician has an easel and three giant cards—two jacks of spades and a queen of hearts.

He lays the cards face down on the easel. Everyone sees where the queen is—but when the cards are reversed, the queen has changed position.

This is repeated with astounding results, as will be explained in the routine. First let us study the construction of the cards.

Each card can be transformed from a queen to a jack or vice versa by a very simple process. The face of the card is divided into thirds—crosswise. One end has a picture of a jack; the center is neutral; the other end shows a queen.

The center is raised, forming a slide or shallow tunnel. A piece of cardboard, two-thirds as long as the card, fits into this tunnel. One half represents a jack; the other half a queen. This device slides back and forth and with its aid both ends of the card appear to be either jack or queen as required.

The edges of the card are raised—like the molding of a tray, so that the slide travels a regular route and goes just the right distance.

Now if a jack is turned sideways in showing the back, it will remain a jack. If it is turned end over in reversing it, the slide will operate automatically and silently, and the jack will become a queen.

Each card is backed with cardboard that resembles the back of a playing card. An ordinary card of normal size may be inserted in the back of one of the giant cards, and allowed to project. This is for a purpose to be described.

The Routine: The magician begins with two jacks and a queen. He mixes them a bit, with the backs to the audience; then shows where the queen is and turns all cards face front.

He puts the queen in the center. In reversing the cards, he transforms the queen into a jack and one of the jacks into a queen. Then he moves the cards about, and asks where the queen is.

Everyone has followed the movements, and a chorus tells him where the queen is located. But when the face of the card is shown, it is *not* the queen.

The magician reverses the cards again, transforming the queen to a jack and a jack to the queen. Then he picks up an ordinary playing card—a queen of hearts—and states that he will attach it to the back of the big queen. But he attaches it to the card which has now become the queen—not to the card which people suppose is the queen.

The changing cards used in "Giant Three Card Monte."

As he mixes the cards, everyone is sure they know the ruse. They are positive that the card with the little card attached is not the queen—but it proves to be the queen!

For the finale, the magician removes the tiny card and reverses the large cards, changing the queen into a jack—so that he has three jacks and no queen. He asks the audience to point out the queen. When a card is chosen, he shows that it is a jack.

He reverses that card, changing it into a queen and uses it as a pointer to indicate the cards on the easel.

"One of those," he says, "must be the queen. Which is it?" Opinions will differ. While the argument is in process the magician places the card he holds (now the queen) between the two on the easel. Taking one of those two cards in each hand, he shows their faces—and lays them on the easel. The spectators are astonished when they see that both cards are jacks. Then the magician shows the face of the center card, and reveals it as the missing queen!

7. THE NEW SWORD CABINET

This is a real novelty—an improvement on illusion which has been exposed at carnivals and side-shows; an improvement which will bewilder those who think they know how it is done.

In the old trick, the magician has a box mounted on four legs. A door opens at the front, and a girl enters. The door is shut, and the magician pushes a pole through the top of the cabinet and out the bottom. Then he inserts cavalry swords through the sides of the box. This proves—supposedly—that the girl has left the cabinet; but when the swords and pole are removed, she emerges from the box.

In exposing the trick, the top is opened, and people are allowed to look in. They see that the swords run about the girl's body, between her arms and legs, without harming her. So the secret of the illusion, through cheap exposure, has become rather well known.

But in the new cabinet, the magician, after he has started to remove swords and has taken them from the front door, suddenly opens the door of the cabinet—and shows it to be unmistakably empty—except for the swords that criss-cross the interior, and the pole in the center! Then he closes the door, removes the remaining weapons, and the girl comes from the cabinet.

The base of the cabinet is several inches in depth. When the door is closed on the girl, she goes to the back of the cabinet, and through a triangular hole, slips her legs into the double bottom, her body being at the back of the cabinet.

At the sides of the cabinet are two mirrors. When the pole is inserted, the girl pulls the mirrors inward and their edges meet the pole. The mirrors and the back of the cabinet form a triangular space that hides the girl.

Swords are pushed in the sides, but they turn in front of the mirrors. The swords that go in the back point downward, alongside of the girl so they do not reach the backs of the mirrors.

When the front of the cabinet is opened, the box appears to

be empty because the mirrors reflect the side of the cabinet and make them appear to be the back. The presence of the pole hides the edges of the mirrors.

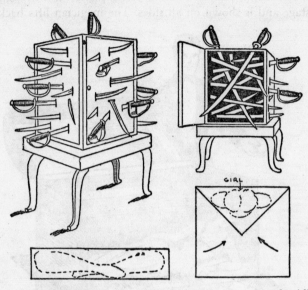

The cabinet before and after the vanish. The diagrams show the girl's legs in the platform and her body at the back.

The side swords are reflected, and give the appearance of swords through the back. The cabinet can be turned around while the door is opened.

When the door is closed, the swords are removed, the girl pushes the mirrors against the sides, and when the pole is taken out, she resumes her original position in the center of the cabinet.

To present this illusion properly, the magician should proceed exactly as though doing the old sword cabinet; and he should emphasize the fact that the girl cannot possibly be in the box with the pole and the swords there. Then pretending to hear someone say that he cannot open the door, the magician should remove the swords from the front and throw the door open.

8. THE GLASS TRUNK

A large trunk, mounted on a wheeled platform, is brought on the stage and is shown on all sides. The magician lifts back the

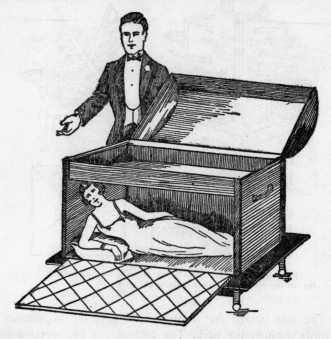

lid, removes the tray, and drops down the front of the trunk, showing that it is empty. Sheets of plate glass are inserted on all sides of the trunk; the tray is replaced; the trunk is closed, and is revolved. When it is opened again, a girl is inside.

The back of the trunk contains a panel, which is hinged to tip forward into the trunk. Set at right angles to the panel is a similar panel, which extends to the back. Thus when the front panel is tilted forward into the bottom of the trunk, the extending panel comes up and forms the back of the trunk.

At the outset, the panel is tipped forward, and the girl is

placed in the trunk, which is then wheeled on the stage. After the trunk has been turned with the front toward the audience, the lid is opened and the girl throws her weight to the rear, tipping the foremost panel up to form the back of the trunk, and leaving her outside at the back, resting on the rear panel which forms a temporary shelf.

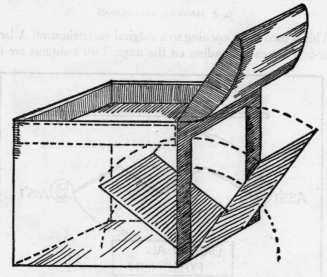

Diagram showing the action of the back panel of the trunk.

No one can see inside the trunk because of the tray. No one can see the girl because she is beneath the lid of the trunk. No one can see up under the trunk, because the platform is thick enough and low enough to cut off the angle of vision.

The tray is then removed, having served its purpose, hiding the transit of the girl; then the front is let down and the sheets of glass are inserted. No glass is placed on the bottom, but one may be placed on the top—where the tray was originally.

As soon as the tray is replaced and the front of the trunk is closed, the girl tips herself inside the trunk. The sheet of glass at the rear is brought between the forward panel and the bottom of the trunk. Then the lid of the trunk is closed. When the trunk is opened again, there is the young lady.

The trunk is wheeled off the stage before the audience suspects that there is no longer a sheet of glass at the rear. This is such a small detail that it is never noticed.

9. A MAGICAL APPEARANCE

This is used as an opening to a magical entertainment. A large four-fold screen is standing on the stage. Two assistants are be-

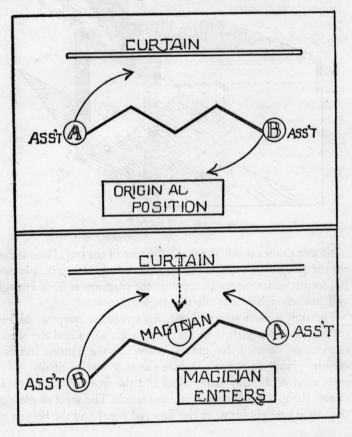

side it. One takes each end of the screen, and they walk in a circle, showing both sides of the screen. Then they form the screen into a square, with the opening toward the rear, and slide it up to the front of the stage, on to a carpet or cloth which has been shown and laid there. A flash of light follows, and the screen opens revealing the magician.

This illusion is very simple, but very effective. It is usually shown with a "drop" or curtain well forward from the back of the stage. There is a secret opening in the curtain—like a panel. In turning the screen around, the assistants carry it back close to the curtain, and the magician comes out in back of it. The assistants fold the screen around the magician, and slide it front and center, ready for the climax.

The magician may also come in from the side of the stage— from the "wing"—in this case the assistants temporarily overlap the wing in showing the screen. He may also come in from behind some piece of apparatus standing on the stage, or from a screen at the side of the stage.

The important factor of the appearance is that the assistants should do their work smoothly and with precision, making the screen into a square the moment that the performer is in position.

10. THE CLEAVER ILLUSION

This is a rather recent development of the torture type of illusion, in which the magician apparently injures an assistant yet does not harm her.

"Sawing a Woman in Two," and other illusions of that sort gained widespread popularity several years ago, and the "Cleaver Illusion," while quite as spectacular as any of them, appeared too late to gain the fame it deserved.

A long box is used in the illusion. The box is divided into seven cross sections, by slits in the sides of the box. The top of the box is also formed by seven separate lids, with spaces between them.

Above the box hangs a rectangular frame, slightly larger than the box, but not larger than the shallow platform on which the

box rests. Double-handled cleavers run across the frame. So when
the frame is lowered, each cleaver enters a slit and goes completely to the bottom of the box, where the frame rests upon the
platform.

The magician demonstrates this by closing the lids of the box
and letting the frame go down, under the control of a rope which
passes over a pulley.

The ends of the box are opened, so that the spectators may see
the action of the cleavers. Then the iron frame is raised, and a
girl lies down in the box.

The cover and the ends are closed. The magician slowly lowers
the iron frame; and just as the cleavers are inside the box, he
"accidentally" drops the rope holding the frame. The cleavers
come down with a crash. The iron frame falls against the platform, and surrounds the box. The girl has apparently been killed.
But when the magician pulls up the rope, out come the cleavers;
the frame is tied up, and when the box is opened, the girl rises,
uninjured. How is it done? Very easily!

The cleavers have wooden handles, and those handles slide
down into the slits in the sides of the box, so the cleavers themselves are hidden from view when the box is closed. When the
girl is in the box, she moves two long shafts, which are at the
bottom of the box. The walls of the box are quite thick, and they
are hollow. In the walls are vertical rods, attached to the horizontal shafts at the bottom; and at the top of the vertical rods
are short horizontal rods. So when the girl pushes the long
horizontal shafts lengthwise, the short horizontal rods fill the slits
in the sides of the box, just a short distance below the top of the
box. The explanatory illustration makes the operation clear. It
shows the entire apparatus.

The metal cleavers are not attached to the wooden handles.
They simply rest in place. As soon as the big metal frame comes
on a line with the short rods in the sides of the box, the rods
catch the cleavers and hold them suspended; while the frame and
the handles of the cleavers continue to the bottom of the box. The
handles of the cleavers are partially in the slits at the sides of the

box; so no one can note the absence of the blades, which are entirely within the box.

The girl is perfectly safe beneath the cleavers as they are held firmly in position. Yet to all appearances, the cleavers have dropped to the bottom of the box.

The raising of the frame is done slowly and regularly; the handles of the cleavers, in coming upward, engage the blades and bring them out. This pick-up is automatic.

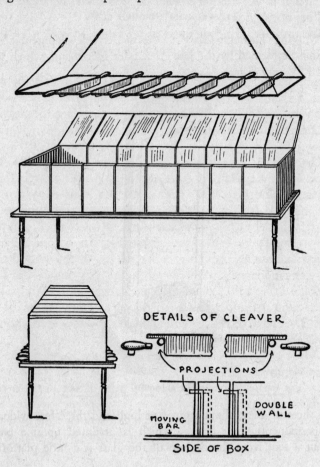

DETAILS OF CLEAVER

PROJECTIONS

DOUBLE WALL

MOVING BAR

SIDE OF BOX

The proper construction of the box is important, as the blades must be held in exact position, so that the handles will pick them up instantly.

The illusion should also be presented with proper precaution. The magician should be sure that the safety rods are in place, and should not let the frame fall until he has lowered it to a position where the rods have engaged the blades of the cleavers.

II. WALKING THROUGH GLASS

"Walking Through Glass" is the modern development of an illusion performed by the late Alexander Herrmann, which was called "Vanity Fair."

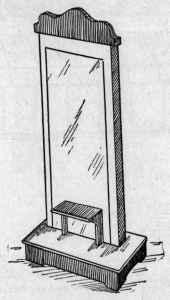

The apparatus.

A sheet of glass, about eight feet high and three feet wide, is set permanently in a frame, which is mounted upon a base. About a foot from the bottom of the glass is a little platform, which extends upon both sides of the sheet of glass. Solid rods connect the platforms with the base beneath, but there is glass beneath the platforms, between the rods.

The solidity of the glass is demonstrated, and a girl stands behind the glass, looking through. A screen is placed about her; and another screen is placed around the platform in front.

Girl in back of glass.

Now the audience can see glass above, below, and on both sides of the screens. The solid wall of glass is between the screens. Yet when the screens are taken away, the girl is on the front platform, having apparently passed right through the sheet of solid glass.

The glass beneath the platform, and between the rods is a separate piece in itself. The large sheet of glass is movable, and slides up into the frame.

Since the solid sheet does not pass below the platform in the center, but goes down on each side, it is obvious that a rectangular

piece must be cut out of the bottom of the sheet of glass—
although the spectators do not know it.

As soon as the screens are in place, the girl slides up the sheet
of glass, and it goes into the top of the frame a foot or more, the
top of the frame being fashioned to receive it. Thus the girl
forms an opening, through which she can pass her body.

Girl passes through the glass.

The motion of the glass is not noticeable. If the bottom of the
frame is made quite deep, and solid, the sheet of glass can be
made so long that the bottom edges will not come into view. In
some cases, the bottom of the frame has been made shallow, and
the performer and his assistant, by standing at the sides of the
front screen, hide the bottom edge of the glass with their legs.

If the girl lifts the glass herself, it is essential to have a safety
catch or some similar arrangement to hold the glass up while
she goes through the hole. To eliminate the danger and delay

necessitated by such a procedure, a lifting device is sometimes
used beneath the stage. Two rods, projecting up through holes in
the stage press up the lower edge of the sheet of glass, and an
assistant raises and lowers the contrivance by means of a lever,
when he receives his cue from the magician above.

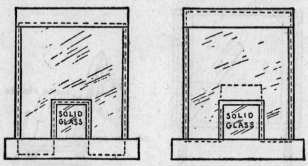

How the glass is raised in the frame.

"Walking Through Glass" was originally presented with a
mirror in the old "Vanity Fair" illusion, and was used as a method
of disappearance, the lady going through the mirror from the
front, and off the stage on a little bridge connecting with the back
curtain.

12. PIGEON, RABBIT, AND GOOSE

In this surprising illusion, the magician has a frame-work
mounted on legs. The frame is about thirty inches square. In
addition, he shows three sheets of paper, each mounted on a light
frame, thirty inches square.

The sheets of paper are shown on both sides. Then they are
placed upon a chair. The first sheet is placed on the heavy frame-
work, and with his hands, the magician shows the shadow of a
pigeon on the paper.

Breaking the paper, he produces a live pigeon through the
paper.

The second sheet of paper is put in position; this time the

shadow image of a rabbit is thrown upon it; and the magician breaks the paper to produce a live rabbit.

After the torn sheet is taken away, the third paper is put in the frame-work. The magician forms the shadow of a goose, and breaking the paper, produces a live goose.

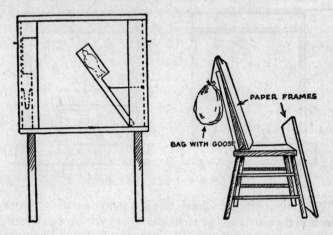

PAPER FRAMES

BAG WITH GOOSE

The frames that hold the sheets of paper are quite unprepared; the secret lies partly in the large frame-work,. and partly in the chair.

Each side of the frame is hinged at the bottom, so that a strip of the side will swing inward. At the top of each side is a container—one holding a rabbit; the other a pigeon.

The first piece of paper is shown on both sides as it is set upon the frame-work. In fixing it in position, an assistant releases a catch and lets the side of the frame-work fall inward. A heavy cord stops it when it has reached an angle of forty-five degrees, and the container, with the pigeon, is directly behind the center of the paper.

The magician makes the pigeon shadow; breaks the paper, and pulls the pigeon from the container, which is open at the front. As he carries the pigeon forward, the assistants remove the paper; but just before doing so, one assistant draws the rod and container back to the side of the frame-work, where the container locks in place.

The same procedure is used for the production of the rabbit; on this occasion, the second container is allowed to fall.

On the back of the chair is a bag containing a goose. It is affixed to a piece of wire which extends over the back of the chair. When the third paper is lifted, the top of its frame engages the wire, and the goose is carried out of sight behind it. This is not suspected, as the paper was shown on both sides prior to placing it on the chair; and the movement is done in a natural manner.

The frame is set in position; the magician makes the shadow of the goose; breaks the paper and pulls a "zipper" cord in the bag. This releases the goose instantly, and it is produced through the torn paper.

13. THE GIRL AND THE SHADOW

This is an unusual illusion. A light cabinet is used, the walls, back and door being covered with cloth. There is a hole in the top of the cabinet for the insertion of an electric light, and the cabinet stands two feet above the stage, on legs.

A girl enters the cabinet, and the door is closed. The electric light is inserted through the hole, which is near the back of the top; and the stage lights are turned out.

The front of the cabinet is so thin that everyone can see the shadow of the girl through the door. The magician asks her if she is ready to go.

She raises her arms, and answers "Yes."

At that instant, the stage lights turn on; the door is flung open, and the girl has disappeared. The cabinet is shown on all sides, and is finally taken apart and carried off the stage.

The cloth front of the cabinet is double and in between is a flat piece of cardboard cut to resemble the girl. It throws a perfect shadow of the young lady. The arms are hinged, and can be raised by a cord that goes through the top of the door and down the side.

The back of the cabinet is hinged; and the platform has a ledge upon which the girl can stand.

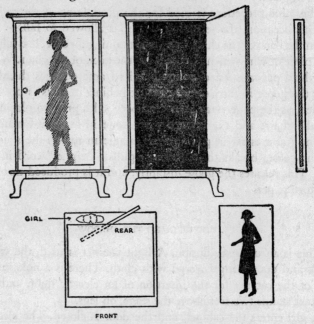

Showing the effect of the shadow illusion; the panel through which the girl escapes and the form in the front door.

The girl enters the cabinet, and immediately takes her position on the back, by swinging its two sections inward, and bringing them back again. This action is unknown to the audience.

The light is put in the top of the cabinet, and is turned on. Then the stage lights are extinguished. The shadow of the girl is seen immediately; but as all the light is in the cabinet, the girl merely steps from the platform and walks off to the near-by wing.

An assistant pulls the cord to make the shadow move. He is standing at one side of the cabinet, the magician at the other. The girl answers the magician from the wing—her voice seems to come from the cabinet. On go the stage lights, and the cabinet is shown empty.

14. THE GHOST

This is a very clever illusion performed with a committee from the audience.

Five four-fold screens are utilized. One is set in the middle of the stage, upon an examined sheet of canvas. It is formed into a square, and a person dressed in a white hood takes his position within it.

The members of the audience are grouped in a circle, and the four remaining screens are placed around the center one—each screen forming the center of a square. The magician's assistants put the screens in place; then they retire, and the spectators form hands around the outer square.

The magician steps within the circle, and states that the ghost has vanished. He takes down the screens one by one, and passes each over the circle to an assistant so that no one enters or leaves the circle.

All the screens come down except the center one; then the magician calmly folds it up and throws it flat on the floor. The ghost has vanished from the circle!

The secret of the trick is very bold but clever. The moment that the "ghost" takes his place in the center screen, he pulls off the gown, and tucks it under his coat. He is dressed just like the other assistants, of whom there are three or four.

The assistants then put up the outer screens. They do this from the inside—all except one assistant, who is at the back, and who starts work from the outside, and walks off the stage almost immediately.

When the screens are in place, a word from one of the assistants tells the "ghost." He leaves his screen, closing it behind him, and garbed as an assistant, he comes out of the outer square with the others—all of them going in different directions, and walking off the stage in an easy fashion.

Thus the "ghost" is gone before the circle is formed.

The outer screens should be considerably taller than the inner, and the center screen should be nearer the front than the back of the outer square, so that no motion of the inner screen can be observed from the audience.

15. FRANCISCUS SCREEN PRODUCTION

This invention of the late Franciscus is superior to all the old-style production screens used on the stage for the appearance of small articles.

An assistant appears carrying a three-fold screen, which is shown on all sides. It is held by handles at the sides of the back, so that the opening of the screen is toward the audience.

The magician closes the screen, and places his hand in from the top. He immediately draws out a silk handkerchief.

He repeats the movement and produces more handkerchiefs; then several glasses which he sets on the table, and a bottle from which he pours a drink.

Then he produces a live rabbit from the screen.

The walls of the screen are made of cloth; the back wall is separated vertically; but the pleated cloth is allowed to overlap. Strips of flat elastic in the border of the cloth enable this side to be separated, yet it comes together automatically.

The assistant's right hand is a dummy hand attached to the handle of the screen. It emerges from the assistant's sleeve, which is padded; but the assistant's right arm is free inside his costume.

In showing the screen, the performer holds it and swings it so that it may be viewed from all sides. The assistant rests his left arm at his side and apparently helps the magician hold the screen with his right hand; in reality the magician supports the screen until he swings it over for the assistant's left hand to take hold.

The assistant's costume is loaded with the various articles. His hidden hand draws them from his pockets under cover of the screen, and he pushes them through the back. So the magician can reach in and instantly produce each article without fumbling.

A great quantity of material is obtainable in this manner. The bottle used is made of metal; and the interior is hollow nearly to the neck, where there is a false bottom, so that a quantity of liquid may be kept in the bottle. The bottle is corked and inverted, and the glasses are in the open bottom.

So when the assistant puts the bottle in the screen the magician can bring out the glasses one by one; then turn the bottle over, produce it, uncork it, and pour liquid from it.

The assistant has the rabbit in a pocket of his costume and pushes it into the screen at the proper moment. After the production is concluded, the assistant carries the screen off the stage, walking to the right with his left side toward the audience.

16. THE VANISHING HORSE

This is the original "Vanishing Horse" illusion; the practical and effective method which I originated and produced some ten years ago.

The disappearance of a horse is a pretentious feat of magic, and it is presented as the climax of a series of mysteries which are dispensed with in this description in order to concentrate on the actual illusion.

A house-like tent stands at the center of the stage, between two artificial palm-trees, which are placed several feet in front of the

WITH HANGING SILHOUETTE SCENE OF MIDNIGHT AND TREES

MOTOR TRACK

PALMS

SWINGING DOOR
WITH BACKGROUND
ILLUMINATED

SIDE VIEW

back curtain, which is a silhouette scene of midnight and trees.

The horse enters the end of the tent; a pistol shot is fired; and the canvas is removed leaving only a skeleton frame-work, and no trace of the horse!

To add to the effectiveness, the scenery is in motion, and the spectators can see it pass by the rear of the frame-work.

Each palm-tree contains a roller, and in the tree on the audience's right is a replica of a portion of the background. A swinging door stretches diagonally across the interior of the cabinet.

The horse, upon entering, is driven out the back as he encounters the barrier. He is accompanied by an attendant who also vanishes, and who closes the swing door along which the duplicate scenery extends from the palm-tree.

This scenery, corresponding with a portion of the moving background, is put in motion at the proper instant, and then the tent is dismantled. The spectators see the duplicate scenery, which rolls into the palm tree at the left; its upper edge is hidden by the cross-beam at the back of the tent.

The eye does not discern that the scenery is further forward at the center, and its exact correspondence and continuous motion add to the illusion. The horse is safely out of view and the curtain falls, leaving the audience in bewilderment.

17. THE DISAPPEARING ELEPHANT

This illusion is sensational because of its large size and its ambitious undertaking—the evanishment of an elephant.

A large cabinet is exhibited. The structure is mounted on rollers. Two doors open at one end, and the elephant marches up an incline into the cabinet.

Two round holes in the sides of the cabinet enable the spectators to see completely through, and the huge body of the pachyderm is visible after the animal has entered the cabinet.

The doors are closed, and the elephant is hidden by roller blinds which are drawn over the windows by men inside. The

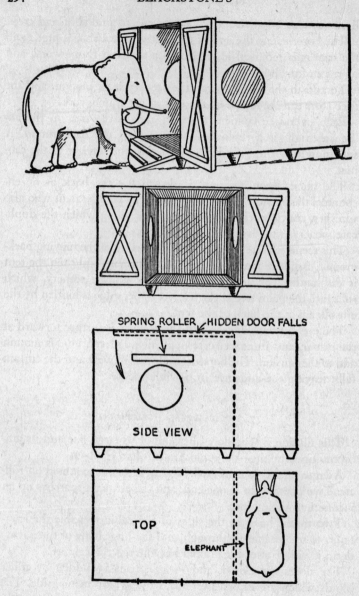

SPRING ROLLER — HIDDEN DOOR FALLS

SIDE VIEW

TOP

ELEPHANT

cabinet is wheeled around the stage to show all sides; finally it is turned toward the audience; the doors are opened, and the roller blinds are raised. The elephant is gone!

The illusion is of simple construction; in fact anything complicated would probably fail to work. The cabinet is considerably larger than the elephant—more so than the spectators are apt to realize.

Its depth is greater than the length of the elephant; and its width is equal to the length of the elephant. As the elephant enters from the side, the spectators do not observe the extreme depth of the cabinet.

The elephant is halted as soon as he is completely in, giving the impression that he takes up most of the space within the cabinet. But as soon as the doors are closed, and the blinds are lowered over the windows, the king of the jungle is urged to the rear of the cabinet, and is stood in a cross-wise position. Here he occupies less than a third of the space inside the cabinet, and a hidden door is swung down from the top to conceal him.

This takes place while the cabinet is being pushed around. When the doors are opened and the roller blinds are raised, the spectators see an empty cabinet. The striped pattern of the interior, which is also on the false back, is misleading to the eye, and the spectators believe that they see completely to the rear.

Not having observed the true depth of the cabinet, prior to the entrance of the pachyderm, the audience cannot make the comparison of distances which might prove a clue to the secret of the trick.

Psychologically, people underestimate the size of the cabinet and overestimate the size of the elephant. Hence they believe that concealment within the cabinet is impossible; while the fact that the cabinet is mounted on rollers assures them that the elephant cannot have made a secret exit.

CHAPTER XIII

MENTAL MYSTERIES AND SPIRIT TRICKS

UNDER THIS HEADING comes various forms of mystery that are akin to magic. The important distinction between these secrets and those of the usual type of magic lies in their method of presentation and the effect that the performer seeks to create.

They can be shown as tricks, pure and simple, if desired; but where a trick is naturally attributed to skill or mechanical deception, mental mysteries are usually considered (by the spectators) to be a form of concentration or even of telepathy; while many people are prone to attribute spirit tricks to some psychic force.

In showing mental mysteries, the performer should take advantage of the attitude of his spectators. It is quite permissible to make simple tricks virtually unexplainable by assuming an air of mystery and talking vaguely about psychology and mental concentration. But with spirit tricks, the various effects should be presented as duplications of so-called psychic phenomena, accomplished by natural means.

There are certain mind-reading stunts that can be classified either as mental mysteries or spirit tricks. It is rather difficult to draw a distinctive line between these two types of magic; hence they are grouped together, in this book.

Without question, this type of entertaining has come into great popularity today; it is a form of magic that is of comparatively recent development, although many of the basic principles have been used for many years. Many magicians are now specializing in mental and psychic effects, and the up-to-date performer should certainly include tricks of this nature in his repertoire.

MENTAL MYSTERIES

The methods described in this section are designed primarily for the use of one person, eliminating the codes and similar methods of transmission used in the two-person mind-reading acts.

I. NAMING THE NUMBER

The performer gives a pad and pencil to a person and requests him to write any number of three different figures. Then he is to reverse that number and write the smaller above the larger. Example: 382, reversed, 283.

When this has been done, the performer tells him to draw a line under the numbers and to subtract the smaller from the larger. After he has made the subtraction, the magician concentrates and then names the result.

First we must note a peculiarity that is evident in any subtraction of this type:

The answer will always be one of these numbers: 99, 198, 297, 396, 495, 594, 693, 792, 891. Of these numbers, 198 and 891 are very uncommon.

The performer pays little attention to his subject until the man is making the subtraction. Then the magician watches him from a distance, and notes his hand or the tip of his pencil.

If only two figures are written, the answer is 99. If three figures are written, the performer has only to identify one (except the center figure which is always 9).

This is an extremely easy matter which can be done on the first trial; and after some experience the performer can catch one of the numbers by a mere glance at the proper moment. Yet he is too far away to see the writing on the paper, or he cannot see it because of the elevation of the pad so no one will suspect anything.

Remember that the subtraction is from right to left. The center number is always sure. There is a distinct difference in the movement of the hand when it makes a 2 or a 6, and one figure caught gives the clue to the whole number.

2. GIANT MEMORY

To perform this mystery, the magician must have a card prepared exactly as shown below.

77	5	70	24	97	91	13	64	89
684268	415617	976392	336954	601123	001123	224606	370774	897639
11	12	90	94	48	60	2	41	99
022460	123583	998752	301123	752796	965167	819099	055055	801123
39	42	4	16	84	37	86	2	68
842684	156178	314594	527965	392134	640448	594370	112358	774156
3	87	21	75	56	49	10	23	32
213471	695493	033695	482022	561785	853819	910112	235831	145945
40	30	59	38	29	72	55	57	15
943707	932572	864044	741561	831459	189763	460662	662808	426842
51	79	66	65	85	26	92	88	71
066280	886404	572910	471897	493257	538190	101123	796516	088640
22	74	46	34	83	81	47	52	19
134718	381909	550550	347189	291011	099875	651673	167303	826224
69	14	93	25	45	6	33	35	67
875279	325729	201123	437077	459437	516730	246066	448202	673033
50	31	82	73	36	54	95	1	98
954932	044820	190998	280886	549325	369549	401123	011235	701123
80	62	8	58	18	76	28	78	7
987527	178538	718976	763921	729101	583145	730336	785381	617853
44	27	53	63	96	61	17	43	20
358314	639213	268426	279651	501123	077415	628088	257291	921347

Chart used in the "Giant Memory" trick.

He gives the card to a spectator and tells him that he has memorized 99 numbers of six figures each—nearly six hundred different figures, and that he has identified each one with a number between 1 and 100.

For example, if the spectator will ask "Name number sixty," the magician will immediately respond with 965,167. This terrific range of knowledge covers numbers from 1 to 1,000,000!

The test starts. Every number that is called meets with an instant response—and a correct one—from the magician. There is a key to the trick that makes it a simple matter of mental mathematics.

Add 9 to the number the spectator calls, and reverse the total for your first two figures. Example: Number 60. Add 9, making 69; reverse, and give 9—6 as your first two figures.

For the third figure, add the first two and give the total. If it is more than 10, drop the figure 1.

Example on 60: 9 and 6 (first two figures) total 15. Drop the 1, and name 5.

The fourth figure is obtained by adding the second and third in precisely the same manner. Example on 60: Add 6 and 5 making 11. Drop the 1 and name 1.

Similarly the fifth figure is obtained by adding the third and fourth. Example of 60: 5 and 1 total 6.

The sixth figure is obtained by adding the fourth and fifth. Example on 60: 1 and 6 total 7.

To make the task easier, use a blackboard. Write the numbers in order so all can see them. Here you have the numbers before you, and you can easily add them according to the simple rule.

3. BOARDS AND CARDS

This is an improvement over an older trick with cards; in this form it is very effective.

The magician gives out six envelopes each containing six different cards. He asks the persons who receive the envelopes to remember one card each, replacing all the cards in the envelope.

Then the magician holds up a board with six cards attached. He asks each person if he sees his card on the board. If the person says "Yes," the magician immediately names the card, even though he does not see the face of the board.

This is repeated with the remaining boards until the cards have been named. Sometimes two or more persons will have a card on one board—sometimes none.

Each board has one card from each envelope. The envelopes are numbered from 1 to 6. Now these duplicate cards are not definitely arranged on the board—they are there at random, but on the back of the board the magician has a tiny list.

For example: 1—JS: 2—10H: 3—AS: 4—9C: 5—4H: 6—QC.

These abbreviations stand for jack of spades; ten of hearts; ace of spades; nine of clubs; four of hearts; queen of clubs.

Each board is similarly arranged.

The magician picks up any board, and without looking at the front of it, holds the cards toward the spectators.

If the man with envelope 1 says he sees the card he mentally selected, the magician simply notes number 1 on the list and names that card. He does the same with any board and any number.

4. THOUGHT FORETOLD

The magician requests that some person mentally select the name of a playing card. Then the magician writes something on a slip of paper and throws it into a hat.

He puts the hat to one side and gives the spectator a pack of cards. He asks him to look through the pack—face up—and to drop his card on the table so that all can see it.

This is done. The magician picks up the hat, carries it to the spectator and lets him lift out the piece of paper. On it is written the name of the mentally selected card!

The magician has two pieces of flat wood or fiber. There are twenty holes drilled in the narrow edges of each—ten holes to a side; and four in each end.

The magician has tiny slips of paper bearing the name of every card in the pack. One piece of wood is used for black cards. The paper pellets are rolled and inserted in the holes with the king, queen and jack of spades at one end, and ace to ten at the side. The other end has king, queen and jack of clubs; with ace to ten of clubs on the other side.

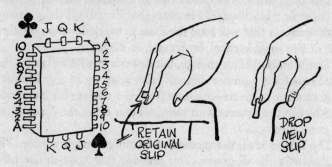

Illustrating one of the index boards used in the pocket; also how the substitution of slips is made.

The other board is similarly arrayed with hearts and diamonds. The blackboard goes in the left trousers pocket; the red board in the right.

Now for a bit of easy sleight-of-hand.

The magician writes anything on a slip of paper—and pretends to throw it in the hat, but retains it between his fingers. While the pack is being spread out he drops the slip in his coat pocket.

The instant the chosen card is revealed the magician puts his left hand in his pocket, if it is black; and his right hand in his pocket if it is red. The index board enables his fingers to obtain the slip that bears the name of the chosen card.

Let us suppose it is the ten of clubs.

In about one second the performer has the slip between the fingers of his left hand. With his right hand he picks up the hat by the brim. As he walks boldly toward the spectator, he grasps the hat at the side with his left hand; thumb beneath the brim and fingers just inside the hat. He instantly releases the slip of paper. It falls naturally in the hat. The spectator sees it there—the very piece (he thinks) that was thrown in at the beginning. He removes it and finds the name of his card!

5. THE MAGIC SQUARE TEST

The magician marks out twenty-five squares on a large sheet of paper or a blackboard. He states that he will fill those squares with numbers that will total the same in every direction on every line of five rows, vertical, horizontal, or diagonal.

This sounds difficult enough, but he adds that he will make that total equal any number desired, from sixty up to five hundred.

A number is given—one hundred and twelve, for example—and he fills the squares with numbers that bring the desired total in every direction.

The first secret is the method of forming a magic square. This is shown in the diagrams. You imagine that your square of 25 blocks is the center of nine similar squares.

Left: A magic square adding 65 in all directions.
Right: How the square is formed.

Put the number 1 in the middle block of the top cross row. Then proceed one square upward to the right—in a diagonal direction, to place the number 2.

As this takes you out of your square, you must transcribe the number in the corresponding block of your square—namely, in the second from the right on the bottom row.

Continue thus—always one step up to the right, transcribing when you go over the edge.

Whenever your diagonal path is blocked by the presence of a number, drop straight downward one square and put in the number; then continue your diagonal journey.

This is done with numbers from 1 to 25. The result will be a magic square that totals 65 in every direction.

Now note five key squares thus:

```
X  *  *  *  *
*  *  X  *  *
*  *  *  *  X
*  X  *  *  *
*  *  *  X  *
```

These are indicated by the letter X. The simple addition of 1 to each of those squares will raise your total from 65 to 66.

Instead of the numbers 17, 7, 22, 12, and 2, those blocks must bear the numbers 18, 8, 23, 13, and 3—which duplicate other numbers on the board.

Add 2 to each of these squares to make a total of 67 in every direction; add 3 to make 68, and 4 to make 69.

Similarly by subtracting 1, 2, 3, or 4 from the key squares you can produce 64, 63, 62, or 61.

The important number to remember is 60, which is the key to the whole system. First subtract 60 from the desired number and divide by 5. That tells you the number to put in the first block.

Suppose 65 is chosen. Subtract 60, leaving 5; divide by 5 and you obtain 1, so you start your progression with 1—a fact which you already understand.

Suppose 70 is given. You subtract 60 and divide by 5—the result is 2, so you start your progression with 2 and end with 26.

If 365 is given, subtract 60, leaving 305. Divide by 5, obtaining 61. Start your numbers with 61, follow with 62, 63, and so on.

Thus it is a very simple bit of calculation to obtain a square of any number that is divisible by 5.

But suppose you get a number like 248. That offers no difficulty. You merely employ the rule given before. 60 from 248 is

188. Divide by 5 and you have 37 as your starting number. But you must take care of your remainder of 3. This is done by the simple process of adding 3 to each of the key squares as you proceed with the progression.

It is important to note that the key squares have no bearing on the others. You merely add 3 to the number which should ordinarily go there, and continue the progression as though you had not made the addition.

With a number like 299, it is better to work from 300. Subtract 60, leaving 240; divide by 5, giving 48 and use that as your number for the original block. But when you come to the key squares, subtract 1 in each instance.

These key numbers will duplicate other numbers on the board, but there are only five of them, and they are quite permissible.

The making of a magic square in itself is mystifying to the average person as few know the rule. But with this tremendous addition of making the lines total any desired number, the effect becomes immense. The rules cannot be learned without a little study, but they are well worth the effort. The performer who does this trick will be credited with amazing mathematical or mental ability. Plenty of time can be taken in calculation.

6. FIVE CARDS AND FIVE PELLETS

Five cards chosen by five spectators; and each person receives a slip of paper upon which he writes the name of this card. He rolls the slip into a ball and lays it upon the card, which is face down.

The magician tosses the paper balls into a glass, and picks up the five cards. Then he orders the balls to be rolled on the table. At his instruction, four of the persons each pick up a paper ball.

The magician drops one of the cards on the table, and puts the remaining paper ball upon it. When the ball is unrolled, it is read, and we will presume it says "Eight of Clubs." The card is turned up—and it is the eight of clubs!

Of course it can be done when all the cards are alike—that's not a bad idea—but in this trick a borrowed pack is used. The secret lies in the paper balls.

First of all, the slips are roughly torn and they vary in size. As no two people will roll a paper ball alike, the result is five different balls, varying slightly in size.

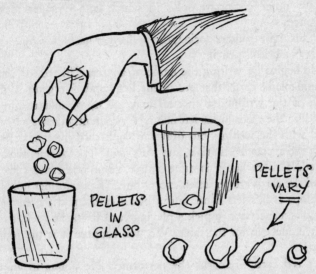

PELLETS
IN
GLASS

PELLETS
VARY

In picking up the cards upon which the balls rest, the magician takes the one with the smallest ball first—and so on—following in order of size—or noting any other slight difference in the pellets.

When the balls are rolled from the glass, four of them are picked up, one by one. The magician easily detects which remains—number one, two, three, four or five; and he tosses the corresponding card on the table.

7. DOUBLE PREDICTION

This is a combination of several methods, used in an unusual mental trick involving a pack of cards, some blank cards and an envelope. The magician writes the name of a playing card, with a colored pencil, on a blank card, and seals the writing in the envelope; he later writes the name of another card on a blank card in black and puts it in his pocket. Both of these cards prove to be cards that spectators choose from the pack at random.

Inside the envelope, the performer has a piece of colored carbon paper, pasted to the face of the envelope. This may be green, red, or any other distinctive color in which carbon paper may be obtained.

In his right trousers pocket, the performer has a card and a very short black lead pencil.

He begins by writing the name of any card in red, on one of several blank cards that are in his left hand. He gives a quick flash of the writing, so that all may see it, without reading it. Holding the cards in his left hand, he apparently draws away the card with the writing, but draws a blank card instead, marks it with the spectator's initials, and puts it in the envelope, which is sealed. This exchange is quite simple, as no one expects it.

All the cards are pocketed except one. The performer holds the envelope in his left hand, and a blank card upon the envelope. He asks a spectator to pick a playing card from the pack, and to turn it face up on the table. We will suppose it is the four of hearts.

"A red card," remarks the performer. He points to another spectator.."You *think* of a certain playing card—but make it a *black* one."

The performer draws a black pencil from his pocket.

"I used a colored pencil before," he says, "now I shall use a black one. Keep thinking of your card—I shall try to get your thought."

So saying, he writes something on the blank card that rests upon the envelope. The spectators naturally suppose that he is trying to catch the person's thought, and is writing the name of a black card. Instead, he is writing "Four of Hearts"—the name of the card first selected, and that is being transcribed in color on the card within the envelope!

Having finished his writing, the performer lays the envelope on the table, and puts the card with the black writing in his pocket. In so doing, he folds it, and pushes it up into the corner of the pocket.

"Name the card you chose," he says to the second spectator.

"Jack of clubs," replies the chooser.

"That's right!" exclaims the performer. "But just to verify it will you first remove the jack of clubs from the pack?"

Putting his hand in his pocket, the moment that attention is on the pack, the performer takes the tiny pencil and writes "Jack of Clubs" quickly on the blank card that is there. He immediately pushes the pencil up into the corner of the pocket, and brings out the card, at the same time turning the pocket inside out to show it apparently empty. He hands the card to the spectator—the name of the chosen card is upon it.

Then the envelope is opened, and the name of the card first selected is found on the card within, the envelope being torn and pocketed.

8. IMPROVED BOOK TEST

One of the most convincing of mental tricks is the divination of a word chosen at random from a book. The performer may ask a spectator to think of the chosen word; whereupon the performer names it; or the word may be discovered upon a spirit slate.

Now there are several ways of doing this, which I shall enumerate briefly before explaining the new system.

(A) Every page in the book is the same; that is, a prepared book is used.

(B) A certain word is at the same position on every page—such as the seventeenth word. The number seventeen must be "forced"; any page may then be used. This also requires a special book.

(C) A card is inserted at the proper page from the top of the book; the performer conceals this with his hand and lets someone push a card in the other end of the book; then he turns the book in stepping to another person. In this case any book may be used. But it is inferior to the others.

In the improved method, both the page and word are forced; but in a very clever and mystifying manner.

The performer first procures cards of three colors—say blue, white and yellow. Then he selects a word that appears quite frequently in the book he intends to use, which is an ordinary novel.

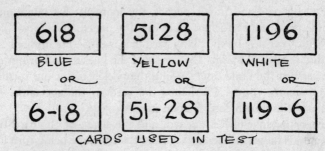

Let us suppose this word appears at 18 on page 6. On a blue card, the magician writes 618. If it appears as word 28 on page 51, he writes 5128 on a yellow card. If it appears at word 6 on page 119, he writes 1196 on a white card. Blue cards where the page number has but one figure; yellow cards for two figure pages; white cards for three figure pages.

Having prepared fifty or sixty cards, all with different numbers, the magician gives these to a person along with the book and retires to a respectful distance.

"Will you select a card?" he asks. "Hold it in your hand but don't let me see the number on it."

A yellow card is lifted.

"Take the first two figures for the page," says the performer. "The remaining pages will give you the word. Count down to that word on the page."

The spectator complies with the request. The word is discovered and it appears on the slate, or is revealed as the performer may choose.

The great variety of numbers on the card will convince everyone that the choice was freely made, especially as a familiar book is used.

It will be noted how this trick works in with spirit effects. The revelation of the chosen word on a slate or in a card on a frame is an effective conclusion; methods of obtaining such results appear later in this book.

SPIRIT TRICKS

One of the most important factors in spirit tricks is obtaining knowledge of what a person has written on a slip of paper. Two specially good methods are presented herewith.

9. THE BEST BILLET SWITCH

The "Billet Switch" is the method by which one folded piece of paper is exchanged for another. Through its use, many fraudulent mediums tell persons the names of their departed friends, and give them other information.

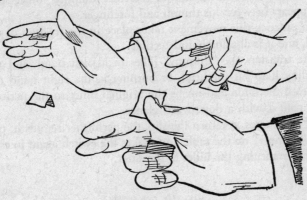

The three movements of the "Billet Switch."

In effect, the performer requests that someone write a name on a slip of paper; fold it and lay it on the table. This is done and the performer tosses the slip into a burner. He seats himself at a table and gazes at the flame or into a crystal ball. Then he tells the name that was on the paper.

Sometimes the same effect is done by the performer holding the slip to his forehead; then replacing it on the table. The spectator receives the slip at the conclusion of the séance, after the performer has revealed the written name.

The whole secret is the substitution of a duplicate billet for the original. This is done so quickly and so easily that most persons will declare the performer never touched the slip of paper.

The slip is folded beforehand and unfolded so that the writer will follow the folds and make the billet the proper size—identical with the duplicate or "dummy" billet which the performer has in his possession.

The duplicate is held between the first two fingers of the right hand, by the edge. The original is set on the table so that it stands like a tiny tent. Holding his hand bent inward, the performer places it over the billet as a shield. He immediately closes his third and fourth fingers, pressing the billet into his hand; and as he raises his hand, his thumb tilts the "dummy" billet so that it appears between his thumb and forefinger.

In practice this movement takes place in the fraction of a second, and it is absolutely indetectible.

He transfers the "dummy" billet to his left hand, and while holding it to his forehead, or burning it, the right hand drops beneath the table and opens the original billet so the performer can read it with a downward glance.

If he chooses to return the slip, the performer refolds it, places the "dummy" on the table and makes the switch again in the action of returning the billet to the sitter.

10. THE INK-BOTTLE

This is another way of getting the desired information from a slip of paper. The magician requests the writer to put the folded message in an empty ink-bottle. It remains there and is removed later on.

The ink-bottle is an imitation, made of wood. It has no bottom. Inside it is a piece of brass tubing. The message goes into the tube. The performer corks the bottle and slides it to the edge of the table with his right hand. The left hand is below the edge, and it catches the tube; or the tube may be dropped into the lap.

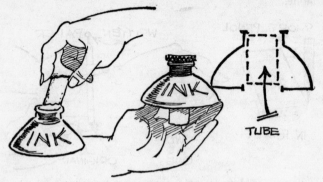

Obtaining the message from the ink-bottle.

Turning away on some pretext—to get a book, or a crystal, or to allow the spectator to concentrate in silence, the performer draws the message from the tube, reads it and puts it back.

Later on he picks up the ink-bottle again, and in lifting it from the edge of the table, pushes the tube back into the bottle.

In the meantime, of course, he can reveal what was written there, or answer any question written on the paper.

11. THE MYSTERIOUS NAME

This trick is done with a sheet of cigarette paper. The magician rolls the paper into a tiny ball, lays it on the table and asks the spectator to name some famous person. The paper ball is placed upon the tip of a pencil. When opened, it bears the chosen name.

In his trousers pocket the magician has a pad of cigarette papers and a very short pencil. When he has rolled up a blank piece of paper he asks for a famous name. The moment it is given, he puts his hand in his pocket and writes the name on top of the pad with the short pencil; he tears off the slip, rolls it into a wad and conceals it between the tips of his first two fingers.

He brings his hand forth and picks up the slip on the table, adding the other little ball to it. He holds the two as one and turns them over. Everyone supposes that he holds the original ball alone.

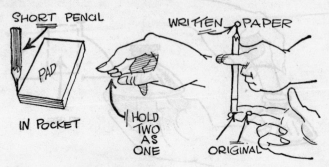

Left: The pad in the pocket.
Center: Exchanging the pellets.
Right: Concealing the original pellet.

In his left hand the magician holds a pencil, point upward. His right fingers retain the original ball of paper, but set the ball with the written name upon the point.

The pencil is of the eraser type: but the rubber is missing. The cavity from which it came is partly filled with wax. The right fingers pass to the bottom of the pencil and it is set upon the hidden ball, which sticks to the wax. With his right hand the magician gives the pencil to a spectator. Then he shows his hands absolutely empty. When the paper ball is opened, the name is written on it—and the magician calmly pockets the pencil!

12. POCKET SLATES

"Spirit Slate Writing" is an old trick. The commonest form of slate has a flap upon it—when the flap is removed, hidden writing appears.

The disposal of the flap is something of a problem at close quarters. The pocket-size spirit slates solve it. They are only three inches long by two inches wide.

The slates are shown blank on both sides. Each slate is wiped with a handkerchief. In wiping the slate with the flap, it is laid on the handkerchief flap-side down. The flap drops in the cloth, and is carried away to the pocket. Then the slates are placed together and the message comes between them. Another method is to merely let the flap fall in the hand.

13. THE ABACUS SLATE

This is a flap-slate. A message appears upon it, simply because the flap is allowed to fall on the table behind a book upon which the slate is momentarily stood. But the clever part of the trick is that the message appears in colored chalk—in a color freely chosen by the audience!

The slate is a child's slate with an abacus of two rows above the slate. There are sixteen beads on the abacus, and only four of them are of the color in which the message is written.

Yet when the performer asks a spectator to name any number from 1 to 16, and when he counts to that number on the abacus, he always arrives on the chosen color.

The important point is that he always counts in the regulation manner—top row, left to right; then bottom row, left to right.

The beads are arranged so that the desired color appears at 1, 5, 11, and 15. But if the slate is turned around before counting, these beads will appear at numbers 4, 8, 10, and 14.

If the slate is inverted, the beads will appear at 2, 6, 12, and 16; or at 3, 7, 9, and 13, according to which way the slate is turned. The magician is familiar with the slate. When the chosen number is decided upon, he merely sets the slate in the proper position to count, and he is sure of striking the proper color.

14. THE MECHANICAL SLATES

The mechanical slates are slates upon which two messages appear—one on each slate; yet the slates may be inspected before or after the trick.

A flap is used; but it locks to one slate at the beginning. It covers a message on the slate; also on the underside of the flap.

The slates are tied together. When the performer takes them and holds them above his head, his fingers draw back the ends of the top slate, and the flap is released. His thumbs draw back the ends of the bottom slate, and the flap drops on to it.

When he releases pressure, the ends spring back into position and the flap is locked on the lower slate.

These slates cannot be cheaply made as they must stand fairly close inspection, and their mechanical operation must be exact.

They represent one of the latest developments of this type, and enable the magician to obtain a message without taking the slates out of sight, and without getting rid of anything.

15. THE NUMBER FORCING PACK

When a message is written beforehand on a slate, the magician must be able to force that message on his audience. Forcing packs of playing cards are well-known, the simplest consisting of a pack of cards that are all alike.

But it is much better to use a numbered pack. Then a number, from 1 to 100 may be chosen, apparently at random; or the number may refer to the page of a book, or a certain word on a printed page.

The new type of number forcing pack is unusually clever. Fifty or one hundred cards, numbered consecutively, are shown mixed. Every card bears a different number, plainly stamped in its center. The performer fans the pack and shows all the cards.

Each card has an index corner bearing the number; and a person is allowed to insert a knife in the end of the pack and turn up the card, noting the number. Yet that number is forced!

The simple explanation is that one index corner of every card bears the same number. When the performer fans the pack, this is not observed, because he does not spread that end of the pack. But when the knife is inserted, he sees that it goes into the end where all the numbers are alike.

A card is slightly withdrawn so that the chooser can see the number on the index corner. That is all he sees of the card. It is enough to convince him—and it is enough to do the trick.

16. BLACKSTONE'S PET TRICK

This is a card trick; but it is included in this section as it is a psychic effort, and an unusually surprising one.

The magician lays a pack of cards on the table, and with it a piece of photographic paper measuring about one inch by three-quarters. The paper is examined, and someone is allowed to write his initials upon it. The pack is cut and the paper is laid, initial side up, between the cut portions.

The magician lifts the top portion of the pack and shows the queen of clubs, just above the tiny slip. When the photo paper is turned over, it bears a picture of the queen of clubs! The initials are still upon it, and the person who wrote them is allowed to keep the little card as a souvenir of a real mystery. Here is the secret:

Two slips of paper are used. The performer, in idly shuffling the pack, finds the queen of clubs and slips it to the bottom. Then he lays the pack of cards on the table. The pack is cut before the paper is examined.

Reaching in his pocket he obtains the slip with the photo, and holds it hidden in the bend of the third finger of his right hand. He also brings out an unprepared slip of the same size. This is examined.

The magician picks up the slip and asks someone to write his initials on it. Before anyone can produce a pencil, the magician reaches to his vest pocket and gets one himself. The slip is in his fingers, and he lets it drop into the vest pocket as he brings out the pencil.

Then he carelessly lays the slip that bears the photo with the picture side down. The exchange is so subtle that no one suspects it, especially as the trick has just begun. The initials are written upon it.

The magician calmly lays the slip on the upper portion of the pack, shows his hands empty and asks someone to complete the cut. This naturally brings the queen of clubs on to the slip. When the top portion of the pack is lifted, the queen of clubs is seen; and the photograph is found on the little slip.

The magician should have a supply of these little slips, bearing pictures of different cards so that the result will usually be different.

17. SEALED MESSAGE READING
(*Improved Method*)

The magician passes out small slips of paper, and envelopes. He requests that each person write a question on the slip of paper, sign it and seal it in the envelope. Then he gathers the envelopes in a hat.

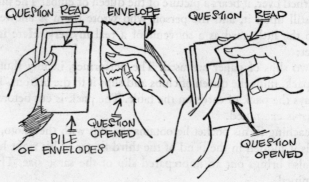

Exchanging the questions in the sealed message reading.

Holding an envelope to his head, he answers the question; opens the envelope, removes the question, reads it aloud and immediately returns it to the writer.

He repeats this with most of the questions, answering each in turn, and returning them all. He also answers a question or two without opening the envelopes containing them, but by returning them to the writers with the request that they open and read them aloud.

This is an excellent mystery, accomplished by very simple

means. Based on an old principle, it has certain improvements that deceive those who may know or suspect the old system.

In the explanation, the old way will be given first. The performer has a confederate who writes a question known to the magician. His envelope is marked so the performer will recognize it. The magician picks up any other envelope, and holding it to his head, answers the question in the marked envelope. The confederate acknowledges it. Opening the envelope the magician reads the question aloud from memory, actually reading the writing on the slip.

He picks up another envelope, answers the question he has just read, and opens the envelope when it is acknowledged. In reading it aloud from memory, he learns another question, and he continues thus until he has answered all he desires.

This simple method is very effective. It is used by pretended mediums. The performer can heighten the effect by making a clever pretense of reading when he is talking from memory; he can also turn the questions toward the spectators without giving them time to glimpse them closely; in fact he can make a real mystery of the trick.

But the additional effects to be described improve the trick enormously.

First: The magician has a duplicate slip of paper bearing the confederate's question. This is hidden among some extra envelopes. When he brings back the questions in the hat, he transfers the envelopes above the duplicate question to the bottom of the pile. He keeps the envelopes in his left hand, the question being on top, turned toward him. The papers are smaller than the envelopes. The slip cannot be seen.

He picks an envelope from the hat, holds it to his forehead, and answers the confederate's question. He tears open the envelope, removes the question and pretends to read it, really reading the confederate's question which is lying on the envelopes.

Now he takes the opened envelope between the second and third fingers of his right hand, and the question between his thumb and forefinger.

He places the opened envelope on the bottom of the pile, and the question on top of the pile, all in the same motion. The question is left there; and the thumb and forefinger remove the confederate's question, the left thumb retaining the question placed on the envelope.

Thus the right hand can immediately pass the question to the confederate, and people can see that it is the question just read by the performer.

Taking another envelope from the hat, the performer answers the question which he has on the pile. He opens the envelope and uses the same transfer as before. This enables him to hand the question he has just read to the writer.

He repeats this all the way through, ending with the confederate's marked envelope. So at the finish he has the confederate's question back on the pile again!

In pretending to read questions after he has opened envelopes, the performer has the preceding question in full view so that he will make no mistakes in reading. He reads from the pile—not from the question in his hand.

The effectiveness of this procedure is obvious. No great skill is required to switch the questions. But the performer should not walk among the audience. He should pass the questions to the nearest person. This is because he does not want anyone to see that he has a question on the pile of envelopes.

Now the additional effect is this—the reading of an envelope without opening it.

The magician gives an envelope to the confederate early in the game. While he is still distributing envelopes and gathering sealed ones in the hat, he cautions everyone to sign their name. The confederate in passing his envelope to the performer remarks that he forgot the signature. The performer has just dropped the envelope into the hat. He withdraws it, and hands it to the confederate with a new envelope, telling him to tear open the old one, sign his name to the question, and to seal it in the new envelope.

But in reality he leaves the confederate's envelope in the hat, and gives him someone else's envelope. The confederate opens it, pretends to sign it, and seals it in the new envelope which bears a tiny mark. On the old torn envelope he writes the question that was in the envelope he opened. No one notices this as the confederate is not too close to other people, and all are busy with their own questions.

The assistant throws the sealed envelope into the hat, and hands the performer the torn envelope, writing side down. The performer tosses it on the table, behind some object, such as a book, and lets it fall with the writing up.

He proceeds as usual with his reading. But in course of action he comes to the envelope with the tiny mark. He experiences trouble in answering the question, and in walking around, or sitting at the table, notes the question on the torn envelope.

Finally he asks who wrote the question he is holding, giving a few words of the question as a clue. The person acknowledges the question. The performer gives him or her the envelope and asks the person to concentrate. Then he answers the question. He tells the person to open it and read it aloud. The person does so, and everyone is amazed that the performer has accomplished the feat. This should be done near the end of the readings, and no special significance should be attached to the fact. It merely creates the indelible impression upon the spectators that the performer is answering all the questions before he opens them— and that is just the effect he is after.

With an audience of more than a dozen persons, the performer may employ two confederates, both of whom forget to sign their names. Each one does the same, receiving a specially marked envelope—envelopes with different marks to distinguish them. Their original envelopes are also marked. One is the envelope which the performer reserves to last as it contains the dummy question.

But the performer can now answer three sealed questions at intervals, returning the envelopes unopened. The first is the one "tipped off" by confederate A. The second is the one "tipped off" by confederate B; and the third is the actual question written by confederate B—a question agreed upon by the performer and confederate beforehand.

On the platform, with a large audience, the performer may use more than two confederates; but too many are inadvisable.

In receiving every question in the hat, the performer should ask the writer if he or she signed the question. Most of them will do so, as they are told to beforehand. But occasionally one will forget. In such instances the performer immediately returns the sealed envelope with another envelope asking that the mistake be rectified; and he always collects the torn envelope along with the sealed one—the same procedure that he uses with his confederates. This proves very mystifying.

The answering of questions is an art in itself. Needless to say, when the performer knows the question, as he does in this demonstration, he can make some sort of an answer. But experience will teach him to give some clever answers.

When someone asks concerning a lost article, the clever performer makes an evasive reply yet gets an "impression" that the article is hidden in a bureau drawer, or in an old suit. Very often lost articles are actually found after such a guess.

There are many other types of answers, and special booklets have been compiled on the subject. But it is not the province of this book to cover such details. The author assumes that the reader intends to present the trick as a form of light entertainment, with no pretense of super-human power, but merely with a desire to create an interesting mystery. The mind-reading "profession" has sometimes produced fakers who use trick methods to obtain dupes. Presented purely as magic, these tricks are legitimate and mystifying.

18. TWO SLATE TEST

This is a very simple, but effective method of obtaining a message without the use of flap slates. The performer has two slates set together—one slate being larger than the other. He marks the outside of each slate with a letter X.

Then he opens the slates and shows the insides blank. He puts the slates together with the blank sides outward and marks them with an X.

When the slates are again opened, a message is found on the smaller slate—replacing the letter X that was originally there.

MARK SMALL SLATE

FINGERS RUB OUT X =

REVERSE SMALL UNDER LARGE

The message is written on the inside of the smaller slate at the beginning. The slates are placed together, the little slate on top. The performer marks this lightly with an X.

Then he turns the slates over; while his right hand marks an X on the large slate, his left fingers rub off the X from the small slate.

Remarking that he will show the insides of the slates, the performer takes one in each hand, the large slate covering the smaller. Under this concealment, the left hand gives the small slate a half-turn; then the slates are opened book-wise.

The half turn has thrown the writing out of sight—the spectators see the side of the small slate that was originally marked X but which is now quite blank.

The small slate is laid upon the large one, the blank sides outward, and the outer sides are marked. The message is now inside, and is revealed at the proper time.

19. THE FIGURE TOTAL SLATE

The magician has a slate which is divided into five sections by horizontal painted lines. He invites various spectators to write numbers in these sections—all except the bottom section. That space is reserved for the total, which is added by another person.

No matter what numbers are written, the performer knows the total, and can reveal it in some mysterious manner!

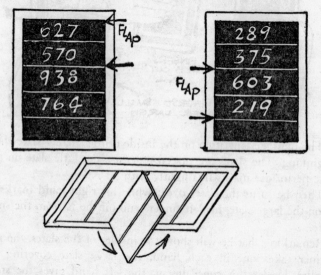

An examination of the slate explains how this can be done. A thin metal flap is used—painted black. It is fitted into the sides of the slate, at the second cross line from the top. This flap may be swung back and forth to cover either the two top sections or the third and fourth sections. Both sides of the flap have a white line across the center to correspond with the white line that the flap covers when in position.

The performer sets the flap so that it covers sections three and four. Then in all four sections he writes numbers, and adds the total, which he remembers. Then he swings the flap so that it covers sections one and two. The result is a blank slate—blank except for the cross lines.

The spectators write their numbers on the slate. The performer turns the slate back upward as he walks to another spectator. This enables him to secretly shift the flap. The result is that the *performer's original figures are added instead of the numbers written by the spectators*. Immediately after the addition the flap is swung back again so that the performer may carelessly show the spectators' numbers. But the total remains in view.

20. CARD AND FRAME MYSTERY

This is an execellent method of revealing a chosen number—a number which is "forced" on the audience by use of the "Figure Total Slate" or some other system.

The performer shows a sheet of cardboard, blank on both sides. He lays it upon a tray and invites some person to write his name upon it.

Then he exhibits a large frame—just large enough to hold the cardboard. The frame contains a sheet of glass, which is quite transparent.

The piece of cardboard is placed against the glass, with the name still showing; it is fastened in position and the front of the frame is shown, with the blank cardboard facing the audience. The frame is set on a special stand and is reversed so the name side of the cardboard again faces the audience.

When the frame is turned around again, the number has appeared on the sheet of cardboard, which is removed from the frame and is given for examination!

The bottom of the frame is hollow, forming a compartment which is filled with white sand. The glass is double—with a thin space between the two layers; and this space connects with the hollow side of the frame.

Two sheets of cardboard are used; one has the number written upon it; the other is painted black on one side to match the tray used in the trick.

These cardboards are shown as one—the inside surfaces being the side with the number and the black side. The magician lays the two sheets upon the tray, and lets the spectator write his name. Then he lifts a single sheet of cardboard. As a result he has the spectator's name on one side, and the number on the other; but he does not reveal the latter side.

After setting the cardboard in the frame, the performer, in clamping it there, carelessly inverts the frame. The sand trickles down into the double glass. Then he can show the face of the cardboard apparently blank—for the sand appears to be the surface of the cardboard.

In putting the frame on the stand, the performer turns the sand side from view, and again inverts the frame. The sand goes back into its secret compartment; and when the face of the frame is shown the number has made its mysterious appearance on the face of the cardboard!

21. FIGURE SWITCHING PADS

An easy method to switch figures is by the use of a small pad. Two types are described here.

(A) Write your own figures on the bottom sheet of the pad. Hold it in your hand while the spectators write their figures on the top sheet. In going to another spectator, calmly reverse the pad, and let him add your figures.

(B) Fold the top sheet of the pad in half—crosswise. Do the same with another sheet, and paste the backs of the folded portions so that they form an inverted T. You thus have a flap which can be swung either way.

Divide both surfaces with four horizontal lines. Put your own figures on one surface; hide it by bending the flap over. Let the spectators write their figures; switch the flap, and let another person add the totals on another pad. Switch back the flap and check up on each person's number; pocket the pad, and proceed with the trick, using the number that the spectator has added —your own total.

FIGURES WRITTEN

638
271
906

TURN OVER PAD

YOUR FIGURES

483
721
839

723
691
486

ORIGINAL
FIGURES

453
723
691
486

BEND
DOWN
FLAP

453
384
510

YOUR
FIGURES

22. THE WRIST PILLORY

This is a device which may be used for cabinet manifestations where the performer retires from view and although imprisoned, causes many unusual things to take place.

The pillory is made of wood, divided into two sections, with hasps at the ends. The performer places his wrists in the holes and demonstrates that he cannot remove his hands. Padlocks are attached to the hasps and the performer goes behind a screen, minus his coat, but wearing a vest.

Immediately manifestations take place. His hands clap loudly and his vest is thrown over the screen; yet the performer immediately appears, his wrists still imprisoned.

The holes in the pillory are not centered exactly. One is slightly above center; the other slightly below. The wrists cannot slip free when the pillories are locked in this position. But when he is ready for the test, the performer quietly reverses the top half of the pillory.

Thus one hole becomes large, the other small; as the wrists are in the holes the difference cannot be detected, and the performer can instantly free one hand. This enables him to clap his hands and remove his vest; yet he can immediately get the free hand back into the pillory.

The pillory can be used in full view. The performer's hands are behind his back; yet suddenly a hand emerges and taps a person who is standing beside the performer. The wrists are immediately shown locked as firmly as ever.

23. THE THUMB PILLORY

This is a miniature pillory just large enough for the performer's thumbs. The pillory is locked to the thumbs by means of bolts that run lengthwise through the ends, with wing-nuts on the ends.

Left: The thumb pillory as it normally appears.
Right: The pillory with one section reversed. Note variation in size of holes.

The performer asks a person to put his arm between the performer's arms, and to shake hands with another person. The performer then strikes the arm in front of him with his hands; his hands apparently pass through the spectator's arm, and he is free; yet his thumbs are still locked in the pillory!

Large rings are tossed to the performer. He catches each ring on his arm, immediately showing that his thumbs are still locked. Then he gives the rings a toss and they fly free—yet the pillories still hold the thumbs, and the nuts must be removed to free the performer.

The "Thumb Pillory" is identical with the "Wrist Pillory" but on a smaller scale. The reversal of the upper half makes one hole larger than the other, as the holes are not properly centered.

First the performer has his thumbs pilloried in a genuine manner. Before the bolts are fastened with the nuts, he asks that the top section of the pillory be removed. The bolts are in the upper half, and the performer uses the lower half to strike them and show that they are solid. This gives him the opportunity to reverse the lower half.

When he is locked in, he finds that it is but the work of an instant to remove one thumb. He masks this movement by tilting the hands upward and keeping the fingers in front of the pillory.

The instant his hands have passed the spectator's arm on a downward or an upward stroke, they are brought together and the loose thumb is slipped into the hole again.

The same action is used in catching the rings and releasing them. A downward and upward movement covers the slipping of the thumb, and the hands are separated very slightly. The practiced performer can execute this trick with rapidity and precision that escape detection.

24. A RAPPING HAND

There are several versions of the "Rapping Hand Trick," a spiritualistic effect in which a wax or wooden hand answers questions by moving up and down, tapping its fingers in a mysterious manner.

For close work, the most practical method is to have the hand placed upon a board, which is held by the performer during the manifestations. The board appears quite innocent; yet the trick lies in it; and the particular type of board described here is new, inexpensive to construct, and easy to operate.

The board is about twelve by eighteen inches in size. It is dark in color, with a roughened surface. Midway between the two ends of the board, but only a few inches from the back, is a tiny hole that passes through the board.

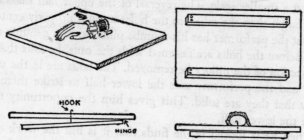

Construction of the board used in the "Rapping Hand." Note action of brace beneath the board.

Under the board are two braces, each eighteen inches long. One is near the front of the board; the other close to the back, and the latter comes directly beneath the hole near the back of the board.

This brace is hinged at the left end. The other end is loose. Running up from the center of the brace is a stout wire that terminates in a slight hook; it runs through the hole in the board.

The performer gives the hand for examination. He shows the bottom of the board, holding the loose brace pressed against the board with his right hand. The brace is fitted with several short screws which make it appear to be firmly fastened to the board.

After showing the bottom of the board, the performer shows the top. While the board is turning over, the protruding hook will not be discerned, as it is very small and black. The performer then releases the brace beneath the board. It drops about an inch, bringing the tiny hook flush with the surface of the board.

The wooden hand is placed upon the board. It has a cloth binding at the wrist; and as the hand is shifted to the proper position by the performer's left hand, his right hand presses up the brace, and the sharp little hook engages the wrist of the wooden hand.

It is then an easy matter to operate the rapping hand. The brace is pushed down or raised by the performer's right fingers, and it controls the actions of the hand.

By counting each rap a letter of the alphabet the hand can spell names; it can count to "forced" numbers; and it can answer questions "yes" and "no," three raps meaning an affirmative, and two a negative.

The braces do not extend the full length of the board; they are trimmed off slightly, so that they are completely hidden underneath.

CHAPTER XIV

HOW TO PRESENT MAGIC

THE PRESENTATION of magic is a distinct art in itself. It is different from any other form of public appearance, yet it has certain points in common with many of them.

The impromptu magician must be an extemporaneous speaker; the comedy magician must be a comedian; the platform magician must be something of a lecturer; and the stage magician must certainly be an actor. Yet this is a good rule that does not work both ways. The best speakers, comedians, lecturers and actors may not be capable of becoming good magicians.

Why? Because there is an important element of psychology in the presentation of magic—something which the magician learns partly by instinct, and largely by experience.

There are many difficulties which confront the magician. He must always do two things at once—perform an effect for his audience and operate a trick for himself. He is telling one story and thinking another. A slip will injure his prestige; and if he slips he will never receive sympathy, but will be the object of ridicule.

To offset these difficulties, the magician has a tremendous power in his behalf. It is a simple application of the rule that "you can't beat a man at his own game." The magician is playing a game with his audience; he knows the game and the audience does not.

Therein lies the charm of magic—the lure that brings thousands to the art. Because of it, a mediocre performer, weak as a speaker and devoid of dramatic ability may thoroughly mystify a group of highly intelligent people. Yet in that strength lies weakness. Encouraged by the ease with which they can mystify, many budding performers are entirely neglectful of presentation. They are ignorant of the most important things they should know, and they glory in their ignorance. They continue to do magic in second-rate fashion, believing that it is their own ability which deceives their audiences, when in reality it is the inventive genius of another man—the one who devised the tricks —that produces the deception.

That is why there are indications of a public apathy toward magic—not because people do not want to see magic—but because they do want to see it, but have been bored too often by weak and puerile exhibitions. The first-class magician does not suffer because of this; for his work is recognized as being of a high caliber. But there are many earnest and sincere magicians who are impeded in their progress because of the presence of the would-be greats who do everything wrong and believe they are doing it right.

The purpose of this treatise is to bring out the fundamental rules for presenting magic, and to emphasize the importance of this phase of the art.

I. PRODUCING MAGICAL EFFECTS

There are three stages in learning a trick. First, learning how it is done; second, learning how to do it; third, learning how to produce it. Some people know how tricks are done, yet cannot do them; and there are many who can do the tricks yet cannot produce them properly.

No matter how simple a trick may be, the magician should consider it from all these angles. First, he should study the trick itself; if possible, watch someone else do it. This gives him knowledge of the effect. Then he should practice the trick until he can perform it; and finally he should plan its public presentation.

Take for example the simple procedure of vanishing a handkerchief with a "pull." A school-boy can do the trick with very little practice; but he cannot present it properly unless he is taught the correct procedure.

The beginner will simply push the handkerchief into one fist and let the "pull" fly under his coat; or he may work it into his hands, and let it go, immediately showing his hands in a careless manner. That is not magic.

The experienced magician will draw the handkerchief through his left hand, and hold it at the finger tips of his right, gazing intently at it, while his left hand obtains the "pull." Then he will work the handkerchief into the left hand, in any easy fashion, letting the "pull" go when the handkerchief is in it. But he will not stop there.

On the contrary, he will keep his hands in motion for a few moments, drawing them further from his body; then he will close the left hand as though it contained the handkerchief, and raise it well away from his body. At this point he will quietly show his right hand empty, and with the forefinger of his right hand will pretend to poke an imaginary corner of the handkerchief further into the left fist. Then with a rubbing motion of his left hand, he will apparently cause the handkerchief to pass into nothingness.

Therein lies the art. Magic stirs the imagination; with the proper presentation, people will believe that they see miracles happen where simple tricks have been employed.

Every trick; every action; every thought of the magician must be toward this end. He must avoid jerky, unnatural movements; he must seek to gain poise and ease of action.

Many tricks have a weak point; and one often hears the inexperienced magician speak regretfully of that fact. When he does so, he is overlooking the real art of magic. The weak points of tricks are the spots that test the magician's mettle—they are the factors that enable one man to become better than another. If tricks work themselves, anybody can do them. It is the covering and protection of these difficulties that make magic an art.

A clever word; a chance remark; a turn of the body; a motion of the hand—any one of these may completely turn the audience's attention at the vital moment. The magician must never be hurried at the crucial moment. That is where he needs all his calmness and poise.

In cultivating ease of action, the work should not be overdone. Let us take a simple example. The magician places an object in his left hand. He carelessly opens the hand and shows it still there, lifting the object with his right hand. With a glance at his audience, he drops it in the hand again—apparently. In reality he retains it in the right. He follows the left hand with his eyes, and the object disappears.

The performer who overdoes the effect puts the object in the left hand, takes it out; puts it in, takes it out; apparently puts it in a third time, palming it instead. All this action is superfluous. It kills the very effect of ease that the performer is seeking to obtain.

These thoughts apply to all effects of magic, from the smallest to the largest. After he is sure he can do a trick, the magician should try various ways of presenting it until he finds the one way which seems best to him—which seems most fitted to his natural actions.

2. MISDIRECTION

Misdirection is the term applied to describe the artful methods of the magician, apart from the actual working of tricks. Misdirection and magic are one. With proper misdirection, a crude trick will become a mystery; without it, an excellent trick will fail.

The preceding paragraphs have brought out the thought of misdirection, for it is essential in producing a magical effect. But it has many other amplifications.

We know that a person's attention can only be centered upon one thing at a time. Divided attention is never close. The magician may sometimes seek to divide attention; but more often he will try to center it upon something—upon something which will protect the secret of a trick.

A typical example of misdirection is when the magician picks up a wand from the table. He has apparently placed an object in his left hand, but it is really in his right. He picks up a wand to touch the left hand. This is a natural movement—but it enables him to drop the object in a pocket of the table.

In brief, the magician must have an excuse—more than that, a reason—for many of the actions he performs. By creating the impression that he is doing an action for one purpose when he is really doing it for another, he is misdirecting the attention of the audience.

In many of the tricks described in this volume, certain actions are given; and those actions are part of the misdirection of the tricks. The student will recognize the importance of such actions.

Another type of misdirection is the deliberate placing of suspicion upon something which is innocent. This is exemplified in the "Ball and Tube" trick in Chapter IX—in fact both forms of misdirection are there.

First the magician pretends that the ball grows smaller and larger. This attracts attention to the ball, whereas the trick lies in the tube. When it is necessary to withdraw the outer tube, the magician squeezes the tube—apparently for a purpose—really to make the "getaway" of the outer tube natural.

In Chapter XIII, the "Wrist Pillory" illustrates the second type of misdirection. The pillory is shown casually; but the magician should appear reticent about the padlocks. This will make people anxious to examine them. The pillory will become a matter of secondary consideration; and after the padlocks have been examined thoroughly, the performer proceeds. In this manner the peculiar construction of the pillory will certainly escape attention.

3. STYLES OF PRESENTATION

There are three styles of presentation: Natural, Humorous, and Mysterious. I am excepting comedy magic which is not an ordinary class, and am dealing now with the usual methods of working.

The natural performer seeks to be himself. This is the best style for impromptu entertaining, especially where the performer is among persons who know him. He does his tricks in a very easy fashion, as though there were nothing remarkable about them. He may even create the impression that the spectators are not going to see anything very wonderful.

When a magical effect is successfully presented in this manner, its climax will be sensational. Some performers can carry this style to perfection. The spectators believe that they are just "seeing somebody do a trick," and they may expect it to be bungled. Their indulgent attitude will be turned to amazement.

The humorous style should be adopted when the magician appears before a fair-sized audience. In a large room or on a small platform, he cannot pose as a master of mystery; at the same time his position is too important for him to try to act in an offhand manner. He must joke with his audience, and employ bits of comedy and witticism, remembering that the spectators are just as anxious to be entertained as they are to be mystified.

The mysterious style is best suited to the stage. The theater audiences will expect to see something remarkable, and the magician can act as though he were a superior being gifted with some supernatural power. If he chooses this part, he must play it throughout. He must assume an air of importance, and preserve that attitude.

The humorous style is also good for the stage performer, especially when he is working at close range. At the same time, any one of these styles may be assumed in any type of performance; but difficulties may be encountered under various conditions.

A man of mystery in a parlor will not have an easy time of it; but if he is sure of himself, he can try it. A natural performer on the stage may also be successful, but the conditions will not be the best.

The "silent act" in which the performer says nothing, is best presented in a mysterious manner. Yet no one should form the erroneous opinion that working in silence is easier than talking.

On the contrary, it is a very difficult type of performance to give, and the magician will often have to resort to pantomime to produce the proper effect.

4. THE OPENING TRICK

The opening trick is very important to the magician. It not only enables him to gain contact with his audience; it also establishes the role which he is to assume.

The natural style of performer should begin with a small trick —one of which he is sure—yet which is very effective. He should mystify his audience as much as possible, and leave them ready for the next effect in his program.

The humorous performer should start with a trick requiring considerable talk, and one that can be interspersed with witty remarks. His purpose is to form contact with his audience, and to make friends with some of the people who are watching him.

The mysterious performer needs a startling effect as his introduction—such as the appearance of the performer from a screen; or the production of various articles from beneath a cloth. Tricks with action are best, and he need not begin his "patter" or "talk" until after he has finished the opening effect.

5. SUGGESTIONS FOR PATTER

Patter is an important part of the magician's work; yet it is neglected more than anything else. This is probably because the average magician does not realize the particular qualities that are necessary.

The tendency is to go from one extreme to the other: either to be extemporaneous, or to rely upon set lines. The result is that some performers talk in a meaningless manner, and others speak as though they were giving a recitation.

The answer is to use outlined patter. After learning a trick, decide upon some interesting talk to go with it, and pick out the salient points of the patter. Use them regularly, and extemporize in between.

This advice is especially applicable to the natural style of performer. The moment that he falls into set lines, he is working directly against his scheme of action. The magician who adopts the humorous style must have a great many more catch lines or bits of phraseology than the natural performer, for he needs to keep up a constant flow of talk.

The mysterious type of performer will often lose effect by adhering too closely to memorized lines, because the moment he becomes a character instead of a personality, he will lose his hold upon his audience.

Yet there are many magicians who use the same patter every performance, and do it in an easy, convincing manner. The answer is that they have reached that stage through constant usage; they have developed their outlines into finished talks; and the reason that their patter is so effective is because they have learned to retain the comments that create an impression on an audience.

Good catch-lines, or "gags," are frequently gained by accident, while performing before an audience. The performer who has no patter will never think of a catch-line while he is working; the man who sticks to the same lines will never have the opportunity to make additions.

Some magicians get their patter from special patter books by different authors; and they have a habit of choosing different styles of patter that conflict. They try to be serious with one trick and humorous with another—the result is they are failures in both.

Two types of magicians who are boring to their audience are those without enough patter, and those with too much patter. The man who lacks patter produces handkerchiefs in silence, does various actions for no logical reason, and loses the necessary contact with his audience. The man with too much patter tires his listeners with verbose comments on his tricks, and takes too long with each effect.

Another fault is the "killing of time"—stretching out a trick merely to lengthen a program. People want action today. They regard magic as a form of entertainment, and they want to see a variety of effects.

In designing his patter, the magician will always find something to say. He can tell certain things that he may do; he can call attention to various articles. Such patter is merely the starting point. To this outline he adds comments and catch-lines until he can show the trick in presentable form.

By studying the performances of other magicians and referring to patter books, he can gain valuable suggestions. Borrowing patter outright is only harmful to the magician who does it. He should seek to get ideas—various comments which he can adapt to his own style of presentation.

In choice of patter, the important matter is what not to say, rather than what to say.

Avoid the time-worn phrase of "Ladies and gentlemen"; do not say "I thank you," after every trick. Do not call a glass an "ordinary glass."

There are certain tricks, of course, which have stories connected with them. There the performer has every reason to follow a regular line of patter. Refer to "Blackstone's King and Queen" (Chapter VIII); to the "Ball and Tube" (Chapter IX); and to the "Repeating Handkerchief Vanish" (Chapter X).

The magician should seek to create other thoughts of this sort about the tricks he performs, and the more originality he uses, the more effective will his work become.

The opening patter is often troublesome. It should be as short as possible; in fact the best way to avoid the difficulty is to virtually eliminate it.

The natural style of performer will do best to begin his talk with his first trick: "Here is something that will puzzle you—an interesting experiment with a pack of cards—" or whatever he may be using.

The humorous magician can say more: "I shall now entertain you with some problems in sleight-of-hand, proving that the hand is just seventeen and a half times quicker than the eye. Observe that my hands are empty—and that there is nothing up my sleeves except my arms. I couldn't do without them—in fact I've had them ever since I was a boy. My first problem involves a silk handkerchief which measures twelve and three-eighths inches by eleven and five-sixteenths. Be sure to remember those dimensions, because they have nothing to do with what I am going to do—"

The mysterious magician can usually dispense with opening remarks, entering immediately into the first effect of his program.

6. ARRANGING A PROGRAM

In choosing the tricks that he is to perform, the magician should be sure that he likes each trick and can do it. If a performer thinks little of a trick, he should leave it out. No matter how much he likes a trick, he should not attempt it if he cannot perform it well.

The choice of tricks is dependent upon three conditions: (A) the place; (B) the audience; (C) the performer.

(A) For close range, pocket tricks or card tricks should be used. Never attempt effects that require large apparatus—especially those pieces that cannot be passed for examination. Use as many ordinary objects as possible.

On the platform, or in a large room, both small tricks and large ones can be used, but be sure that everything is large enough for everyone to see it. Avoid tricks that are performed primarily for one person. Remember that everyone must be entertained.

This applies to the stage on a larger scale. Work in the audience as little as possible. Avoid small apparatus just as pocket tricks are avoided on the platform.

(B) Card tricks are best suited to audiences composed entirely of men. They appreciate other effects also, but are suspicious of anything that looks too mechanical.

Women like colorful tricks—productions of handkerchiefs, flowers, and ribbons.

Children are particularly pleased with tricks that involve animals. Never attempt too difficult tricks for children. They are easy to deceive, if properly handled, but they "catch on" to certain methods unless great care is exercised.

(C) The performer must also consider his own interests. If he is performing at a club, or some place where people may be on three sides of him, he should use self-contained tricks that require no additional parts, special tables, etc.

On a platform or stage, he has more range; and he also has facilities to pack or unpack his apparatus.

He will find that mental tricks and spirit effects are suitable for both men and women, and are very effective in connection with a long program.

7. CONCLUSION

The best attire for a magician is either a regular business suit or a tuxedo; the former for informal affairs; the latter for platform or stage.

There are many other factors in the presentation of magic. Proper enunciation; arrangement of tricks so that they do not conflict; and dozens of minor matters which have some importance. These, however, would require a lengthy discussion; and some of them would not be of general interest to the student.

But to both amateur and professional, the matter of presentation is important. Common sense is the great asset that will solve any difficulties. Always listen to criticism, whether you like it or not.

Actual performing gives the experience which is so necessary to the magician. But no one should believe that he will be perfect or even good after a few performances. When a magician believes that he has no room for improvement, he can rest assured that improvement is actually the one thing that he needs more than anything else.

Self-confidence and resourcefulness are two things which must be cultivated. The magician must be sure of himself; and he must be ready for any emergency. If a trick goes wrong, he should pass it off as nothing, and proceed with something else.

Over-confidence should be just as carefully avoided. Some magicians underrate the intelligence of their audiences. It is a fact that people are easily deceived. Any magician can learn that by experience; but it is also a certainty that they are quick to detect a slip.

Real effort should be put into magic—into studying it, learning it, practicing it, and performing it. The art is fascinating and enjoyable; and anyone who devotes time to it will be repaid for the effort.